THE WRITE PATH II: HOPE

Israeli and Palestinian Youth Finding Hope
and Empathy Through Writing

Steven Aiello
&
Bob Vogel

Publisher's Name: Bob Vogel and Steven Aiello

ISBN: 979-8-988317-8-4

For permission requests, please contact the authors at:
vogel@lasalle.edu; debateforpeacemun@gmail.com

Table of Contents

WE ARE FROM
Written by *Israeli and Palestinian Students*

We are from the land of our forefathers
We are from pens and paper
We are from love. We are from passion
We are from our differences. We are from our similarities
We are from sadness
We are from laughing and crying until we cry and crying until we laugh
We are from letters and words, beauty and pain
We are from overcoming fears
We are from insecurities
We are from creativity, imagination and fantasy
Yet we live in a world that feels too real
We are from boundaries and restrictions
We are from tired of fighting
We are from fighting for our voices to be heard
We are from peace and fight, and from day and night
We are from silence. We are from chaos
We are from many traditions. We are from many cultures
We are eight people
We are from seven languages.
We are from six cities. We are from eight women
We are from three suitcases left in Spain.
We are from two religions. We are from one land
We are from a land that was meant for peace but has never seen the white dove.
We are from here and there and everywhere
We are from the holy land.
We are from appreciation
We are transformed from lives.
We are from expressing our deepest gratitude
We are from Writers Matter.

DISCLAIMER

The Writers Matter program is a non-political initiative that provides a safe and supportive environment for individuals to express their thoughts and emotions and have their voices heard. Through writing, participants can explore complex feelings such as fear, anger, grief, emotional stress, and uncertainty—particularly those experienced as a result of the Israeli-Palestinian conflict. Through structured writing activities, Writers Matter has helped participants reflect on their experiences, process their emotions, and gain new perspectives. This reflective process supports emotional well-being and fosters personal growth.

DEDICATION

This book is dedicated to the brave Israeli and Palestinian teens who, even as the world around them burned, reached for the pen instead of the sword. Through words, they found one another. Through stories, they remembered their shared humanity. It is also for every young voice still writing, still hoping. May their courage, compassion, and unshaken belief in peace light the way for those who follow.

"Let peace be louder than fear."

"שהשלום יתגבר על הפחד" *(Sheha'shalom yitgaber al hapachad)*
"ليكن السلام أقوى من الخوف" *(Liyakun al-salam aqwa min al-khawf)*

ACKNOWLEDGMENTS

We would like to acknowledge the following individuals and organizations who have continued their support of Writers Matter whose encouragement, support, and funding made our vision a reality has made this initiative possible:

- To the students and teachers who comprised the first cohort of the Writers Matter program, which began just weeks after October 7 amidst an ongoing war.

- PTS Foundation: Tony and Pam Schneider

- Berstein Family Foundation: Jeff and Dana Berstein

- Kessler Family Foundation – Howard and Michele Kessler

- US Embassy in Israel for supporting Debate for Peace and for years of backing programs that bring people together.

- Risa Levy, Cultural Affairs Specialist at the US Embassy Jerusalem Public Diplomacy office.

- Professor Evan Fallenberg (Bar Ilan University) for helping our students refine their writing

- Rebecca Taylor, Editor of *Jewish Renaissance*, and Anniyah Rizvi, Editor of *Words with Weight*, for publishing writing from our students and amplifying their voices.

- Noor, Hala and Dr. Zeina Barakat for judging the Writers Matter: Hope Competition

- The Women's Federation for World Peace, and the Intercultural Museum in Kielce, Poland, for giving our students a platform to share their writing.

ABOUT THE AUTHORS

Bob Vogel, Ed.D.

Bob Vogel, Ed.D. has a doctorate in Educational Psychology and Organizational Development from Temple University. After 43 years teaching at La Salle University in the Department of Education, Bob retired and currently serves as Professor Emeritus of Education. Previous to his tenure at LaSalle University, Bob taught for the School District of Philadelphia.

In 2005, Bob was Founding Director of the non-profit Writer's Matter, which helps young students learn writing skills through personal journaling. The program serves 4000 students, 100 teachers and more than 30 schools participating yearly. Since its inception, Writers Matter has served over 35,000 students.

His most recent books are Wondering: Feelings, Emotions and Building Resilience, Honest, Becoming Me and The Write Path. More information about Bob's publications and Writers Matter can be found at bobvogel.org and writersmatter.org **Contact Bob at vogel@lasalle.edu**

Bob lives in Philadelphia with his wife Marlyn and has two sons and three granddaughters.

Steven Aiello

Steven Aiello grew up in a Jewish Italian American family in Brooklyn, NY, where he attended ultra-Orthodox Jewish schools. After 18 months of post-high school yeshiva studies, he became an Israeli citizen in 2009, completed a master's in diplomacy, and served for two years in the Medical Corps of the IDF before studying Islam at Tel Aviv University. He is now a PhD student at the European Wasatia Graduate School for Peace and Conflict Resolution

In 2017, he founded Debate for Peace to bring together Arab and Jewish youth in Israel via Model United Nations. Since then he has run over 30 MUN conferences for approximately 5,000 students and led over two dozen Jewish-Arab youth delegations, including winning Best Small Delegation at YaleMUN 48 and Yale Model Government Europe 12.

Steven is an executive board member of the NGO CSD-NY, Middle East regional coordinator for the Bosch Alumni Network (BAN), and dialogue facilitator for Asfar, an intercultural education NGO. He is passionate about sports, travel, debating, Model UN, reading, and comparative religion. He lives in South Tel Aviv with his wife, Daniela, and their dog, Waya. Contact: **Steven at debateforpeacemun@ gmail.com**

Student and Teachers Bios[1]

Israeli and Palestinian Teen Writer Bios:

Rachelle is a 16-year-old Christian Palestinian girl from Jerusalem. Rachelle loves writing because it is one of the only ways that help her understand herself and her feelings clearly: "when I write all my thoughts down on paper, I feel as if I've discovered something about myself that I have never known, because I have a problem with comprehending my own thoughts sometimes, and so writing has been a huge help for me ever since my childhood."

Jack Lubavin is a 17-year-old Israeli Russian teen who enjoys writing, studying cinematography and screenwriting, and working on movies in his free time. Jack loves Theater, writing, travelling, and hanging with friends. The most important thing for Jack is helping others.

Tasneem is a 16-year-old Palestinian living in Israel, from a northern village called Deir al-Asad.

Rita moved to Israel 3 years ago from Russia (Saint Petersburg) and studies diplomacy in Tel Aviv school. In her free time, she likes dancing, playing the piano, and learning languages (three so far).

Tom Yaari is a 14-year-old student living in the center of Israel who has been writing stories since she was 8 years old. "I feel like it allows me to express myself."

Mohammad Shibli is a 17-year-old who adores nature and loves conservative ideas.

---

[1]   Additional writers have chosen to remain anonymous, or only be recognized by initials

Maia Assaf is a 16-year-old writer, poet, and peace advocate from New York City, now living in Herzliya. Maia pushes herself to her limits, constantly learning and connecting with people around the world, believing that words have the power to create change.

Zainab Arabe is 17 years old. She likes cats, is a second child, and has a hobby of drawing, is passionate in writing, likes nature and her dream is to be an architect with a side just of a director.

Mahdi Omar is a young Palestinian Arab and passionate 17-year-old from the village Tuba-Zangari in northern Israel. He is a rising actor and director who shows his love for filmmaking and cinematography while also working as a fashion model as a side hustle. He also enjoys traveling solo, reading and baking. On the political hand Mahdi yearns for peace between the Palestinian and Israeli people and hopes for a day when both nations can live in peace.

Shahar Liba is a 17-year-old Jewish girl, who grew up in Israel. She likes to read books, learn new languages, have good conversations and laugh to her heart's content.

Arielle Zuck is a 15-year-old Ashkenazi Jewish Israeli girl from Ramat Hasharon. She's an aspiring writer, musician and actress. She enjoys singing, playing guitar and piano, writing stories and songs, reading, traveling, drawing and crocheting. Anything artistic, really.

She finds the human mind fascinating and wishes to learn more and explore it through her writing and her reading.

International Writer Bios

Doğa is a 15-year-old Turkish girl studying in Turkey. She has a passion for writing and listening to music and wants to be a great engineer one day. She is into mathematics, fashion and makeup.

Lamija Saltagić, or Miya L. L., is an 18-year-old student at Third Gymnasium in Sarajevo, Bosnia and Herzegovina. She is studying Information Technologies (IT), though she hardly believes it will be her future career. During the week, if she's not in the school library or hall, she can be found in the corner of a nearby coffee shop, Caribou. There, she writes in her notebook, perhaps recording her feelings or maybe observing people passing by and guessing their stories. Her best friend and loyal companion is Mika Mercutio, a Yorkshire Terrier.

Endina is a 15-year-old girl from a small country in the Balkans. She is a science enthusiast with a deep passion for astronomy and physics. Exploring the mysteries of the universe, from black holes to quantum physics, she is always eager to learn more about how the world works. Her curiosity drives her to ask big questions and seek logical answers. She also enjoys reading books that keep her engaged, she loves spending time in nature and is a big fan of winter.

Elif Ulubek is a 16-year-old Turkish student who likes reading and writing. She is curious about science and enjoys debating and arguing with people about world issues.

Amina Šeko is a sixteen-year-old girl from Sarajevo, Bosnia and Herzegovina. She finds herself in the world of literature and likes to express herself through writing, while reading in hope of understanding, feeling and learning from others.

Noam Stein is a 17-year-old Swedish student with a passion for immersing himself in diverse cultures, playing guitar and living life to the fullest.

Sanskriti Srivastava is a lively 14-year-old Hindu girl from India who thrives in the beautiful surroundings of Kigali, Rwanda. Captivated by the ocean's mysteries, she channels this passion into her writing. Writing allows her to reflect and express her creativity, from crafting essays on climate change to weaving together poems and stories. Her beloved dogs enrich her life, grounding her while she pursues her dreams.

Asja Kreševljaković lives in Sarajevo, Bosnia and Herzegovina and is 18 years old.

Julie Saleh is a Palestinian Christian, from Jerusalem and Nazareth. She is a passionate dancer, who finds both peace and resistance in the movement and rhythm of dancing. She enjoys hiking, writing, babysitting, listening to music, driving, and debating and politics as well as traveling so she can experience the world from her own perspective.

Nicoline Alexandra Eleonor Ostenfeld is an 18-year-old Swedish Danish writer born and raised in Malmö, Sweden. She aspires to pursue a future in cardiovascular pathology, where her goal is to make an impact alongside achieving something that she can be proud of. In her free time, she enjoys reading, writing, and figure skating, which allows her to express herself in a way that words cannot describe.

Duru Özkan is a 16-year-old Turkish girl who enjoys creating things. She creates journal pages and likes to write different types of pieces. In her free time, she likes to spend time with her friends or family, read and go on walks.

Teacher Bios

Amal Buqai Kayal lives in a village called Judeida-l-Maker, close to Akko. She is a wife, mother, and teacher. She lives in the land of prophets and messengers from God who taught creation what justice, peace, tolerance, and love are, but where people fight for decades to achieve them. Amal is one of the Writers Matter facilitators.

Abeer Watad was born in October 1990 and is a Palestinian Arab woman from Baqa al-Gharbiya, Israel. She is married and a devoted mother of two boys. Abeer is an English teacher, passionate about the power of language to open minds and bridge worlds.

Beyond the classroom, she is a gender researcher, driven by a deep curiosity about identity, equity, and the lived experiences of women in her society. A lifelong reader, she turns to books for both knowledge and comfort—believing in their quiet strength to transform, heal, and inspire. Abeer's students are featured in Part IV of this book.

Ella Ben Emanuel is a teacher of diplomacy and English, as well as a mother, grandmother, actress, comedian, and writer. She believes in the power of words to heal, foster empathy, and create worlds of possibility. Ella lives in Jerusalem.

Robin Flam is an English Teacher and MUN Advisor who moved to Israel in 1970 from Pearl River New York as a young child. Her mother was active in the civil rights movement in the United States, which deeply affected her. Robin tries to implement her desire to live in a just and friendly world into her teaching, by participating in activities that cultivate coexistence, while teaching how the right words and really listening and understanding and caring about others, is the path to a peaceful world.

Julia Mor is a high school teacher from Rishon Lezion, Israel. She loves to read, write, debate, travel, bake, and spend time with her family and friends.

Shatha Halabi is a Druze English teacher, writer, and peacebuilder who believes in the power of words to foster understanding and connection. She believes that stories ignite empathy, emotions drive learning, and every voice is valued. With a deep passion for writing and peacebuilding, she uses education as a tool to inspire critical thinking and kindness.

Elena is a high school teacher. She has been writing poetry and short stories for years, not considering herself "the real poet". She regards writing as a way to capture and reflect reality, stay resilient and enjoy life more.

Sassie Yona is a wife, mother, daughter, sister, friend, and educator. She enjoys expressing herself through poetry, and believes that there will be peace in her lifetime.

Naftali Salz was born in the late 70's to a USSR immigrant family. He has lived all of his life in Ashkelon, a coastal town next to the Gazan border. From that vantage point he has seen the various stages of the conflict evolve from amity to animosity. Trained as a mechanical engineer, he underwent retraining as a math teacher and later an English teacher. His work is often a reflection on fissures in the Israeli social structure, often hidden ones.

Monique Vielbig is a mother of three, an educator and a mentor to many young minds. Originally from California, she has been living in Israel since 1999.

Inna Yoffe Veytsman was born in Leningrad and immigrated to

Israel in 1990. She is married, raises twins and resides in Netanya. In addition to her acquired Hebrew, Russian and English are her primary languages. In addition, she is enchanted with French, which she studies at her leisure.

Writing Competition Bios

Kristen Abu Nassar is a 17-year-old Arab girl who lives in Nazareth. Kristen loves the world of music, sports, film and poetry, in addition to being passionate about traveling the world and living life to the fullest.

Lama is 16 years old from Kissra village in the north of Israel. She aspires to become an engineer.

Zohar ben Kimhy is a 17-year-old Israeli student who likes to read articles, magazines and interviews and sometimes to write. She's interested in fashion design and painting everything that comes to her mind.

Moataz Abu Ahmad is from Nazareth city. He really enjoys writing and debating and also really likes English and drawing.

Maria Muhamdat is a 16-year-old girl, born and raised in Shefa-Amr, studying in Comprehensive C. She is passionate about music, creative writing and reading in Arabic and English, and is inspired by anything related to cultures.

Sivan Ben-Ami is a 17-year-old boy living in Magshimim, Moshav near Petah Tiqwa. He enjoys writing in his free time.

Lidor David is a 17-year-old from Zichron Yaakov, a town in northern Israel. He is an avid debater competing on Israel's national debate team. Lidor founded 'Youth in Action - Empowering Political Literacy in

Israel' a non-profit to make political education accessible to young activists. Alongside high school, he is also taking university courses in political science to deepen his understanding of the field. In his free time, he enjoys cooking, exploring new cuisines, and finding creative ways to make dishes plant based. He's passionate about education, politics, and creating positive change.

AbdAlrhman Shded is a 15-year-old from Baqa al-Gharbiyye who loves a challenge. He's passionate about physics and always curious about how things work. Horse riding gives him freedom, and working out keeps him energetic. In his free time, he enjoys music and films. Whether pushing himself or learning something new, he's always looking to improve.

Madian Marana is a 16-year-old Palestinian Muslim from Israel. She is an IB DP student at YOUnited – Givat Haviva International School and a dedicated young peace activist. Committed to fostering peace in the Middle East, she actively engages in dialogue and initiatives that promote understanding and cooperation across communities.

Abigail Rubanenko is a 15-year-old Jewish girl from Kiryat Ono, Israel. She is a student at Ben Zvi High School, where she excels in a gifted class and participates in the Mashatzim (young squad leaders) program, leading and organizing community service activities. Abigail is passionate about medicine and dedicates time to volunteering with Magen David Adom (MDA). In her free time, she enjoys listening to music, exploring art, and diving into a variety of interests. She aspires to pursue a career in the medical field, where she hopes to make a meaningful impact.

Rotem is a 16-year-old Israeli peace advocate who grew up in Jerusalem and likes music.

Special Shout Out to our cover artist - Maria Fakher Kayal:

"I am Maria Fakher Kayal, I am 9 years old. I live in Judida-Maker. I am in 4th grade. I love painting and singing. I love to meet new people. My best friend is Lydia. I see all the people on the planet as one hand together. There are 4 religions in Israel. Each one completes the others and all of them give a nice and amazing view. The uniqueness of each religion blooms in a beautiful way. All of them together decorate the life of the whole planet and make it the best place to live."

Digital Resources

Writers Matter Website

Bob Vogel's Personal Website

Debate For Peace Website

Moment Magazine -Jewish and Palestinian Teens Write—and Brave the United States—Together

Jewish Exponent - Professor Robert Vogel Helps Jewish and Arab Students Come Together

6ABC News - Students from Israel visit Philadelphia to share stories of living through war'.

Worlds Affair Council

Video – Virtual Conference

Storytelling and writing. UN event, October 2024

I Wonder – I wonder Stories

Introduction

The Write Path II: Hope

The genesis of this book begins with the dark day of October 7th, and the terrible war that it ignited. On October 10, 2023, we began holding daily Zoom calls to allow students—both Arab and Jewish—to meet online and support one another, as well as engage with those abroad. Soon after, I was introduced to Professor Bob Vogel, Founding Director of Writers Matter, and we began meeting weekly via Zoom. Through the use of selected writing prompts, the students began to articulate their feelings and emotions, work through their trauma and share their thoughts with others. The writing sessions lasted for ten weeks and eventually led to a speaking tour in the U.S for the students and teachers where we read our work and had conversations with over 500 people of all ages and backgrounds.

Joining the program wasn't easy. It took immense courage from the students. Emotions were high, and the toxic communication on social media, an outburst of antisemitism around the world, and suppression of Palestinian voices within Israel combined to silence many. My fellow teachers told me that they admired the idea of continuing to meet, but they couldn't send out invitations to the programs I was running because they feared complaints from parents. One parent called to complain that I had allowed his daughter to "meet with the enemy." But we kept meeting. Gradually, the group opened up and communication between the students increased as they expressed their desire to hear each other's voices.

In April of 2024, we raised funds for students and teachers to travel to Philadelphia and Washington, D.C., to share our stories. Our speaking tour was empowering as we met with middle and high school students, members of the World Affairs Council, and numerous adult groups. We experienced unbelievable interest from people eager to hear young voices from both sides of the conflict. These students were trying to process their suffering together and find ways to deal with their collective trauma.

The first year's program led to our first publication: *The Write Path - Jewish Israeli and Palestinian Youth Finding Commonalities and Mutual Understanding Through Writing.* This book served as the ultimate vindication for the students and teachers. It provided a unique window for outsiders into the changing lives of Jewish, Palestinian, and Druze students post-October 7—feeling unsafe on the streets and having little personal contact with friends, they needed a safe space to express their emotions and feelings. This new reality was emotionally challenging, and finding coping mechanisms was crucial. Writing about their lives and sharing with others proved to be an effective strategy.

Unfortunately, the war waged on. Most of our displaced students were able to return home, and the rockets gradually decreased in frequency. But it was often one step forward, two steps back. A second war front erupted on the Lebanese border, making meetings in the north no longer safe. When that ended, the 55-year reign of the Assad family came to a shockingly swift end, bringing even more uncertainty. The Houthis began launching rockets and drones at Israel, while attacking ships in the region. Iran and Israel engaged in a set of tit-for-tat bombing attacks. The first Iranian attack in April 2024 occurred while we were in D.C.; when the second attack was launched in October 2024, a few days before Sukkot, I tried to get home in time, only to find myself outside watching the night sky light up surreally as dozens of drones and rockets sailed in all directions.

At the same time, in Gaza, the situation went from bad to worse. Beyond the death, there was sheer destruction, with nowhere untouched by war, and many families left homeless. After 18 months of high-intensity war, Gaza had been utterly destroyed—yet Hamas maintained a stronghold on power, threatening Israelis and Gazans alike. Perversely, reliance on aid to survive only further empowered Hamas, as it seized the aid and controlled its distribution or sold it at exorbitant prices.

Even now, as we write this, after weeks of relative quiet, the second ceasefire has fallen apart. Just in the last 24 hours, two Israeli soldiers were killed in Gaza, and the government announced a call-up of thousands of reserve soldiers to prepare for another large-scale operation, while Ben Gurion Airport was hit by a Houthi missile attack. And always, we are reminded that there are still hostages - daughters, brothers and sisters—being held underground, with a clock ticking.

During this challenging time of collective and personal traumas, Writers Matter has grown to encompass a larger community. We have created a space for Arab and Jewish, Israeli and Palestinian, teachers and students to meet, processing their own pain and emotions through writing while daring to feel the pain and emotions of others. Each of us faces unique challenges, and together we support one another, refusing to give in to the external pressures that we seek to divide us. Each piece in this book took incredible fortitude and a leap of faith to create, and by reading and spreading it, you can help empower our writers.

Our group has also become international, expanding to include youth from Europe, Asia, and Africa (see Part II).

Methodology

After the initial writing cohort during the first months of the war was led by Professor Vogel, Steven and Amal initiated and led several teacher training courses using similar prompts to the students. The teachers were then able to use writing prompts in class with their own students. Several alumni of our first cohort were then given support to create their own peer-course, which they taught via zoom, with the final meeting in person. We are currently working to prepare facilitators for our Gaza-based writers' group.

Book Structure

Part I: **Student Writing** (Israelis and Palestinians)

This section contains the writing of the Israeli and Palestinian teens who participated in our Writers Matter workshops. Their writing is rich and varied, reflecting the diversity of the group. They wrote about family, identity, and more—all in the shadow of war. One prompt, "A Letter to the Other Side," reflects the challenge of using writing to process personal experiences while engaging with others. Students were also paired to write "We Are From" pieces, expressing personal narratives together.

Part II: **Global Youth Perspectives**

Here we hear from young writers in Bosnia & Herzegovina, Kosovo, Rwanda, Sweden, Turkey, and the Philippines. These international partners became a lifeline when our students were stuck at home, desperate for distractions from the war. With the success of our writing program, we were able to "pay it forward," offering workshops to youth abroad. Using similar prompts, these students brought fresh perspectives and highlighted the shared and distinct experiences of youth across continents.

Part III: **Teachers' Voices**

This includes contributions from educators who joined teacher training workshops Amal and Steven led in the spring and fall of 2024. Jewish, Palestinian, and Druze teachers from across the country wrote and shared pieces, just like we had with the students. While the workshops aimed to give teachers classroom tools, it became clear that the writing itself was vital for the teachers' own well-being. Deep emotions emerged, sparking meaningful discussions and new prompts, such as "This Scar is From" and "Where I Am Now." Group writing also fostered cross-community understanding and connection.

Part IV: **A Tragedy in Baqa al-Gharabiya**

In November 2024, tragedy struck the Ibn al-Haithem school in Baqa al-Gharabiya. On November 3rd, Steven stood beside the school's English coordinator, Abeer, and Principal Zeyad Abu Mokh, handing out certificates. Just three days later, he received devastating news—Principal Zeyad had been murdered in the school parking lot. This devoted educator became yet another victim of a wave of violent crime plaguing Arab communities. We turned to writing to help the students process their grief and shock. Their pieces–marked by pain and resilience-are dedicated to the memory of Principal Zeyad Abu Mokh.

Part V: **Hope Competition**

We move to a message of hope. Writers Matter sponsored a writing competition that paired students from different backgrounds to co-author pieces on the theme of *hope*. Writing with a new partner, especially from the other "side," was difficult. Many struggled to connect, find a shared voice, or even write about hope at all. But ultimately, we received twenty submissions from forty students, from short stories and poems to a children's book about displacement and fictional tales of forbidden relationships between Israelis and Palestinians. A panel of Israeli, Palestinian, and international judges selected six finalists who received cash prizes. These writings reflect a shared yearning for a brighter future together.

Part VI: **Writing from Gazan and West Bank Youth**

The newest Writers Matter group was just being formed as we sent this book to publication. We include here writing from our nascent Gaza and West Bank youth writing cohort.

Final Thoughts

Finding hope amidst chaos, destruction, and hatred is a daily struggle. It is easier to ignore the pain of the "other," to cling to a binary of good vs. evil. The truth is more complex: millions on both sides are suffering. There are no winners in war—only loss. Yet this project has shown us that writing can nurture empathy and compassion. Our path is long and uncertain, but we have lit a beacon. We will keep writing. We believe in the strength of our voices, and in the power of listening. We must never give up. *Hope is our future.*

Part 1: Israeli & Palestinian Students

In this section, ten young Jewish and Arab writers from across Israel share their stories. They reflect on their identities, childhood experiences during times of war, and what they are grateful for. They write letters to their younger selves, messages to those on the other side of the conflict, and express their wonders, hopes, and fears. In some pieces, they even write together threading a fragile tapestry of complex, intertwined identities.

I Am From

Zainab

Hello, it's me
I came from a country that has never been free

A place of land that is desired by all
A place that contains anyone and everyone

I came from a small place on this earth
So small not even the size of an American state

It has two names, but it depends on the person who says it

I came from a place whose religions are diverse
Where Muslims, Jews and Christians lived

Until
One decided

Appropriation starts
Displacement, war, death....

I am in a place where voices are never heard
Small, big, young, old. All!
Are muted for what?

If we stayed before in the past
Where there's no war

Each one would have his place
Everyone could live in harmony
Isn't that the best?

Tom

Where am I from?
From the little girl I used to be.
The one who danced in the park, the one who talked a lot, maybe too much.
The one whose biggest nightmare was to be inside four walls.
The girl that lived on the stage.
Cause the show must go on
The one who didn't care to be perfect, just free.
Is that where I'm from?
The girl I was before tests became a thing, before I needed to be,
I learned to do my own makeup, learned to dress and talk.
I'm scared to get out of my four walls.
And the show needs to be over
But I'm still from this little girl, right?

Mahdi

I'm from,
I am from stability, empowerment and hardship
I come from a place of power, love and so high above.
I come from a womb of a mother who fights so hard to protect
what's hers.
I come from a place of rebirth, life and a protected hive.
I am no ordinary human though I am a fighter, a fire that glares for
every desire.
I am from myself and myself I keep.
I am from confidence, success and no time to sleep.
I reach what I want and what I want, wants me.
I am from shifting, I am from progress and I am from light.
I have sight.
And I fight for what's right.
Though I'm human, moreover I'm a soul.
I am from happiness.
I am from freedom.
And my freedom shall be mine.
I come from a place of protecting myself.
Some would call it narcissism, some would call it optimism.
I am from belief, I am from relief
But let's not forget that before I was from grief.
And to not go back is chief.
That's where I am from, I am from mindfulness, I am from endless
nights of prayer that I built every layer.
I am, I am and I am.
I am from revolution so I find every solution.
May I become from fame.
May I be of success.
And may I be from a place of rewards and endless awards.

Arielle

I am from sadness and anger.
I am from hurting and suffering.
I am from my mother, who many say I look like.
I have her hair and I have her spirit.
She always finishes first and so must I.
Not because she told me so, but because that is how I think.
I am from my father, who is kind but angry.
He lashes out and sometimes I am afraid I might do the same.
Sometimes he cares, and I try my hardest.
I do not have their eyes.
Theirs are green, the color of life and the color of our world. The plants that give us life and support us. They are what help us breathe and eat. Green provides.
My eyes are brown, the color of the dirt beneath graves and underneath our feet. The dirt we walk on every day without giving it a single thought.
I am from sadness and anger.
I am from hurting and suffering.
I am from myself, but sometimes I wish I wasn't.

Jack

I am from Israel, oh, you want me to be more specific. I am from Kfar Saba, even more? I'm not giving you, my address! OK, OK, I'll try.... I was born 17 years ago from my mother's tummy; I came there from.... You know... fun business. They came to Israel from Russia, so I'm from a Russian speaking family, for 4 years I didn't know Hebrew. I am from a group of people who believe that school is big bullshit, it won't help most of us.

You know, I am from a fantasy world, at least that's what my bullies said for 14 years straight, I am weird, I am too kind, I'm a dreamer, I imagine stuff, I don't believe in God (but fairies are real), I write imaginary stories, which you already noticed because you are reading it.... which makes you come from a fantasy world as well.... I... I'm from a lot of places: Jew, LGBTQ, Israeli, Russian, writer, actor, bullying, my parents, justice fighter.

Whoa, that's too much, my head is spinning. But you know the beautiful thing about it? That's what makes me -me.

Shachar

I am from my past where I made mistakes in every corner I went to. I am coming from a place where I didn't know. Where I didn't understand, where I didn't get why and how things happened. From where questions did not get answers.

From where I was told to find answers on my own.

I am from the place where curious minds were left to starve thinking of something more.

Little by little did it change, once starved now fed.

Travelers started coming, coming to share their stories around the fire at night. Stories of sorrow, stories of laughter, stories of where they came from.

Stories that made me grow, made me understand, made me see beyond.

Now when travelers come with stories, they also bring questions. Now I give answers, now I know what they need.

So now I travel to somewhere far and unknown, and on my way answer those who ask.

Now when I sit around a fire at night and I'm asked where I am from, I tell the place where questions did not get answers, of the time I didn't know, of the place that let me be, of the place I call home. Of where I was made to be a forever learner.

I am from a place where curious minds never had enough and always wanted more.

Children of War

Mohammad

Being a child in the war is hard
I sit in my room safe and still
 while Gaza burns against its will
I see pictures, hear the cries
and wonder why the world denies
but even under this endless night
Hope still beats in Gaza's heart
While I look at my side others see the hostages and just cry
they say bring them back
any price to revive human life
I dream of a time when this will go
when no more bombs or graves are made
when the children can run and play and we can live in peace someday

Jack

Ah, ah, ah, staying alive… staying alive… I'm not crazy, just a child of war. The weird part is still being stressed from sirens, just a child of war. It's not a title I want to have… but that's the reality… hearing the alert for a siren and not thinking "uhhhh run" is amazing, thinking "just one more moment, if a bomb fell, I will die either way", just a child of cruelty. Being able to travel, telling about my country and realizing… it's not normal you guys, we live in a reality where a million children live in war. The jokes that we make are too mad even for the darkest humored person. If someone hears "don't ever tell someone you're from x, your life depends on it", they will listen, but we? Don't make the children of war laugh, we are proud, we laugh at fear.

Listen, I know it's scary, but I like to think of it that way, we are the children of ancient Greece. We defend, not attack. We are the children of Ares, God of war, Athens, goddess of wisdom and war strategies. Don't forget that Iris, goddess of pride, is our close family member. We are broken, yet the strongest country, just because of that, that we are the children of war.

Mahdi

Rumble, Destruction and Torture.
That's what comes to mind when I see those pictures of war, a war that's not too far from me, A war that if I walk an approximate of 15 minutes I will be able to see with my own eyes, a war that has destroyed houses - the war that killed the most courageous people and has plucked the innocence from children's eyes.

I sit here in the north, watching the chaos unfold on two fronts.
To my south, Gaza yearns for comfort, its people caught in an endless cycle of bombardments and blockades. To my east, Syria remains a broken mosaic of war, a conflict so loud and relentless that it echoes through the mountains.
I am roosted in between, watching and wondering how long it will take before the cracks in the world around me creep closer to my feet.

It's strange to live so close yet feel so far away.
It's strange to feel afraid, knowing they feel the same way.
It's strange knowing those children of war dreams like I do.
It's strange knowing they laugh.
It's strange knowing they are loved.
It's strange finding out they're human…

Every single thing seems so surreal, I feel weird and I teared up.
I feel stuck having no luck,

I feel caught knowing they are not taught,
I pushed my hand to dig them up but nobody grabbed onto it, it felt like the sane thing to do then figured out nothing is sane about this.

Everywhere I look, I see the cost of war.
It's in the lines on my grandparents' faces, the worried whispers of neighbors, the new broadcasts that never seem to end and even follow me everywhere I go.

And yet, despite all of it, there's still a small flicker of light and hope within me. Maybe because I'm young and free and haven't learned how to let go of it. I hope for a day when the rumble of bombardments is replaced with laughter, for them, for us, for all of us to live in peace. When the destruction gives way to rebuilding. When courage isn't measured by who survives the longest but by who dares to make peace.

I hope for a country full of joint hands and for a country full of love,
May we all know peace,
May we all have it,
May we all feel it,
And may we all live long enough to experience it.

Arielle

It's suffocating, I think.

When the war had just started, I was away from home, away from all my friends and my cats so I ended up too depressed and too miserable to even get out of the house we were in.

I found comfort in my phone. Instead of doing schoolwork, I played video games on a laptop and texted my friends. It didn't make me feel better. It was just a distraction.

For a very long time, I couldn't take my eyes off the news. I had to always check what was happening on the internet, on social media, on the web, and the TV. I had to know everything. But knowing everything didn't help. It didn't make me feel any better. If anything, I only felt much much worse. I was digging a bigger hole for myself to fall into.

I had a family member who was taken away from his home into the deep tunnels underneath Gaza. I never knew he existed before the war, but I cared so much.

I went with my mother to do things for the hostages almost every week. In between playing more video games and doing my hobbies, I'd have a few hours where everything was quiet in my mind. I would take a close look at the sculptures and art they had on display at the square. At the images of all the people who were taken away from their homes, from their families, and placed deep into enemy territory, where they were not humans, but simply animals. Objects to use for the enemy's interest.

But then I'd see what happened on the other side. People around me didn't feel sympathy, because to them all these people were cruel to our people. They would kill us without a second thought if they had the chance. But they were still people. They are still human beings.

It's become too much for me to bear, now. If I can, I will shove it as far away from my brain as possible. I'm able to have that privilege, and I hold it dear in my arms.

I wish to be able to breathe.

Zainab

Lately, after 373 days of War, I'm tired and sick of seeing all that. Living in fear and uncertainty. Whether I will live or die. Kids too young to understand what war is are scared every night. The bombing sounds and the sirens sound. It's all terrifying. I hope we can live peacefully. I hope we can live.

One of my most important years, I don't want it to be ruined. I wanna live till I graduate, till I have kids, Till I get old. I wanna live for the day that I die from old age, not from war.

The world is really ending.

Climate change is getting worse.

The Sahara Desert is getting flooded with water

Weird stuff is happening

Europe is getting hotter; that's not a good sign. Everything is changing, it's worrying and frightening.

Hurricanes and volcanoes. Earthquakes and floods.

The ozone layer is also getting worse.

I wish people would be more aware of the impact of war

The air pollution. People's lives. The earth is being hurt as much as we are

I wish there was no war, no fights, just peace. I wish this world would be healthier, stop producing and start planting. Start to make the world green again instead of making it black and white.

These are just wishes. But I really hope it will come true one day and every bad thing will vanish forever.

Tasneem

This is the kind of child who never got to live their childhood, who has faced a harsh life since birth. These children are present today, in this moment, in Gaza — under bombings, under fire, surrounded by rubble and destruction. There is no life where they are. Even the animals in Gaza suffer from pain and hunger.

Are they guilty of anything? Of course not!

I wonder: what kind of heart does a person have to kill without mercy?

And I am shocked by those who see what is happening and remain silent.

If you talk about rights, then these children were either born already killed or born as orphans. Some of them see their families die before their very eyes.

Their mental state is terrible — fear and exhaustion, the loss of a father's and mother's affection. Even their closest relatives have died.

I ask: what is people's response to all this?

Is it because Gaza faced oppression that it is being bombed?

Even if Gaza is being bombed because it resisted–what is the fault of the children?

This is a massacre, not a war.

This trembling we see in a child under the age of six is something we only see in horror movies — and we are deeply affected by it. But now it is happening in our reality, and people remain silent and calm, as if we've become numb, as if death has become just numbers.

Every child in the world — regardless of nationality, background, or who their family is — has the right to live with dignity, to play with their siblings, to sleep safely in the arms of their mother and father. What we are witnessing is the murder of childhood, either directly by weapons or slowly through hunger.

I hope all this sorrow ends, that we live in peace, and that the news one day speaks of projects that embrace children, provide them with food, safety, and peace.

Gratitude

Jack

Dear God, (?) Please hear my prayer, as the day ends, I want to thank you for all the miracles you've done- I'm thankful for having a home, a family, education and health. Thank you, good night.

AND....

I'M DONE.

What do you mean, no? I have nothing to thank for- I don't even believe in God. I mean yes, I'm thankful for having a roof over my head, but I can't call it a home. Yes, I have a family and education but they caused so many problems... but at least I had them... and health.... thank you for not killing me, or making me really sick, but I am mentally and physically not well.

If you look at things as obvious, so nothing to thank for, although my life is not perfect, we need to remember to thank the world for not being in a worse situation.

So, guys, let me thank some people: thank you friends for becoming my second family and helping, thank you mashatzim and krembo[1] for letting me take a big part in them. I have a girlfriend- thank you, good grades- thanks, theater- merci. But the weirdest thing for others, and even to the fingers who are writing it, I am thankful for my bullies for making me who I am.

So thank you Jack for being strong and persevering.

Zainab

I'm thankful for being a female
Having long hair and a sense to feel
I'm thankful for being alive

---

[1]   Youth movements in Israel

Around a family of seven
Wish we all go to heaven

I'm thankful for having friends
They are such a blessing for mental health

I'm thankful for my parents
They always make sure that I have good health

I'm thankful that I will be called "mom"
A name of pride for giving lives

I'm thankful for being raised well
I'm thankful that I believe in God
I'm thankful to God
Without God nothing would be there
Not me being a female
Or my friend on this earth
Not my parents or my dreams
Nothing at all like the air in space

Tasneem

I am thankful for being alive and for having my family with me,
I am thankful for my ability to overcome life's challenges and for the
mistakes I have made as they allowed me to see the world more clearly.

Shahar[2]

I am grateful for my life
I am grateful for this adventure
I am grateful towards those who did me wrong

---

[2]   Shahar is the Hebrew word for "dawn" or first light.

13

I am grateful to those who did me right
I am grateful for everything life has given me
I am grateful for my name that helps me bring light to each day. I am grateful for my imagination that helped me with this creation.

Rachelle

Sometimes, I feel I'm not thankful enough,
Though deep down I know I am.
Still, there are moments I fail to see
The treasures lay within my hands.
I'm grateful for the blessings given to me—
A home, a place to rest, a family whose love i hold dear, loyal friends, good health
And countless gifts I often overlook.
Yet, always, there's this thought within my mind,
For some I love bear burdens they don't deserve.
Their cries echo where hope feels distant,
Their struggles weigh upon my nerves.
Why do I hold this life so safe
When will my people face tomorrow unsure?
Some may deserve far more than I
Yet it's their pain I can't endure
How are blessings chosen, scattered, split,
And how is the fate that we bare decided?
For every joy I have, I wonder
Why are there burdens left for them to wear?
My people— beautiful, unseen, family whose names I'll never know.
I think of you with every breath, your dreams sown into the soil of my gratitude
And through I'm thankful for all I own,
For every gift, every joyful time—
In quiet moments, all I feel is a boundless longing just for you.

Mahdi

I am thankful for the cool breeze on a hot summer night,
Oh, the cool breeze that makes you feel alive,
the breeze that makes you feel loved and the breeze of those who
loved you back.
Oh, but the breeze of success is also so ecstatic, No the breeze of you
looking in the mirror and actually loving what you see is gorgeous as
well. That's the breeze I am thankful for.

I am furthermore thankful for the times I've stubbed my pinky toe on
the wall – not because I enjoy the pain, but because of what it represents.
In those moments of sharp, unforgiving discomfort, I'm reminded
that life has a way of humbling even the strongest of us. It's such a
small thing - a toe, a corner, a split second of ache and yet it can bring
everything to a halt. It's the kind of unplanned chaos that mirrors
life itself.

Coming of age has taught me that life isn't made up of big, dramatic
moments alone. It's the small, often painful ones that shape us. The
unexpected setbacks, the unkind collisions with reality, the moments
when we feel most human. It's a metaphor for the times I have rushed
too quickly into something without thinking, only to be stopped in
my tracks.
 I have learned to be thankful for these moments. They force me to
pause and reflect on my surroundings, on my choices, and on how
far I've come. That's what I'm thankful for.

I am thankful for my shoes - not just for where they've taken me, but for
what they've endured along the way. Every scuff, every crease, every
worn-out sole tells a story of movement, growth and perseverance.
They've carried me through long days and late nights, through
moments of triumph and stretches of uncertainty. And as a runner,

my shoes have carried me across miles of open roads and winding trails, through the crisp morning air and under the burning afternoon sun. But they've also been there during harder runs - the ones where my legs felt heavy, my lungs burned, and my mind begged me to quit. They have absorbed the weight of frustration of the countless moments of breaths of gratitude I took.

I am also thankful for my desk lamp, not just for the light it gives, but for the quiet moments it creates.
In the late hours, when the world feels still and the weight of the day has settled, my beautiful black colored and curved desk lamp glows softly, illuminating more than just my textbooks and notes. Its -
A steady presence, casting warmth over my work and reminding me why I push myself to excel. Under its light, I've solved tough problems, written essays that felt like small masterpieces, and dreamed of a future as bright as the space it lights up. My desk lamp is a symbol of how I've learned to appreciate the small, ordinary things in life. It's seen the doodles in the margins of my notebooks, the playlists I have curated for study sessions, and the moments I've paused to just breathe and be grateful for this fleeting time of being young and alive.

I am thankful for all the moments life has presented us with - whether they're satisfactory or unpleasant. I am thankful for my soul and those who give it an aura of comfort.

Arielle

I am thankful for — what? What am I thankful for?
I am thankful for my friends, that is what I want to say. Thankful to the people who love and respect me, for the ones who wish to cause me no harm. Thankful for the way the sun rises each morning and the moon wakes up to greet me at night to light up the darkness. Thankful for the things I am able to do, for the life I was given; for

the hobbies I collect, and for the ability to have them in the first place.

But being thankful isn't something we can always do. Gratitude and love aren't things we can always express and show the world — show the things we are thankful for. How are we supposed to? Are we meant to say *"thank you"* over and over and over again without an end, only to receive nothing in return? Are we supposed to be thankful for every little thing we own, because people out there don't have it at all, but for us it's so simple and so ordinary that we can't even give it a second thought.

I am thankful for what I am. I am thankful for the opportunity to live. I am thankful for it all.

Letter to My Younger Self

Tasneem

I ask you not to give up, and to face life with strength
I want you to give your parents all the love, kindness and support you have both emotionally and financially and to be their role model and pillar when they grow old
I want you to continue your path to succeed even if you lost everything along the way

Arielle

Hey, little me.

I know life is hard. I know it's always been hard, and no matter what people tell you, it never gets better. I know that every day feels like a dreadful task to you, and I understand deeply how much you cannot stand the thought of continuing your life this way.

I can't tell you I don't feel the same way you do. I can't lie to myself or you because it won't convince either of us. It will only make us feel a thousand times worse.

I know you want to believe there's something more to this, and I do too. And I know that no matter how hard you try, the thought that you could live a life that isn't full of internal suffering feels unreal.

I feel the same way. Sometimes I don't, but when I do, it feels like the end of the world.

I understand how lonely the world can be.

How it feels like no one is around to help you or to be with you, how everyone is faking and just telling you something that is completely the opposite of the truth that they hide in their chest and behind your back.

I know you get all anxious when you walk past people and they look at you oddly, as if you were a creature from another planet, or they start giggling and chattering between them and you have this feeling that tells you they're saying horrible things about the way you look or walk or dress.

I know you have a hard time trusting people because your fears take over your entire mind like an evil entity and you cannot convince yourself the words, they tell you are simply lies.

But I can tell you that it gets better.

You learn to differentiate.

You know when it's not true, when it's just your anxiety that is filling the void of your brain and not the truth. Because the truth is real and you just have to look for it.

You have to stop comparing. You ought to tell your friends how you feel, because if you don't it'll only get worse. They'll understand, maybe even try to improve, and figure out how they can help you feel better.

You ought to stop trusting every whisper that comes out of the monster's mouth because it only wants to make you feel worse.

The world is cruel.

Humans are complex and difficult.

They're like chef's salads, with good and bad things chopped and mixed together in a vinaigrette of confusion and conflict.

We might never truly understand them, and you might never truly understand yourself. But that's okay, I guess. That's life.

From your older self

Mahdi

Dear Mahdi,

I want to start this letter by expressing my deepest points of gratitude for you who have taught me what it means to grow and evolve into a beautiful human being.

You introduced me to what love actually feels like and how to find the good in every hardship I go through.

Ebullient that's what you were. But remember September 1st of 2019? Yes, the first day of seventh grade.
Where you thought life was absolutely the worst.
Moving into a new school, trying to build new habits to fit in as this stereotype of a Bedouin male teenager, forced to grow so fast even though sixth grade was 2 months ago…
How did that even happen? How is being thirteen so different from being twelve?
Why were you always being forced into liking this nature of what's so called "manliness"?
You couldn't even fathom what your actual likings are. These were the thoughts going through your little head. But being forced to grow taught you the most complex things of all.

Aspiring that's what you are working towards, Success will find you, Success will have you, Success will carry you and success will absolutely **love** you.
Life will give you tasks, life will give you burdens but life will never give you work that she knows you cannot do.

Radiant beauty that's what you're accomplishing, but not the kind that's only the cover though the kind that's the whole book, yes people actually love you and look up to you!
People go to you for advice knowing you have gone through experience, people adore your jokes and people adore you whole.

Masculine that's who you're becoming, but not your village's stereotype of masculine.
not the smoking, girl lusting masculine but the gentle, heart-warming, kind and loving masculine.

Astonishing that's what grandma calls you, you are now one hell of a lucky man you won medals, you won contests and the most important of all YOU won yourself.

Hard Working that's what they only see, but inside you have hidden a battle with yourself, a battle with love, a battle with hate and a battle with what's yet to come.

Delusional, that's what they call you sometimes, but you have learned that it's their own insecurities talking to you, you have learned that people are so afraid of other people's success and always rush to hate and drag them down rather than working towards their own.

Inspiring, illuminating, iconic and impressive and all of the above (except for the D part) THAT'S what you are and way more.
Oh, dear Mahdi, you are everything we have prayed for.

Jack

Hey sweaty, get out, don't be scared. I just came here to talk to you. It might sound crazy, but I know who you are, not in a creepy way. So, I wanted to tell you, you're important. People are mean, but the soonest you'll realize that you are perfect the way you are, the sooner you'll be whole. No, don't cry, I didn't mean to upset you. Let me just tell you a story, like the ones you enjoy writing- long ago the zebra felt bad for not looking like a tiger, she had many many haircuts and dyed her hair, but nothing helped. You know why? Because it's the zebra's nature and she shouldn't feel bad about it. What she needs to do instead is go talk to someone, because even the black and white that she once had were no longer the same after keeping all her feelings in her tummy. Who Am I? Well, just a fairy who came to help. You know, you will someday feel better, even change your name in a few years, and your new name will be Jack.

Hey, I think it's time for me to leave, but don't stop writing, this is your strongest tool.

Zainab

Dear Zainab, I'm your older self. I'm not that old yet. But I went through a lot not just through my experiences but also through other experiences

One piece of advice to me, to you, to everyone:

"Don't overreact" and "don't overthink." Don't over anything. Why? There's a lot of reasons. Overthinking may lead to misunderstanding, and you will have difficulty trusting anyone even if they are completely innocent.
Don't over think Zainab just live the moment and forgive, forget and let go.
Why shouldn't you overreact? People don't deserve your kindness.
Don't overreact, be mature and everything will go smoothly yeah smoothly
So, no reaction, no problems, no fights.
You will be happier, relaxed and have no worries about anyone.
No one can say anything about you
You will be the mature, respectful one
The ideal in the eyes of people
BUT don't be so polite, when danger or disrespect occurs don't step back, don't be polite, instead fight and give them what they gave you "the same treatment" it's the only fair thing and if it's needed cut the relationship with them. You're not alone, you have yourself and only yourself, you have always been your own best friend, your own superior.

Little me little Zainab, love yourself and be grateful every morning and night that you are still alive

Love you.

A new year is about to start. Maybe next year I will have other opinions. I'm gonna be an adult now. I wish we could have our dream come true, my younger me.

Mohammad

I wish I could sit down with you and talk about the changes I've seen over the years. The world we grew up in feels like it's shifting in ways that don't always make sense, and I can't help but feel uneasy about where we're headed. There are three big things that weigh on my mind: how society views health, what's happening to masculinity, and the way family and tradition are being treated.

First, I've noticed that something as basic as health is being turned upside down. There was a time when being healthy was something we all strived for, a sign of discipline and self-care. But now, it seems like the focus has shifted to praising unhealthy lifestyles in the name of "body positivity." While self-acceptance is important, we shouldn't ignore the value of striving for a healthier life. Glorifying habits that harm people in the long run does no favors to anyone, and it's troubling to see this celebrated as progress.

Then there's what's happening to men. Masculinity, which once stood for strength, responsibility, and leadership, is now being questioned and criticized at every turn. Instead of encouraging men to be strong, protective, and reliable, society seems to push them toward softness and passivity. Men are told to suppress their natural traits rather than embrace them, leaving many confused about their role and hesitant to step up when needed. This isn't progress; it's a loss of something vital.

On top of that, the way society handles gender and abortion feels troubling. Gender, something once tied to biology and reality, is now seen as completely fluid, leaving many confused and struggling to find their identity. While understanding and empathy are important, ignoring basic truths only creates instability. And then there's abortion, where the focus has shifted so far toward personal choice that the value of life itself often feels overlooked. These are delicate, deeply human issues, yet they're often treated like political tools rather than the profound moral questions they are.

And finally, family and traditions that hold communities together are being thrown away. The idea of family as a mom, dad, and children is often dismissed as outdated, and traditions that once gave people a sense of belonging and purpose are being replaced by fleeting trends. These changes leave people disconnected, unsure of their roots, and uncertain about their future.

If I could give you one piece of advice, it would be this: don't let the noise of the world affect the values that truly matter. Strive for health, not just for yourself but for those who depend on you. Embrace what it means to be strong, responsible, and dependable as a man. Honor, family and tradition are the foundation of a meaningful life and a strong society. And remember to approach the various issues of gender and life with compassion, but also with clarity and conviction.

Stay true to what you know is right, even when the world tells you otherwise. These values are worth holding onto, and they will guide you through the confusion of changing times.

With love and hope,

Your Older Self

Letter to the Other Side

Arielle

Is it quiet over there? Or is your void of sorrow and loss filled with the noise of bombs and gunshots, collapsing buildings, and collapsing families?

How are you able to go on in a world so cruel that even humans aren't capable of stopping themselves from hurting each other?

Do they really control every part of your life?

Do the women really suffer as much as we are told?

Why are we only taught to hate ruthlessly those who are different from us? Why can't religions who come from the same origin learn to live in peace and accept one another? Why are humans so evil?

I want to believe there is a future where we get along. Where we do not kill each other. Where killing a person on the other side doesn't grant you glory and the love of an unknown entity we might never see with our own eyes.

I want to believe we might be friends someday.

Do you want it as well?

Reply to Arielle's letter by Zainab

No–It's not quiet at all. Even when it's quiet outside, it's not quiet inside. It's frightening, hearing and seeing all these shattered bodies of kids and women. War was never like this. It's hard and suffocating living like this. Are we controlled you ask? We don't even have the right of speech, sad, isn't it?

From the other Arabs' perspective, we are the betrayers. They say, "why are you living with the enemy?" It's not like we have a choice. We were born here and we will stay and keep living here. It's not like we have anywhere else to go to if we are displaced, homeless refugees whose only wish is to live. We stayed in our homeland, and we will not leave.

Women are suffering for what? War was never meant to be cruel! No! Our religion that keeps us alive and resilient teaches that "a war is between the two armies and not the civilians;" we were taught "don't kill kids, women or elderly." If hate wasn't there, we would be living in peace together but instead hate and strife is always stronger. Greed and intolerance is overpowering the kindness and understanding in this world. I wish that we can reach a point where there is no killing, no war, no political parties or divisions, no hate, just peace. Where we can be friends, share things and maybe, just maybe, be happy.

Jack

Hi, I'm Jack. I have some questions that I actually don't need the answer to if it's too much. *Stress laughing* hahaha ammm… so I see you as equal, but I really want to understand, you live in Israel, why call yourself Palestinians? Why not even Israeli Palestinians? I think that we grew to be afraid, all of us. We are just children, why do we need to think about it? My parents used to change sides when seeing you, I don't know why, we are all humans, no? You got hurt on 7.10 just like we did… SO LET'S JUST SIT, WAIT… wait… let's sit and have a talk, see each other, look into each other's eyes? Whoa, you have really beautiful eyes, blue. *stop* our country is separated to hate between us, so maybe instead of hating you (laughs) we'll hate others together? (Sad smile)

Mahdi

A letter to the divider of both sides
Dear Ice Wall,
You rise between us, a cold and lifeless sentinel, dividing the land we both call home.
You are not just stone and steel; you are the silence that keeps us apart, the frost that chills any warmth we might share, you separate the olive branch from the blue star that overlooks it. You are the silence that stifles our stories and the distance that hardens our hearts.
Yes, I write to you not with anger, But with a heart heavy with questions.

As a child of this war, I often wonder: do you hear the songs of hope we whisper beneath the noise of conflict? Do you feel the longing for a day when we no longer need walls? You claim to protect, yet all you truly do is divide.
But as an olive picking soul, a child growing up in the shadow of your cold embrace. My people's roots run deep, like the olive trees that have stood for centuries, bearing witness to both our joys and our tears. The olive branch is our symbol of peace, but it is also a reminder of resilience - a resilience tested every day as we rebuild what war has taken from us.

Do the children beneath the blue star know this heart wrenching ache that those kids picking olives feel? Do they see their humanity? Or has fear blurred their vision? I do not know their world, only that it is out of reach for those on the other side. Do they ever dream, as I do, of a day when the wall crumbles and the olive branch can climb to meet the blue star without fear?

Ice wall, you are not just a barrier of stone; you are a barrier of stories. You make it easy to forget that on both sides are people who bleed, who love, who grieve. But I cannot dare to forget. I cannot hate. My heart carries the weight of too many stories, too many faces, too many

27

dreams that long for peace.

I write this letter not to curse you,

But Dear Ice Wall, I dream of a day when the olive branch and the blue star no longer need you. When you melt, I hope you carry away the bitterness you were built to preserve and the bitterness of those who built you.

I hope bridges rise in your place, where hands reach across and where children can grow up unshackled by war.

Until then, dear ice wall, I will hold onto my dreams, rooted as deeply as the olive tree.

And I will carry the love of the stars with me, even when you try to freeze it.

Sincerely,

A child who reads under the olive tree.

I Wonder

Shahar

Wondering. Wondering? Wondering around in a big forest called life.
While looking at the bright stars up at night.
Wondering thoughts that keep you up. They creep you! They freak
you! But you're stuck.
Anxiety and worry slipped in; you're stuck.
You have to give in.
Wondering and wondering with no place to go.
No goal, no answer, with nothing to hold on.
Hold on, hold on, why didn't you run?
Had you taken any action you would have been done! Wondering and
wondering is all that you do! Leaving you sad and alone like a balloon.
If you were to take an action, you would have left with a smile. And
more than a few candies to remind you of those good times.

Tasneem

I wonder how people show their true selves when they get angry
I wonder how life can treat good people
I wonder how people can ignore the ones they love because of a
mistake they made
I wonder how people can kill people just because they are not of their
religion

Rita

I wonder how friends' connection work
I wonder why we love and why we hate
Why our hearts feel pain and they love
Why people trust and why do they believe

I wonder how our hearts decide
The quantity of feelings that we want
To share or to hide
 the truth we want to realize
and truth that we ignore throughout our lives
I wonder how friends' connection works
And I wonder who loves me in this world

Tom

I'm sitting in my room, I feel the air leaving my lungs, I'm staring at the phone, "Please answer.... Please "I'm begging you
I'm not Breathing, please answer,
Why won't you answer?!
"I need you please", my air is running out, tears are choking me.
My phone rang, she finally answered.
"What do you want now? I'm busy", Mia asked me. I need help, please. There is no response, she doesn't return a message. I need help, please answer me ...., there is no response, she doesn't return a message. Fine! I'm done with you, but I know I can't leave. And I wonder what I did wrong. I've been here for you, I supported you. Why can't you do the same?! I sometimes wonder, what happened? How did we get so far apart? We used to talk every night, we used to talk about everything, what happened? And I wonder, what happened to us? And if we can ever fix it?

Zainab

I wonder why people get greedy when they have everything someone else lacks.
I wonder when will we ever feel complete?
They say "it's our nature"
But nature was never greedy

Light and warmth are provided by the sun
We are never gonna freeze
Plants clear the air and provide food
Humans cut trees to build houses that have no life, just houses no homes
They produce unhealthy food and pollute the air
Wild animals, fish and birds all lived happily on earth
Till humans greedily attacked them all
Those innocent creatures, never harmed without a threat, are being hunted in a huge number leading to extinction
A saying in my language says, "humans are the biggest enemy to themselves". They didn't lie- Humans are a threat and an enemy for everyone, not just themselves
I wonder when life will ever be peaceful
When will all the rotten things disappear
But I remember that this life won't be too long
We should do better so we win the afterlife and live in heaven

Mahdi

I wonder,
I wonder if peace will roam the world like everyone wishes to.
I wonder if global warming can actually be fixed after all the damage humans caused.
I wonder if a wailing mother crying over her dead children's bodies will actually see them again.
I wonder and I wonder and I wonder
What happens after we die?
What happens if we humans learn how to live in peace?
What if we actually lived in peace, would the earth look any different?
Would suicide rates decrease? Would the numbers of missing children decrease?
Would "evil" disappear?
Those are all questions that go through my head every day. Single. Day.

And as a 17-year-old they shouldn't.
I should be thinking about video games or prom or even my next outfit,
But no, instead I wonder about the things I wonder about
Like how can I lead two different countries at war to peace?
I still wonder if I can send every message, I'm willing to, to the world.

Arielle

I wonder.

I wonder a lot.

Too much, maybe.

I wonder how we humans came to be, and I wonder why I said that thing the other day and if I should've said something else. If that thing that I said was wrong and if I hurt the person I spoke to by saying those words.

I wonder why I act the way that I act.

Why do I like drawing instead of sports?

Why do I hang out with the kind of people I do?

Why do I have such a hard time feeling anything that has to do with hate?

Why do I let people hurt me again and again and again despite knowing better?

I wonder why I wonder so much because I hate wondering more than anything. It makes me crumble under every thought as it gets worse and worse.

I hate wondering, yet it's what I do almost every night when I go to bed, every morning when I wake up, and every second of my life.

When I find myself not wondering, the moment I make the realization, I begin to wonder.

I wonder what would happen if I were to stop wondering.

Jack

I wish to have a beautiful dress, glass hills and a wonderful ball. Oh, wait I got confused with a fairytale, this world is not a place where wishes come true. But, what if... just considering... I wish... I.... I WISH LIFE WAS NOT AS BAD! *Heavy breathing* I'm sorry... You know, sometimes I wonder, why do we hate each other? Why are we... why can't we not hate? I don't need an answer. *sigh* I know the answer, we all always knew. If the world was perfect, then we wouldn't have a meaning, if everyone loved each other.... if there were no fights. but it's impossible! I WONDER IF IT'S POSSIBLE TO HAVE NO SUICIDES! NO SKIN COLOR! NO MONEY! I wonder, what if the world wasn't hard, if it wasn't hard to smile, to breathe, to work in my dream job, to have a family, have a house. I wonder if a reality with no wishes is real.

You know, maybe I have one wish, that wishes were a real thing and not just a stupid fairytale.

"Imagine there's no people, it's easy if you try..." Dear fairy godmother- bibidi bobidi boo, no pain will be in you.

Partner Writing: We Are From

Jack and Tom

We are different, on two different sides, living in the same world. From a young age we learn that fairy tales exist, the perfect world, with a good ending. But in the end, we all wonder, is it really possible. Are people even able to live without fighting? Can a fairytale end happily when we are both alive. I wonder. I wonder. If our differences are that bad. If we are able to live side by side.

Will a Knight in shiny armor come and save us? Is our witch that bad? Did you watch Wicked? It's not related! Well, it kinda is... two sides, two stories, different but best friends. Even the wizard, wanting to make Oz perfect, ended up ruining everything with hate. I wonder why I'm not in bed right now, sleeping and dreaming about perfection. And I wonder why we are like this.

Rita and Mahdi

We are from,

We are from the north and the south,
From being stuck in our house. Love or hate served on a plate,

We are from escaping and overcoming,
From words and thoughts that are numbing.

We are from thoughts we never say,
From words we will regret, do so or get a threat.

We are from light but thunder some say were stuck, some say were under.
From parts that are broken equally unspoken.

We are from the same roof but not so same,
From knowing different and feeling diverse,
But living in combat does disperse.
We are from understanding life in different ways,
From planting seeds that we might waste,
From loving people that we hate,
Oh, take me to that freedom gate.

Oh, we are from.

We are from celebrating different dates,
From coming home in different shapes,
And putting on our hero capes.

Oh, we are from the same problems we need to solve,
And from them we should evolve.

"Do not stand at my grave and weep. I am not there; I do not sleep.
I am a thousand winds that blow, I am the diamond glints on snow, I
am the sun on ripened grain, I am the gentle autumn Rain."

From light comes we and we come from light,
We are from a big land that needs urgent sight.

Shahar and Zainab

I am from Iksal.
I am from Yavne.
I am from Friday prayers.

I am from shabbath rest.
I am from my mom's grape leaves.
I am from my mom's couscous and schnitzel.
We are from the characteristics
of powerful women.
We are from writing feelings where
our dreams are healing. We are
from big and loving families.
We are from Israel.

Arielle and Mohammad

We are from a place that offers a space for religion and race
A place that is supposed to give democracy and free speech a warm
embrace.
A place of diversity, of culture, and grace,
Where religion and race each have to find their space.

Children's laugh fades to fear where the Israeli bombs are heard sharp
and clear
Borders lock yet in the darkness voices still rise,
Voices that still wait for their demise

A place where faith is woven into the air,
Yet sometimes, it feels like too much to bear.

A refuge that is ours to take,
But giving to others would be a mistake.

We dream of a place we can all belong
Where no one's faith dominates the song
And a place that will forget our rights and wrongs.

The rivers murmur, the winds allude,
To battles fought, old wounds renewed.
Neighbors watch with wary eyes,
As hopes for calm begin to die.
The land we love so strong and proud now hears the whispers of a troubled crowd
For hearts to mend, we need a future we can defend.
But first, we ought to learn how -- on each to depend.

Children's laughter fades to fear when the Israeli bombs are heard sharp and clear.

On the other side domes are in the air, sirens calling "beware, beware".

War offers space for scars and life equals smoking cigars,
Yet peace offers a way to end the pain, stop the strife, and honor every human life.

Musings

Jack: A Black Heart

For some reason my heart is black, I mean that people who are "different than me" are a weird concept. But you know what is the weirdest part about it? I am nonbinary and still judge genders based on how people look... I feel disgusted when I see 2 boys or girls kiss, but I like both and have a girlfriend? So how does this work exactly?

I feel bad for my thoughts, I just wish I could erase my mind and start over. I am a coordinator in "Krembo Wings"[3] and have autism and still my mind makes sounds of "eww". I want to believe I am a good person but every time I see an Arab I get scared, a feeling that I don't choose to feel and I know it's wrong. And still, I protect them when my friends say that all of them are terrorists. So here is the important question? Am I stupid? If I told anyone about those feelings, I would be considered weird, weirder than I am already considered. Looking in the mirror, why is the mirror not broken? Why am I still considered nice, perfect to protect the outsider, freedom fighter, when my thoughts are absolutely against it. Someone stabbed me with a knife, by someone I mean- my mind.

As I am writing I also start to doubt my writing skills, "I am a screenwriter goddammit, how can my writing be that bad!!!"

So dear thoughts, you can get lost, because even if you still exist, I will still be the good person that people see me as.

Zainab: Broken Hearts

A cold person isn't heartless. It's just a person who has a broken heart

---

3   A popular youth service movement in Israel

and happiness and kindness are trying to escape through the cracks
of their broken heart.

Mohammad: Nature

Mother Nature, did we leave you behind.
Do you ever intend to return to the times of sun worship, not hiding
it from?
to earth that is sacred, and rivers that were wild and unconfined.
before we forgot how to love you.

I love you always but yet I hurt you.
Not by preference, but with the weight of a world which takes and
does not give.
Instead of advocating for you, I contribute towards hurting you.
trapped in the cycle that sees devastation as progress.

It is not me; it is everyone.
We cry, why should I transform when the world fails to change.
And then I see, if it is not me, then I am the decay.
If I remain idle, I am the problem.

Mother Nature, do you still hear us?
Do you still forgive us, even though we keep failing you?
Will you heal, despite our foolishness, or will you turn away from us
and leave us to reap the devastation we have sown?

Guide us back before all that is left is silence.
Show us how to appease you once more.
before we lose you forever.

Orit: The Dove

Dove, flying through the sea of dreams.
Restless, searching for those who their desires will fulfill.
Always looking for those determined and eager to excel
Endlessly passionate people, who want to achieve and learn.
We should all learn from those people, who so grandly succeed
So the dove can finally sleep in peace.

Rochelle: Drowning

I was drowning in more ways than one,
Lost within a sea of sorrow,
A sea you warned me of, time and again,
Yet still, I drifted—
Clinging to a thin thread,
Full of guilt and aching for forgiveness.
Beneath the surface, my secrets lay heavy,
A burden unseen,
For hiding there was no longer an escape.
And if I spoke, would judgment follow?
Would shadows trail me wherever I turned?
I was trapped,
Bound by the silence of my shame.
Then, through the depths, I heard your voice.
Soft as light breaking through storm clouds.
"Why are you here?" you asked,
And your words, tender as they were,
Broke through my helplessness.
You gathered the bullets of my despair,
Each one wound I thought would never heal,
And stitched the broken pieces of my heart.
With threads of hope.

You bore my pain as though it was your own,
Though your wounds ran deeper than mine,
You held me with love.
Those words cannot contain.
And in your love,
The thin thread I held grew stronger.
Through the piles of shame that bound me,
Your hand reached out for mine.
It lifted my soul from my despair.
Filling me with warmth
I had never been close to feeling.
You became my refuge,
A shield against storms
In your presence, I found peace—
A stillness I thought unattainable.
For as long as you have loved me,
Nothing else in this vast universe mattered.
As long as you were here.
The weight of the world fell away,
And no force could break me.
No shadow could overcome the undying light you gave,
And no weapon formed against me shall ever prosper.

Shahar: A Painted Sky

The sky is painted in orange, yellow and blue. In those calm and warm
colors that remind me my time was well spent.
Smiling and laughing with all of you.

Maia

History Class

History classes, a mere box to check off on your busy schedule.
before trudging along to calculate the area of a circle.
History classes were spent learning about wars,
branded with a reputation that shifted humankind—
wars from which entire empires crumbled,
empires that fundamentally altered the world as we know it,
nations wiped off the face of the Earth.
remain mere subchapters under an era.

Yet somewhere along this sadistic path,
I became a firsthand source.
As history repeats itself,
those sources historians marked as most valuable.
wanted nothing more than to be stripped of that title,
laced with wounds that scarred souls.
My bones tremble, haunted by the thought
of a foregone outcome:
in a century that will eventually turn into a millennium,
I lie decayed six feet under the surface.
New kids will sit in history class,
watching the clock,
with bored expressions painted across their youthful faces,
its hands grazing the hours ever so slowly.
They will learn about this war—
the one that belonged to me.
They will memorize dates that authors deemed crucial,
the names of individuals who earned a bolded label
through inhumane actions that led them to be viewed as
unconventional.

Spending hours cramming for exams,
ones they long to pass while thinking of their future,
frustrated that this war, my war,
takes up so many dreadful chapters in the textbook.
A year will pass, and those students will disregard.
the wars that came after me.
The facts forgotten, only to be learned.
by another underdeveloped frontal cortex—
a bittersweet cycle,
a cycle that never makes room for the truth.
So she remains never learned.
Our story never reaches the altar,
displayed with photos they say marked history—
but really, they summarized it.
And we stand hopeful at the border,
the Day of the Dead surrounding us
with leaders crossing on red velvet carpets,
gates closing shamelessly on us.
To be forgotten is torment,
but to never be known is a line crossed.

A hypocrite I would be to harbor anger,
for I once skimmed the stories of those before me,
carelessly flipping through used pages,
only pausing on faces that felt strange.

In moments, I fantasize about the days.
when my consciousness granted me permission to be detached—
an ignorant bliss that slipped through my childlike fingers long ago.

So much time spent glorifying possibilities

that my reality descends into torment.
I once believed that God, the universe
bore a grudge against me—
until I realized the grass isn't always greener
and "what ifs" often become living nightmares.

I rise every single morning with freedom.
I wake up at all.
So I will proudly be part of a tragic history
I wish it could be rewritten with a "happily ever after".
I will assist in documenting who they were
because I see them as a vivid dream
in the back of my mind—
those who perished into dust,
their last breath dancing with the wind.
And those who will live to pass along the story,
that will be translated vaguely through time.
They will become open for interpretation,
symbolic.

Countless stories, lives that were more real
than any characters written by Kafka or Dostoevsky,
Jane Austen or Hemingway.

The names of those who waged war will go down in history,
written in bold, highlighting an important phrase—
It almost feels disrespectful.
They'll be remembered,
while those who should have never been counted
in the statistics of the dead
will become just a number.

So next time you sit at that desk—stop.
Time will forgive you.
Learn a story beyond the ones they teach you.
Because before you know it, your voice is silenced,
your story untold.

May the story of my people never be forgotten,
but may my name be known
by at least one child who learns about this war
when I'm no longer here.
If they forced me to play a role
in their malicious games,
if these men stole my youth for personal gain,
then damn right, my name will be spoken
on the lips of those who come after me.
I'm taking my rightful place in history.

Part II: International Student Writers

In this section, we hear from thirteen young writers who joined our weekly sessions from Bosnia and Herzegovina, Kenya, Kosovo, the Philippines, Rwanda, Sweden, and Turkey—alongside their Israeli and Palestinian peers. Their writing explores diverse identities, personal scars and pains, musings and wonders, musical inspirations, and the similarities and differences that shape their lives.

I Am From

Endina (Kosovo)

I am from
I am from a beautiful place,
A place where wrongs remain untold.
Though I never lived to see it all,
The voice of people still unfolds.

I come from lands of mountains high,
where joy and music fill the sky.
Belief is what we seek to find,
when hope is lost, cast to the tide.

I come from a place where food is shared,
Yet the hunger in our hearts is always there.
I hope I'll come from a place you know is loved,
Because it had its people fighting for it.

Noam (Sweden)

I come from different worlds, with dark pasts and deep cultural roots of sorrow, but simultaneously with a big joy for life.

I was born and raised in a city built on new encounters and revolutionary innovation, from parents with diverse backgrounds.

I am from a mom, born and raised in an unfamiliar country, from immigrant parents, one fleeing from persecution, and the other one in hope of a brighter future.

I am from a dad, born in one country but raised in another one. This was a new country, built of immigrants with a dream, to create a safe haven for a vulnerable and persecuted group of people.

I come from a past where my parents met in the most unexpected place, the largest city on the planet.

I am from a family where diverse cultures are intertwining, a family that is open to changes, and a family that is resilient.

I am from a family that travels, explores, and is open minded to all people and cultures different to our own.

I am part of a family spread over continents, countries and barriers, a family where face to face encounters is rare.

I am from a family celebrating love, kindness, and peace in the community we call earth.

I am from a family not part of one country, not part of one group, but instead part of life.

Maria (Philippines)

I am from a country full of successes, yet also triumphs—the Philippines. I am from a region with a culture that would warmly give smiles, attract, and invite neighbors of differences.

I am from traveling, exploring, and walking through noisy streets that are filled with talk and laughter. I am from being exposed to the festivals and rich traditions that celebrate our heritage.

I am from my grandparents' treasures, giving me the chance to have such great parents to be entwined in my life forever. I am from that family of five, woven with diverse stories that we come together with inside the pillars of our house.

I am from the aroma of spiced and cooked food filling the air from the magic of my mother, dishes as testaments prepared with care. I am from the hardworking hands of my father, keeping us held up with resilience. I am from the shared stories, interests, and knowledge of two of my sisters, leaving out no one.

I am from many things, but all from one place—a place that holds my heart, my history, and my future, reminding me that no matter where I wander, I carry this essence within me, a compass guiding me home to the Philippines.

Amina (Bosnia & Herzegovina)

I want to escape it. I want to run away from it. It makes me sick and scared and it follows me wherever I go. All I see are blurry lines and a vague vision of what the world could be, but it keeps spinning and nothing is clear. People and places are blurry and I'm only sure of what I feel. The breeze that so graciously feeds my brain and the hand that holds me tight. The rain that washes over my face and the salty tears that flow with it. The kiss from a human and the kiss from the sun. The ground that keeps me from flying and the bed that keeps me from dreaming. The stories that I fall asleep to and more so the ones that wake me up. I feel the cold that gives me illness and the warmth that makes me dizzy. I feel the people that I hold and the words that they give me. I feel it because it's real and it's real because I made it that way. I am from the fear of making nothing real. From spinning on this ride until my body is left alone, and my soul is wondering. Wondering why I am running away. Why can't I sit with it? Why does nothing make me so scared and I yearn for something, anything? But when I lay my head on the cold ground and close my eyes forever, I'll see that the world is steady and I was the one spinning. Nothing is very clear and real now and it's my comfort because I know it. We all return to what we know. I am from nothing, and to that I return.

Sanskriti (India/Rwanda)

I am from a place where people start their day early in the morning,
I am from a place where the population is the largest with excessive pollution,
I am from a place where cows and dogs run around the streets,
I am from a place where diversity floats on the wind with different cultures together.
I am from a place where all festivals are celebrated with fun and respect.
I am from a place where there is a lot to do with family and friends,
But I am from a place that is not always perfect but also filled with obstacles.
I am from a place where study is prioritized more than a child's health,
I am from a place where dangers rage at every step you take,
I am from a place where criticizing is normalized in society,
I am from a place where women are mostly never safe around men, even their own family.
However, I am from a place where there is still support and understanding in people,
Now, I am from different countries in the world due to shifts.

Starting from a country where my life rages with my childhood memories and fun,
Now, I am from a place with a drastic history that is unforgettable.
I am from a place where safety and cleanliness are there with every step,
I am from a place where nature is taken care of and a main part of tourism,
I am from a place where the country still is developing,
I am from a place that minds its own business and is isolated.
I am from places that had different versions of me with a lot of teaching and love.

Nico (Sweden)

I am from two worlds,
Two worlds that intersect yet stand in stark contrast. I am from a world where all the colors of the rainbow are allowed to shine as brightly as they want to. I am from a place where I am allowed to shine as brightly as I want to. I am from a country that allows me to be who I want to be.
I am from a good heart.

But I am also from a place of ignorance.
I am from blissful ignorance, from a place dazzled by its own brilliance, colors so bright they cannot see one another.
I am from a country that chooses to ignore suffering, clinging to a fragile, ephemeral peace, like a naïve child.

I am from another place—near, yet impossibly distant, just a border away.
I am from a life that has never felt truly my own, a life unwanted but mine to carry.
I am from wanting to run away, and leave all my academic achievements behind, leaving them to be nothing more than vanity.

I am from a feeling of not belonging in the place I should belong. Close, but not quite close enough. Similar but not quite the same. The equivalence points never reached, the titrant always turning blue. I am from unheard words, dismissed thoughts, voices disregarded.

I am from a place where people are like fireworks, we rise, then shine brightly for a short while as we try to imprint the world with our existence and then fade with death.
I am from wanting to be the largest, most spectacular and outstanding firework, only to die the fastest death.
I am from a place that encourages that. A place that is a creature under the hands of Greed.
I am caught in between the two worlds, finding a place for myself in both, yet truly at home in neither.

I am from sitting in the passenger seat of my own life, an unknown identity.
I don't know to which world I belong.
But I wish to believe I am from a good place.

Nahla (Kenya):

I am from a hidden past. A hidden identity. Do I really know where I am from? I was told Nahla is your name and wherever you are is home. I ask myself a lot of questions.... the main one being my origin, my real self. I'll never really know because the past I'm told is one I don't want to believe and the one I want is mainly peer pressured and not the real me. I hope I get to know my past.

Lamija (Bosnia & Herzegovina)

I am from a place where flowers cannot grow,
where birds rise only to fall, wings broken mid-flight.

A place that sparkles to the outside eye,
Yet shadows lurk with knives hidden tight.
I grew up in fear, … a fear of standing apart,
of being cast out, for sins I could not name.
What if I'm different? Am I a sinner for that?
I offered you love; you returned only lies,
anger, a game, a hollow disguise.
It was joy for you.
Nobody else.

I am from a place where pride is worn like a crown,
yet we build ourselves up by tearing others down,
where power is drawn from insult and scorn.

I came with love, but you taught me hate,
and now, as I turn my back on it all,
don't dare try to stop me,
for I am done with sorrow.
I am done with feeling small.

Duru (Turkey)

When I was little, I liked to imagine that I came from a place that's filled with rainbows and unicorns where the sun never sets. In reality I come from a place where the sun only comes up once in a while. I don't know why I didn't like the place I came from as a kid. Every night we ate dinner together. Sometimes that dinner table was filled with laughter and joy. But sometimes it was filled with silence cutting through the air like a knife. We used to play games or watch movies once in a while. I remember loving the time I spent with the people that make me who I am today. But now I barely see them. I can't recognize where I come from, let alone the people whom I love the most.

I didn't appreciate the good times back then and only focused on the bad stuff, which led me to want only good things to happen. But what I hadn't realized was that, in order to have a rainbow you need the rain too. Since I know that now, I can easily tell you where I come from. I come from a family that's loving and caring where everyone looks out for each other. I come from a household that's filled with fights and arguments that took days and months to forget. I come from a place warmer than any sun could ever make me feel.

Now I'm proud of where I come from and the person that I have become.

This Scar Is From

Amina

Cloudy, gray sky is an omen for rain. It comes so we know how to get inside, and if we don't, it's our fault we get wet. It hurt a lot when you left without warning, and it hit me like a train that you weren't coming back. You left forever; you left a scar. You left behind kind words and warm hugs, people and places. Everything you loved and worked hard for you left like you hardly worked and loved. But I forgive you. We can forgive scars only when others give them to us. The most pain and hurt we do ourselves. You were just a small cut at first, and I liked you so much I kept cutting my skin to see more of you. But now I can't stop bleeding, you're all over me and I can't see myself. This scar isn't from losing you, but from having you. I won't lose you. I won't heal, as I love looking at the pain you and I have caused me. It brings me greater joy than the one I'd feel letting you go. I forgive this ugly world for everything because you are in it. This is a rough life because you live it. These cold hands because you hold them, and this misgiving hour, because only you know when. Cloudy, gray sky is an omen for rain. It comes so we know to get out of the house and water ourselves like flowers, and if we don't, it's our fault we never grow.

Sanskriti

This scar is from my overthinking.
It comes from replaying the most painful moments far more often than the good memories.
One small mistake in a day becomes a spiral, pulling along every regret and misstep I've ever made.
I wonder if this cycle will ever end—or if I'll find forgiveness, even from myself.

This scar is from being an only child.
No one to confide in, no one to look up to—just me, surrounded by silence,
Waiting for the day I no longer feel so alone in my home.
People assume that being an only child means getting everything you want, being spoiled and indulged.
But material gifts don't replace the warmth of genuine love.
Instead of envy and judgment from others, what about understanding?
Being an only child doesn't define the way I think,
but the loneliness and assumptions have left their mark.

Julie

I have three main scars, one from myself, one from family and friends and one has haunted me from the second I was born and it is being a Palestinian.

The scar from family and friends is a scar that I've been struggling with for years, which is eating without feeling guilty, or without anyone making me feel guilty. From age seven I used to ask my mom why I'm not skinny like those other girls? Why is my belly too fat? My mom comforted me then. Years later my dad asked why my belly was so big. To this day I can't accept my body, every time I eat something I shouldn't it makes me feel like that same day. To this day, I was never happy with how I looked, I hated my body. Every single time someone comments on how I look it's like putting a knife inside a wound and twisting it, and I have to smile and pretend that everything is fine and that comment was funny.

The second scar is my favorite, it's hard to call a scar even but sometimes it's one of the reasons I want to fall and break and sometimes it's why I live, it's what's keeping me alive, this scar is being a dancer, especially one who started her path in teenage years. I always feel that I'm behind and no matter how hard I run it's like I'm running towards something that keeps running away. But when I'm selected and just hearing "good job," it's like everything fades away. Being a dancer healed my wound, healed the ones that weren't seen, but at the same time it opened a bigger wound and that is never being good enough.

The third scar is who I am, a Palestinian living under the Israeli occupation, I walk in the streets of my country, my city, my home, where I'm from and I don't feel that I belong, every time I walk near the old city I feel like a stranger in my homeland, I also feel anger and sadness, and at the same time guilt. When I travel anywhere abroad, I feel at home more than I ever felt at home here. When you walk in Jerusalem you can feel the tension in the air, automatically you go to survival mode, imagining scenarios in your head in case something happens,

When I walk, I make sure not to put my hands in my pocket so I'm not a suspect in their eyes. When I'm at work I have to see the broken eyes of a customer whose brother is arrested for an unknown reason, where his lawyer or family can visit. This scar is who I am, a Palestinian living under the Israeli occupation.

Every day I realize more that I don't have scars anymore, I used to, but every once in a while, a scar reopens and it doesn't seem like it's gonna close any time soon.

Anonymous

This scar is more of an invisible scar. I call it my first scar. I got it before I saw the light. Still in Mamah's womb, I was unwanted, rejected and almost denied life. An unsuccessful abortion. Brought into a world where the first people I met were actually family but not friendly.
I rarely speak about my scar to avoid more pain. I prefer hiding it from everyone. It's better if I hold up my smile and shoulders high as I make myself a better future. I imagine my scar is invisible.

Maria

This scar. This scar is from the years I have spent yearning for friendships that never truly wanted me, from trying to level with people who didn't see me for who I really was. It was a deep scar. This scar was from the times I gave too many pieces of myself to those who didn't care enough to hold them.

This scar is from wanting to earn their respect, their affection. It was from trying to blend myself into their world, also from realizing that I was losing myself in the process. It was from seeing myself being a smaller person with every failed attempt to connect but continuing it as if it was the right thing to do.

This scar is from the cut that the lonely feeling scraped into me. The more I reached out, the smaller I seemed. This scar is from the length of time it took me to stop looking outside for validation, the time it took me to turn inward. This was once fresh, from the neglect I did to those who truly saw me. It was a scar, from a healed wound on seeing the ones who really knew me and still chose to love me– my family.

This scar became one from leaning into them, with all their flaws and love that offered me comfort and understanding I once tried to find elsewhere. This scar is from the reminder that I never have to shrink to fit into someone else's world. This scar is from removing the masks, the pretense, the chase for approval.

This scar is from that painful but valuable journey. This scar is from knowing that some people may never even be meant to be. Despite that, this scar is from the healing that came when I allowed myself to be reminded of my family.

When I look at it, this scar is now from a lesson. It is from the importance of knowing who truly your back has, who will always meet you where you are, even when the world seems to turn away. The scar is there, but it doesn't mean it still hurts the way it once did.

This scar is from learning that true connection starts with yourself and the ones who have always been there, waiting for you to realize you don't have to earn their love– you just have to be yourself.

Lamija

Childish story indeed but for me it was a hurricane.

"The ice will melt, and my heart will long for you and your love. I didn't care about the competition, just for that one moment. Seeing you lean against the door frame, gazing into her eyes as the final flight of a swan, I felt myself suffocating once again. The melancholic melody brought back every small moment I shared with you. Dignity above all; I'd sooner falsify a song than show tears. The victory was not ours, but the night flowed with letters and words, and I felt every flame which burned them.

I swore to let you go, but it's a sin to kill a muse." (The Letter 63. by Miya L. L.)

The victory was indeed mine, for every cut made a sparkly night. The song I was meant to sing that day, just three verses, was Never Enough by Loren Allred. Its lyrics captured my feelings perfectly:

"I'm trying to hold my breath.

Let it stay this way.

Can't let this moment end..."

He, a soul I adored, sat right in front of me with a guitar in his hands and a girl by his side. My heart ached, but my face stayed cold, and my voice was steady. When the words "Can't let this moment end" passed my lips, I remembered our November.

I had asked if I could keep you company, and you responded with a sneer: "Of course, why are you even asking?" I replied that I didn't know and called you "weird". But that "weird" wasn't what others whispered behind your back to mock you; it was something softer, born of childish thoughts.

You read Life Is a Dream by Pedro Calderón de la Barca, and I read Romeo and Juliet, the balcony scene. I loved the silence we shared. Then a friend, who thought only of herself and her ego, interrupted. Our moment was no longer the same, but your glances grew more beautiful; until that, too, was stolen by rumors.

I'm sorry I was a fool, as much as you were one, too

Doga

It sounds ridiculous now but this scar is from your love. Learning to find comfort in your absence by pain, mostly. Maybe because loving you was painful. So, to remember our times together and not forget you I must feel pain, I thought. Then, I found a blade in my room. It looked shiny and new as ever. As the blade went through my skin and my blood started to run down my hands, I felt like you were there, right next to me. I remembered our times together. And how happy and sad I felt at the same time. I never enjoyed that but it made me feel safe. After the wound started healing, the scar remained. Now every single time I look back at it, it reminds me of you. Carrying you on my body, basically having you with me everywhere I go doesn't feel comforting anymore. I know what I did was wrong and I indeed regret it terribly. Maybe the best that I can do is to let you go and accept that it's over between us. I moved on but you still somehow remind me. With a single notification on my phone or even just me walking past the places we have gone together. But I am not bitter anymore. Because I know that the love in me will never fade away.

Adir

Was it easy to take?
Cause you were there,
and I was no longer.
No one there was looking after my sake.

And those new scars of an old fear,
This emotional reminder of a great wall,
Blocking love in and out at all.
The silent scream of my youth falling as a tear.

And all along you had the nerve to act as if righteous,
As if it was a mistake that you could wash away,
And if you are sad, I hope it'll forever stay.
Sort of a scar for it to be just.

Do You Really Know Me

Lamija

People judge before they meet.

I didn't want to be a stranger to you, so I tried to get closer, even though fear clawed at me. But I wasn't afraid of you; I was afraid of someone hurting you.

There were moments when, as a child, I dreamed of hiding in your embrace, safe from the world. Perhaps because you seemed to carry the peace I never had but desperately chased.

In the silence, which was never awkward with you, I wanted to stay, to forget everything and wake up in a better tomorrow. But you laughed at my scars, the ones the world gave me, and the ones I gave myself.

Laugh all you want. It doesn't matter. You laugh because you don't understand. You don't know that you've been my muse; the reason for three books, nineteen poems, six compositions, and sixty letters. Laugh, because what else could you do?

Call your nemesis friends, and I'll be a fool or a madman. I was foolish enough to believe you would stay.

I loved your smile. Now, we walk past each other without 'Hi', and you 'll still say you know me. Yet, I still see when you're hurting, even if you'll never notice I care.

Call it boredom, I'll call it love. I cared, I loved, and I'll keep loving. Even now. Even tomorrow. And you'll keep hating, because you never truly knew me.

I wonder what you'd say if I asked you, "Did you ever really know me?"

Nico

Do you really know me?

You thought you did. Everyone believes they know someone, in some way or another.

You declared to understand me expertly, to know precisely how I felt. Yet, you never saw the truth. You chose not to. You only knew the version of me you created in your mind, the one that fit neatly into your idea of what I should be. Instead, you clung to your own delusion, treating me as an accessory to your life, a reflection of your misconstrued desires. I didn't exist for you to mold, control, or display when it suited you.

The day your rage consumed you—rage because I wouldn't come to you, wouldn't comfort you, wouldn't assure you everything would be fine after your tirade of insults and degradation—I was terrified of you. The memory of that moment, when everything around me seemed to shatter in your fury, replayed endlessly in my mind.

Did you know?

Did you know that the one you deemed a threat, someone you said was only after me for their gain, took my side as soon as they learned what you'd done?

Did you know that they stayed with me for hours because I was too scared to go home, knowing you'd be waiting to know you'd be there, waiting for me?

Did you know that the people you dismissed as untrustworthy, the ones you said would betray me, were the first to stand by me when they'd learned what you'd done?

What if, next time, it wasn't just your words that wounded? What if your anger found a new way to hurt?

No. You didn't know. And you simply don't want to know. Because to you, I was no more human than a flower in a vase, mere vanity

- a prize to be displayed. You wanted me to be your most valuable possession, just so you could have someone to soothe your ego. You'll never change—I've long since realized that. Some people are just impossible to please. As soon as they get what they thought they wanted, they always want more. I know that. You know that. Though you'll never acknowledge that. But you don't know me.
And I'm glad you never will.

Noam

Do you really know me?
I met a person with big aspirations.
A person who, from outside, was blazing with confidence.
A person who, from the first second you meet him, makes an impression of robustness.
I thought he was kind and knowledgeable about various aspects of life.
I thought this person had a plan laid out in front of him, a plan to succeed in life.
But after a while, when I got familiar with him, the truth emerged
This was not a person filled to the brim with confidence.
This was not a person with some grand ambition, striving towards something.
In reality, it was someone standing on the edge of the abyss of adulthood, hoping for the best.
It was a person who, with mixed emotions, stumbled into the unknown, into the next chapter of life.
Then and there, I realized that this person was me.

Where I Am Now

Noam

Where I am now.

I am in a place, at a certain period in my life, where everything depends on carpe diem, to seize the day. My teachers always tell me to do this, do that. They give me assignments piling up on each other, layers upon layers forming a high tower. They tell me that the only reasonable way to reach one's aspirations in life is to perform in school. The same sentiment echoes from my parents.

And to them I respond:

Yes, no one can deny that school is important, but does school really reflect carpe diem? For me, carpe diem means doing whatever comes to mind, if I want to learn to play an instrument, then I should do it. If I want to travel and experience dazzling adventures, then I should do it.

I am now in a place where it is difficult for me to reconcile what my brain conveys with what my heart says. My brain tells me to seize the day and use the few hours of light I have to study, to please the outside world and do what I expect of me. Instead, my heart screams for me to enjoy life, to do the things I have dreamed of, to seize the day. Sadly, reality has caught up with me, and now the dreams are put off on a shelf, waiting for me to implement them. I am now living a life ruled by society, constantly balancing between my dreams and the expectations placed upon me.

Maria

I started looking for her. Running in the shadows and finding the light, if ever she is actually shined by a light.

But I saw her blurry figure at the end of a bridge onto another, waiting for the right time to cross it. She was at a turning point, standing between the end of something familiar and the beginning of something unknown.

She felt heavier, afraid that she'd fall with the weight of bigger choices she is now carrying. Each one felt like it was shaping a version of her that she is yet to understand.

I saw something by her side. Failure accompanying her. I saw it whispering doubts in her ear. It's the opportunities she let slip, the moments she knew she could've done better in. Was it the one preventing her from crossing over? It stings, sometimes more than she let on. But I saw the "failure" still standing beside her– I realized, it wasn't the enemy. It was teaching her.

The teacher knew that there were small victories. The moments she spent late nights poring over papers and pages, feeling like it's all too much, only to see the results come back better than expected. She stood there, seeing the subtle reminders to keep moving forward.

And, she did. Step by step. Where is she now? I tried to analyze myself. Then my vision became clear. She is in the in-between of someone she no longer was and also not yet of who she will be. She was in an imperfect place of doubts and hopes. She is still growing, still figuring out what's next, and that's okay.

Lamija

I was standing in the cold. Snowflakes were falling, and I stood there without a jacket, gloves, or a hat. I felt nothing, yet uneasy with myself. I was not cruel… I wanted something impossible, so I stood in the cold, hoping to reach the world. Now I realize how cold it was.

"Painting is a process," you said, and I laughed because I never knew if it was real or not. But then: "Painting is a process of love," appeared on a piece of paper. It is love, but there is no place for you and me. Now, as I write this on my way home, two years later, snowflakes are falling again, making a beautiful view. It's cold, but this time I feel joy because I've let the burden go.

Don't confuse me anymore.

Nahla

I look at myself in the mirror. A pretty smile. A pretty face. A scarless skin. I am a happy girl who loves where she is. My achievements are what make me happy. I am moving towards my goal; being independent. I am now taking small and large steps to my independence era. I am proud of who I am becoming. At last, I can walk straight and say I am me. I am who I am.

I am myself. I am who I want to be.

Julie

Where am I now?

Where I am, a question that goes through my mind every day, where I am, where I'm going, where I'm headed, am I dreaming?

For over a year a genocide has been happening kilometers far away from us, from me. I wake up go on with my routine, (working, studying, eating...), then all of a sudden a moment of realization strikes me: in Gaza, children are facing death every day, dying from hunger, shaking in tents, looking for anything to eat to fill their empty stomachs, that their parents are trying to fill as well, wishing to have an egg for breakfast, or even smell it.

Every single day there are new horrifying stories, another war crime committed against my people. It's getting worse every single day, hour, second. All these crimes are streamed all over social media and the internet. Day after day there is new horrifying footage from Gaza, there are testimonies, and I just wonder, is it possible there is no humanity left in the world? The world knows about Hind, a 6-year-old who was hit with 72 shots in 6 seconds. The world knows about the father who got a birth and death certificate on the same day for his twin children, they know about Abood, who was kidnapped and tortured. I wake up every day to a heavy heart, just a two-hour drive a tragedy unfolds, and yet we are incapable of lending a hand. It's a cruel irony that in the parallel world we live in, I'm privileged to live a decent life and others are deprived of the most basic human rights and need to live. Where am I? I'm here, yet my mind is with those children, women, and men, who are facing death, hunger, a genocide.

Endina

Where I am now
It's a shadowed place, yet I still find the light.
That's how you survive, isn't it right?
Surrounded by people, but the warmth feels fake,
I climb endless stairs just for you to say,
Kind of lost myself and that is actually okay
Even though you tried to stay, but never really did.
But I made it through despite those who got in my way.
That's how it goes, the price I had to pay.

Asja

Where I am now is someplace unimaginable to my four-year-old me. I envy her innocence. Where she spent her days was grandma's couch, watching cartoons and eating red raspberries. Grandma is dead now. The last time she called, I did not pick up because I was busy. Where

I am now is regret. When I was a young girl, I was insecure about not having a chest. I padded my bras. Now I hide my breasts under baggy clothes. Where I am now is a corner hiding from a man following me home. Wherever I was, I wanted something more. Longer time to watch cartoons, bigger chest, smaller chest, more attention, less attention. I always wanted to, but I never learned how to have or be.

"Love me more," I cried to him while cutting the flowers in his garden. I only wanted to keep the hydrangea. I saw myself in its grandiosity. I cut the red flowers, the yellow ones and the hydrangeas were the only ones left. I looked at them and felt repulsed. They were dull, boring, and lifeless. However, what bothered me the most was that there was nothing else to cut. I kept moving my fingers, opening and closing the scissors. I heard the metal blades sliding with one another. Where I am now is frustratingly staring at the hydrangea. The petals look pathetically blue. I want to rip it out of the soil with its roots.

Oh God, I cannot focus on that anguish. I am too cold. In this cold, I can just look at them. Suddenly, they seem calm, peaceful, and kind. My cheeks are rosy, lips frostbitten, hands frail. My eyelids are dropping, and I want to sleep. Where I am now is embracing the warmth of a blue hydrangea flower.

Sanskriti

I am in a place where failure and success determine your worth as a person.
I am in a place where people may share the same thoughts but quickly turn against each other.
I am in a place where bullying is not just normalized but celebrated as something remarkable.
I am in a place where racism is disguised as humor, making a mockery of different races.

I am in a place where being different in any way makes you a target for ridicule.

I am in a place where jealousy thrives, and genuine appreciation is nowhere to be felt or found.

I Wonder

Asja

I wonder if I will ever give him almond chocolate. My cousin returned home a month ago. He always brings sweets with him. This time he brought chocolate with almonds. I love almonds. The first time I tried them; I couldn't describe the taste. I remember how firm they felt in my fingers. However, at the first crunch, its flavor unfolded. Gentle. I could imagine the smell of almond trees, dancing with the breeze. There was comfort in that imagery. Presence of something greater than this, yet pure. I always feel that gentleness when eating an almond. However, the almond chocolate did not capture this. It was too sweet. There were four pieces of it. The three chocolates were eaten the next day.

One night, I was studying late and I noticed the last piece. I wanted it for a sugar rush, as it was late and I needed to stay awake. I craved it. It was during the week we didn't talk. I remembered him and put it aside. In February, we were on a trip. We spent most of our money on eating. I thought he'd enjoy the almond chocolate. I felt purity again through resisting the sweetness. When I'd finished studying, I thought about how I'd look giving him a chocolate out of the blue. Fragile? The thought of it scared me. However, I didn't want anyone else to eat it.

In order to keep it safe, I have moved it to my room now. It's on the table. I saved it for him. Though I'm still scared my brother might come in and eat it, I am hiding the chocolate so I can give it to him. However, I "forget" to bring it each time I know I will see him. Because when I do, something withers within me. I know how he views me. I know what he's seen. He saw unspoken words written all over me.

Even worse, he's heard colors I've spoken. I didn't hear them myself. That's what scares me. The sweetness of chocolate can't veil the sick branches. Maybe, I should find a new hiding place. I'd hide them in my gloves. I wonder if I will give him the almond chocolate before it reaches its expiration date.

Elif

I wonder,
I wonder If I could be someone else
in the mirror of your eyes.
Erase the lines I've drawn with pain.

The warm memories seem to be so cold,
their glow turning into shadows.
a chill settling where the music once lived.

You see me now,
as a headache pulsing in your temples
a cockroach scurrying beneath the light
an itching sweater clinging to skin
I am everything you despise.

It hurts,
the way the sparkles in your eyes
dim and scattered like ashes
each time I speak.

And I wonder if an old broken record
once you loved to hear

can ever be more than
something you'd rather throw away.

Julie

I wonder whether I'll cease this endless running,
Running towards a dream that sleeps further away
Escaping from problems that keep sweating away
I wonder if I will ever stop running, every day,
will I ever be able to seize the day.
will I ever be able to pause and take it all in,
To breathe, to feel.
but I know the cost to feel everything at once. I tried for a moment.
It ached me more than the endless escape.
I wonder if I will ever surrender and let go of the rose with thorns
that I chose to hold.

I wonder if I ever would reclaim the happiness I felt as I was a kid
The simple life I once knew, where the sun rises and sits each day.
I wonder whether the smallest things which brought me joy will ever
bring me joy again.
I wonder if I will ever feel it all.
But why do I wonder when I feel nothing, but at the same time I feel
everything. So, I wonder…

Duru

A wish. Just one wish. I wonder. For what should I wish? Love?
Health? career? Wants? Needs? What? For what shall I wish? I don't
know. There are so many options. Why can't I wish for all, or wait can
I? Do I actually have to pick one? Can I pick more? Maybe infinite
wishes, but no that's just ungratefulness. Okay what about saying
them all in one breath?

no... they are still more than one wish. What about three wishes like Aladdin when he rubbed the old lamp? I can't rub my cake though. That would just be weird. I guess I can make one wish. I wonder who made this rule. Is there even a rule? I don't know anything. I just wanted to make a wish, just a wish, one wish...

Noam

I wonder why so few people find happiness.
I wonder why people can never settle for what they have, why they always yearn for something more.
I wonder what people define as happiness.
I wonder why some people go to bed with an empty stomach day in and day out, while others live in abundance, throwing away what others would desperately desire, as if it has no value. I wonder why I am one of the lucky ones, one that gets to go to school without paying any fees.

Why am I the one who worries about what shoes to wear to school, while others, much younger than me, go barefoot in search of work? I wonder why people like me seem to think that most others live like we do, as kings and queens in a democracy with free speech, and with laws that protect our lifestyles.

At the same time, I wonder why my society, my reality, is the one painted gray, the gray reality where the majority of people live in an illusion of what they think is happiness. In this same illusion, we place our elderly in slaughterhouses waiting for them to die.

Why are we the ones complaining about our lives, how hard they are, and about the chaotic world around us, burning from hopeless wars to the environmental crisis, while we live in our grand castles, unaffected by the flames.

I wonder why we, who have the resources to make our world a better place, choose not to.

I wonder how my reality coexists on the same burning planet others call home.

I wonder why people view our world through the lens of bright colors. How can they find happiness in the smallest gestures despite all the misery?

For me happiness is appreciating life, appreciating what you have.

And therefore, I wonder if I can become one of the lucky ones, not just in material wealth, but in finding true happiness by appreciating life.

Sanskriti

I wonder if I will break free from overthinking and finally feel free.
I wonder if I'll ever achieve something meaningful in life.

I wonder if I'll be able to make my parents genuinely happy and proud.
I wonder if there will ever be a turning point, a moment that changes everything for the   better.

I wonder if the weight of my insecurities will ever be lifted or if I'll always carry them with me.

I wonder if I'll ever find my true purpose or if I'm destined to keep searching endlessly.

I wonder, and I keep wondering, every day about life, its purpose, and my place.

Amina

Close your eyes before turning off the lights, the darkness that comes after is much brighter than the one you'd see had you kept them open while it was shining.

When I was little, I used to wonder how my parents knew the names of all streets, or why my skin wrinkled when I bathed. I wondered what would happen the day after, when I woke up, and I waited for the morning to live. The world around me was so big and it looked like an astounding place where humans are heroes. I wonder when I stopped wondering. When did I wake up disappointed? The leaves fell to the ground and the snow followed them. I was left there standing, unable to see any good. Nothing I ever knew of on the ground; I gave up my last hopes. I never wonder because I think I know it all, when really, I know less than I ever knew. The little girl in me is now long gone and it's better that way. She wouldn't like the world her new eyes see. Looks are deceiving and humans are cruel. I wonder what she would think of me. Doing to others what I'd hate to be done to me. Giving into the mess of existence. I'm now less than I ever was. My hair is longer and I grew taller, but my brain is eating me alive and my heart is smaller. Will I ever wait for the sun to rise instead of the moon? When the snow melts, and leaves start hanging from trees again, I will follow the path that's now uncovered. The same one that I walked before it snowed, before I knew nothing. Maybe I can learn again. Learn to see, to be the better that I'm looking for, to live for the child I once was. To wonder.

Opened eyes will get used to the dark even if they saw the brighter picture, but eyes that are closed to avoid disappointment will never know of the colors they could have seen.

Maria

I wonder.

Most of the time, I sit still always caught in a fragile moment of thought. Before doing something, there are pauses in between, wondering where each of my choices will lead me. Each move, small or grand, is onto a vast unknown. It's an intricate one between cause and effect.

I've been onto the idea that everything happens for a reason. It's a comforting belief but also the cause of my weary questions when life feels chaotic. This is because the pieces of my story fit together like a puzzle. Each heartbreak leads me to a picture far grander than I can envision. And then there's karma. Good or bad, I believe in it too, in the unseen occurrences of deeds that affect the scales of life. An action I do in this world, it is watching– always finding its way back to me, even if it's just a whisper carried through the wind.

So, I wonder every time. What significance will this specific action have in my life? Will this even cause anything? Is there a reason for this to happen?

Each step I take already feels like a question, even at its peak of attempt. Am I stepping into opportunity or consequence? Am I moving closer to joy or a lesson I didn't know I needed? Fear and curiosity drive my mind. A quiet reverence for the mystery of it all.

I wonder if life is less about the right or wrong of my actions and more about the sincerity behind them. Because if karma is watching, perhaps it sees or so I hope beyond the surface. It's less about punishment and reward and more about balance. The scales don't tip to judge but to guide.

So, I wonder, not with dread. I actually find a quiet kind of strength. For even if the answers remain elusive, the act of living for a reason, with purpose, in curiosity, and care becomes its own reward. I keep stepping forward, living in a life that, in its wondering, I strive to find a meaning.

Lamija

I wonder if we would be close in every other life. Would it always be you leaving first, or would it be me sometimes? Will my smile always end in tears beside your bed, saying goodbye with one last kiss on your forehead and a few whispered words? I wonder, after all these years, when it will finally end; because I miss you just as much as I did that cold, rainy December night. Without a doubt, you are one of my worlds, if not my entire world.

For us, everything always begins in October and ends with the last breeze. A breeze that takes one soul, then another, leaving behind empty, lifeless bodies. I feel cold, empty, but I'm still standing. I smile at the memory of our days and fill my nights with tears, where only you and I can be together once more, at home.

Now, I am alone, searching for those eyes everywhere. The child you left behind is still here, wearing the same green sweater, the same pink shoes, waiting for you to walk out of any room. Then, everything starts to collapse. She cannot speak, and there's no one to pick her up and say, *"Hey, hey, it's okay..."* The voices are loud, and I can't tell if I'm cursing myself or the world. But you would have known.
I wonder, does any of this make sense? Probably not. Not to those who have never loved a different soul.
The snow is falling again. I look up at the sky, just as I did back then, smiling as I whisper those words. I wonder if they ever found you, my beautiful Second Star to the Right.

Nico

I wonder, does the moon know it's loved?
Does the moon know it lives with purpose; does it know the love and adoration it receives, the countless pieces of art written and created in its beauty?
A single rock, floating in solitude amidst a vast darkness—shining so brightly when nothing else does. A borrowed light, a reflection, nothing of its own. I wonder, how many of us are like the moon? Lonely, silent, yet dazzling only in the emptiness of night. Do we

burn so others might see, only fade when their world fills with light? The moon, in actuality, is nothing extraordinary, just a simple rock, made of oxygen, silicon, magnesium, and so on. Earthly materials. Uninteresting materials. Plain materials. Just stone and dust, the remnants of a violent past. A scar in the sky. Yet it draws poets, painters, dreamers, and lovers to its cold surface, offering them nothing but a reflection. The moon is our muse, an unfeeling witness to the longings we pour out, as if hoping its pale glow might soothe our restlessness.

Perhaps that is the moon's cruelest beauty. It gives us nothing of itself, and yet we give it everything. Our words, our songs, our stories. Perhaps it mocks us in its silence, knowing we will always return to it, hungry for inspiration, searching for meaning in its emptiness.

The moon is loyal to the Earth, bound in quiet devotion, circling endlessly—not out of love, but because even in its loneliness, it has nowhere else to go.

Perhaps, it is as the Palestinian poet Mahmoud Darwish wrote; "Maybe the moon is beautiful only because it is far." Maybe its beauty would vanish if we touched it if we truly understood it.

Maybe we love it because we can't have it. Because it will never love us back.

I wonder, if the moon ever looks at us—at the chaos, the greed, the fragile hopes we scatter across the earth—and feels grateful it is so far away.

I wish I were your moon.

Endina

I wonder, when you look into my eyes,
Do you see the pain or does it fade away, like a moth to the flame?
Really, tell me, do you feel the same?
It is a hard thing to say but I cannot help but think.

78

But no, you will not tell me. Is that right? Why? I cannot figure it out. Whether you love it or hate it, you should have stayed. That is what I wonder when the storm comes rushing in.

You know I wonder what would happen if I quit because the game is starting to lose its grip.

And yet, I still find myself drawn to it, waiting for my dreams, though I know they do not fit.

A Song That Moves Me

Sanskriti: *Blue* by *Billie Eilish*

The blue song by Billie Eilish drifts like a slow-moving tide, its whispers slipping under the skin, wrapping around the soul in a cold embrace. It is not loud, not demanding; rather, it hums softly in the background, a gentle lullaby for broken hearts. The sound is like ink bleeding into the water. Deep, dark, and spreading into corners you never meant to visit.

There is a quiet sorrow that rides the melody, a feeling of being suspended in a space between breaths, between thoughts. The piano notes fall like raindrops in a room with no windows, each drop heavy with unspoken things. Billie's voice is soft, like a confession, a fragile thread of truth woven through the weight of a thousand unvoiced emotions. Each word feels like a secret she's sharing with you alone, a whispered understanding that somehow, in that moment, the world makes sense in its sadness.

The blue is not a color. It is a feeling like sinking into a sea of stillness, where the water is cool and the world above seems too far away to touch. It is in between the places where you are not lost, but you're not found either. It is the quiet hum of loneliness, the way the dark can be comforting in its silence, wrapping you up like a blanket, both protective and suffocating.

There is a quiet beauty in this blue, the kind that lingers after the song ends, a soft presence that stays long after the words fade. Billie sings like she is caught between being and nothingness, her voice heavy with an emotion too precious to put down.

In those moments when the world feels too loud, her voice tells me it's okay to be lost, to float in a space where nothing is clear but everything feels right in its own broken way. The blue is peace, a surrender to the uncertainty that sways like a breeze through the heart.

What moves me is how the song lets me breathe within that blue, cradling the sadness gently without rushing to escape, the song helps on sad days when nothing else helps. It's not about rising above it, it is about sinking in and finding stillness in the silence. Blue does not ask for anything, it simply lets me be and close my eyes to the blue world under the sea. And in that, I find an understanding of what it means to exist in the quiet spaces and enjoy the quietness around me, where light does not reach. And sometimes, that's enough to know that even in the bluest moments, I am still here, still alive, still happy, still striving for more.

Lamija: Chopin's Waltz

I do not have a favorite song, just as I do not have a favorite animal, color, or plushie.
Things simply happen. Sometimes, they meet your expectations; other times, they happen when you least expect them. Fear and love might be connected there, but in my life, everything feels unexpected, just like that evening.

Sitting on the shore with a notebook in my hands, writing and drawing. Sun was setting when I heard a light breeze of jazz. My heart skipped a beat… The pen started moving on its own.

A couple was dancing, coming to life, when suddenly, a tap on my shoulder asked for the same dance.

Listening to those playful notes, staring into hazel eyes, unclear faces, and swaying to the breeze of jazz, we ended with Chopin's waltz on that sweet, sweet night.

P.S. Chopin's waltz was never meant for dancing.

Asja: The Gnossus in Gnossienne

How do I recall hearing Gnossienne no. 1 by Satie for the first time? It has always found a way to tiptoe into my life. When I was a kid, I remembered the colors I saw of it. Dark red mixed with deep green- a forest to get lost in. I could hear its hums with each tone, each crumbling leaf and unknown farewell. The scenery was dark. However, its otherness made it safe. While I would not be able to indulge in this melody when I desired it, as I was unable to recall the name of the composition. It always found me. These were moments of delight. I would curiously turn to find where it is playing from. However, the closer I got, the more of the composition would pass. In the moments when I came closest to uncovering it, it would slip away. This is how I knew it was love- the relationship between this melody and me. We did not know each other, yet I learned about myself through it. I did not know who wrote it, when, how or why, but I knew the emotion of it. I felt its stare on my glance, overpowering. In this gaze of each it revealed the emotions put into the process of making art, the process of making love, the process of life and of death. What the artist pours into it, what I pour into a touch, a laugh, or a kiss, is not of ours anymore. The feelings encaged within our bodies slip, unknowingly. It shows that lingering anguish is part of the world. We can run and cry, scream, and revolt, but it will always be surrounding us. In that feeling of being adrift, I was the Minotaur in Knossos. However, through the need for comfort and discovery, I was also Theseus. The composition mirrored my inner conflict. The mix between a beast and a human, the worldly and heavenly. However, which is heavenly: the human or the beast?

82

The beast kills because it does not know the reason, the human kills despite it. That is why we kill thinking it will bring something greater, as observed in the tragedy of all our revolts. I think Theseus killed the beast because he saw himself in it. The composition describes that moment of acknowledgment. The stare. Theseus looked at the Minotaur and saw the similarity of their eyes. While different beings, they both knew fear, they both knew neglect and both knew longing, both knew expectation. It was not a matter of survival in those brief moments, but an intrusion into one's mind that was truly frightening. The beast faced the unknown and the hero faced what was known to be evil. We kill, thinking we know what is right. Theusus thought he killed a beast, just as Raskolnikov did when he swung both his arms, holding the axe and finally splitting the brain of a woman he deemed hopeless. Both these men killed holding shining objects, reflecting light. Both held power and heroism in their hands. However, only one fell to their knees. If we do not feel the guilt that made Raskolnikov sick and shameful in front of a woman devoted to God, despite her life being sinful- are we any different from the beast? We refuse to look. We refuse to look at ourselves thus the world becomes the mirror. How do I recall hearing Gnossienne no. 1 by Satie for the first time? I remember its colors because they are part of our human nature. The combination of bloody red with nature's evolving green moves me to be still. It moves me not to stare, but to see. Gnoissienne taught me how to be still knowing that through that I will be deemed a beast, that others attempt to conquer in pursuit of their fleeting fantasies. The Minotaur did not choose his fate. Regardless, he withstood it. The beast's emotion, just like ours, embodies chaos through that acceptance, which can only be captured frame by frame, through art. Whereas the heroic figures expose our primal selves, which seek their reflection in everything but the mirror. The mirror of Gnossienne made me realize we are in a constant battle between the beast and the hero. However, the righteousness of each is exposed in their passing.

Nico: *Violin Concerto in D Minor, Op. 47: I. Allegro moderato* **by Jean Sibelius, and** *Clair de Lune* **by Claude Debussy**

Bow to the strings.
Let the melody bleed its sharp truths steadily as the breath I force
into rhythm, a waltz with and against myself.
One, two. One, two.In, out. In, out. Until all that remains is *silence.*
Silence.
But the silence did not soothe. I was numb, scared, as broken, and
terrible as the weight of your gaze. A gaze that burned, that never
softened— because I was not enough.Not truly. Not ever. Never.
Silence. How I craved it, yet it betrayed me. I wanted to feel
something, anything— everything and nothing, all at once. I needed
the music to fill me, to course through my veins like lifeblood, to
surge with the furious tempo of my heart. These notes, this concerto
of grief, they once spoke of you.
Your words meant nothing, they contained nothing of value, because
to you I contained nothing of value. A sheer act of desperation, a
conditioned return game of cat and mouse - throw anything at the
wall and see if it sticks, a suicide mission where I either played
into your hands or became the villain that orchestrated this animus
symphony of cacophony.
And so I saw the truth: To you, I was always replaceable. I could
have been anyone. And yet, the music plays on. The keys sing
beneath a musician's fingers, their trembling voices rising and
falling, as if they, too, bear the weight of this ache. The bow dances
against the fragile tension, dragging notes like confessions from
the depths of my chest. Each note a plea, a scream, a whisper— an
echo of something I cannot name.
This music, this storm of sound, is the only thing that is understood.

It rises and it falls. It shatters. It mends. Gentle and fierce. How many times have I not sought solace here? How many times have I not begged these notes to carry the burden I cannot bear? The flowers I once nurtured— those fragile blooms of hope— have long since withered, their petals scattered to the wind, no longer touched by the weight of time or your neglect.

Silence.

This music was never for you; it was never about you. The melody twists, cathartic, as if it knows a secret. My secret. As if it knew the truth I once refused to admit that I was not grieving you.

I was grieving the *me* that once believed in you.

New petals now bloom under the care of someone else, cradled in the stillness of a hope yet to take form.

Noam: David Bowie's Starman

I feel like a Starman, inspired by David Bowie's song.

Every time I hear it; I'm filled with happiness and hope . The music calms me, helps me focus, and sends a warm tingle through my stomach. When "Starman" plays, I feel untouchable, as though the music creates a protective barrier around me, making anything seem possible. I am not sure whether it's the catchy strumming guitar or his unique, bewitching voice, but regardless, it conveys a magical message about freedom and following your heart. Bowie's Starman offers salvation from the feeling of being locked in, trapped by societal norms. It's a magical spell that frees you to let loose—just as Bowie did with his alter ego, Ziggy Stardust.

As the Starman said: *"let the children lose it, let children use it, let all the children boogie"*. These words urge us to be aliens, to reject the norms and structures of the adult world and create our own paths. Thanks to Bowie's Starman, countless young people have been inspired to embrace their true selves, to express their values and thoughts, and to challenge an already corrupt society.

Thanks to Bowie, I too, am a Starman—embracing my true self and finding freedom in his music.

Partner Writing - Writing Together

We Are From

Endina and Lamija

I am from a place with many siblings, a place surrounded by mountains, a place that has endured much suffering, yet a place filled with incredible music and food. Our culture is rich, but our hearts are richer.

Given a million chances and a million choices, never would I choose not to be who I am.

They can try to change me all they want, and they may try to break me down, but in the end, I'll stand tall in the rain.

It may not be the greatest place, and I accept that with grace. But I love it, because in the end, we're all running the same race.

I am from a place where people pass by with blank faces, looking forward but holding on to the past. Our country offers music and food to satisfy every soul's desire, but sometimes, we make fools of ourselves.

If I had the chance to fly high, I would; but not by sacrificing myself, like swans at the lake.

They may love my name, but not the reflection in the mirror, because no ego loves its own reflection.

No matter how it begins or ends, people will stay; people who carry a love for music and dance.

We are from places where music and food can lift you to the sky, yet people still struggle to make sense of it all.

If you come around, we will embrace you with love because family is a line but you are from everywhere alike.

You may meet us and think, *"They're just people, nothing special."*
But I am here to tell you it's much more than that.

We are from two countries, not vast in land, but enormous in the hearts of places from where we stand.

Nico and Sanskriti

We are from places where cleanliness is prioritized.
We are from places where the waves enter our nerves.
Waves of the shared experiences from the people around us.
We are from shared experiences of disdain from strangers.
We're from places where strangers judge us, as if we were fish
climbing trees.

We are from places where we are told to not use AI, but marked
using it.
A resource being used against itself.
We are from a place where adults expect us to be an infinite resource
of perfection.
But, also, tell us that not everything in life can be perfect.
A perfection that is expected but never to be reached or appreciated.

We are from places where we are expected to socialize with
strangers.
They can either be too young or way too old, which makes it worse.
Strangers forced within close proximity under the guise of closeness.

We are from places where the internet is our main way of communication
to our loved ones far away.
Meeting them once a year then leaving with tears in your eyes.
An ephemeral feeling of belonging and happiness.

We are from different worlds, but our shared struggles connect us
like branches from the same tree. N
We are both from the same imaginary world.

Asja and Nahla

We are from a hidden past, overshadowed.
Our identity is known to people buried, but still waving.
Where we are from, nothing ever changes—same leaders, same
vain promises, quieting the smile behind the grave.

Where we are from, people are hopeful, wanting to dream the
dreams of the future.
However, our past is like a scab politicians can't stop picking at.
We are from people who choose to elect leaders that make our
wounds bleed, ships sink, pockets empty and live hard.

When we look outside the window, we see our hometowns as
beautiful places.
The site is bitter.
We can smell them, hear them...
We breathe them.
Their smell of our cities is of a mother's touch, but the hands of
leaders are those of a drunk.

We are from a place where we feel like kids.
Kids await a beating if they don't follow the rules.
We are from a place wanting to grow, dreaming of being brave
and standing up.
We are from a place of wanting to do the right thing.

We are from a place where politicians keep picking at our scabs,
hoping to see green in the blood.
We are from hoping to see the roses of the blood bloom.
Maybe then we can define our homeland with a smile.

We Wonder

Lamija and Sanskriti

Looking at the mirror's broken glass, seeing a reflection that was once whole, I wonder where did I go wrong? I try to move between the blades as they cut through, breathing slowly, careful not to reveal where it hurts. I wonder when it will stop hurting.

Words can start wars, but fulfilled ones can end them too. I wonder when will I finally be enough? Not in your eyes, but in mine. When will love to stop feeling like a lifelong lie, earned only through comparison? I wonder when will I stop putting them first? It's the same question as, "Why give someone's life to a love that's not meant to last?"

When will I be enough if I have already given up on finding that mad silhouette? I cannot change the truth I have struggled to accept. I searched for you in every glance because the past haunts me, and I am still just a child.

I wonder how time flies, like birds taking flight.

The birds that took flight, when will you come back with the world's sight?

When did the little girl who was free get captured in the cage of her emotions and soul?

From gazing up, longing to match their height,

To now looking down, wondering when I took flight.

From wondering why others possessed it,

To hold it yourself, uncertain if it's a gift or a curse.

I wonder when did the days of looking up – asking when I will grow,

Become moments when others look at me, asking when they will grow, too?

When did school become a jail with limited joy,

When it once was freedom and laughter every day?

Human nature has always been to wonder, and I have been wondering since I was born.

The world, with all its mysteries, beckons curiosity from every corner,
Making you question every part of it.
Sometimes, wonder feels like the gentle touch of a feather.
Other times, it stings like the rough scrape of rusted nails.

We wonder if the world will crumble upon our shoulders or vanish alongside us?
We wonder when we will escape the harsh reality of the world, when will it end?
We wonder if love is a lie or if it can ever truly last?
We wonder if we will survive the semester or if the semester will consume us?
Why fill our heads with the ash of empty marks,
When could life burn bright, like a fire in the cold night of the forest?

Elif and Nico

We wonder,
Beneath the weight of stars
If meaning lives in space
Between what we are and what we seem.

We stumble,
Through mornings heavy with routine,
Tracing paths worn smoothly by others
But yet, still yearning for something new beneath the stars,

Each smile,
A mask we wear too whole,
Perhaps, a protection to hide our scars,

And still,

We wonder.
Not for the answers we fear,
But for the hope that asking means we are alive.

We wonder,
Wonder - childlike wonder, when did we stop wondering?
Beneath the endless stars, we wonder—why this, why us?
The silence of the universe answers only with more questions.
In our ache to know, we find beauty. Wonder fills the void, not as
emptiness, but as hope—overflowing, unending, alive. To wonder
is to live—to reach for meaning in the void, to let questions breathe
life into our search.
Perhaps wonder itself is the answer.

Musings

Lamija: Differences

*"The Difference" was originally written in Bosnian, and I've translated
it into English. It was inspired by Shadows of the Pomegranate Tree,
a novel by Tariq Ali.*

"Do you believe that roses are red?"
"I do."
"And yet there are many colors, and you love each one?"
"I do."
…
So why can't you love?
Differences are just fantasies,
Look deeper,
All the walls are the same.
For your name, leave me,
Like a withered rose, without petals to all.

You said you love the field of roses,
But why not me?
Isn't the difference a gift?
Isn't a quarrel a shame?
Look at those eyes,
Like tender buds,
And those lips, dear and warm.
If they were all the same, no one.
Would have their beloved.
If all eyes were the same,
There would be no pearls,
There would be no gold,
There would be no seas,
There would be no diamonds!
But still, it's all the same.
Warmth envelops all,
When I collapse into your arms,
I lose myself in the blueness,
In the restlessness that hides in your eyelashes.
Forget the differences for a moment,
Hold me tightly and don't leave.
Differences will always remain.
But we will live.

Sanskriti: Secret Beneath the Waves

Secret beneath the waves.
The ocean is quite deep, a slumbering sleep,
Resting our secrets and letting our wonders seep.
Beasts of bizarre look, with glistening eyes,
Slide through, in nooks and watery lies.
Towers of corals built strong and tall,
Dwindling in oceans of jeweled walls.

Haunted remains of ships, while ghostly stories remain concealing,
That avalanches of civilizations pried over, but no relics were freeing.
The ocean whispers such a despondent sorrow song,
And it bears more, in memory as it's a billion years strong.
Ones who are bold, unlike the rest,
Are in wait of a treasure that pulses through its chest.
Finding those who belong to this place,
Only good fights in the honor of grace.

Lamija: A Peace

"A peace…"
A peace?
An oddity, a word as surreal as it is within the soul.
It flickers in the remembrance of the foe, a concept leaving only a "sacrifice" in its wake.
"Put a smile on your face, make space a better place," a sentence woven everywhere, yet far from reality. I never wished to be in a hurry; however, it seems it is fated in humanity. I strive, and have striven, to be enough. I smile, even when I bleed; I respect, yet receive in return only "scratches" on my humanity.
Blindly…
    Blindly I gaze into each shadow and spark in the eye, trusting, loving,
        As if I expected that peace…somewhere…anywhere…anybody…
    It took me fifteen years to feel enough, a moment some may never know.
    I am neither angel nor demon, though I have been named both, wearing masks, yet holding what lies within.
I am human.
    I walk through emptiness with colored eyes, cursing my own name, pulling at my hair because I cannot…
    I cannot find peace within. I - I wonder if I ever felt it. Freedom.

It's easy to be "royalty" when riches suffice, but what of humanity, starved for the "little meaningful" things?

"You could give me the universe; I'd still look blankly and flee!" I once screamed in the mirror, pretending it was one I held dear. Years later, I was in front of Truth…

"Why didn't you tell him when he wanted to talk?"

To speak and shatter you, or to stay and plant flowers in silence. I forced a smile on my face, no one would ever guess it hid tears. Why would I destroy something as fragile as a melody of raindrops, simply to feed my own selfishness? — The Letter 63 by Miya L. L. It is easy to be the only one, until you're a peacemaker without peace, a five-year-old with a grown mind.

To be truthful takes time, battling every Giant to find peace.

So, what am I?

An oddity as it is, one who is despised for difference.

I am not a believer, yet if peace serves the soul, so be it. Do not create divides between you and me because I carry what you carry: birth, blood, bones, death.

I do not have an identity, but if you love it, do not create distance because of our "happy places".

Let me be truthful and say, I love the little things: gestures, kindness, nature, love, and the beauty of differences.

But my peace dwells in the quiet of 3 a.m., when the portal to the world of papers and ink opens.

There, one is embraced despite flaws, names, beliefs, masks, and haunting ghosts.

Our peace may differ; that is all right, as long as the difference is beauty.

"A peace?"

"A peace is that which makes unfunctional bleeding lungs functional, slowly. Simply Love."

Julie: The Social Media Trap

Scrolling on your phone, all day
Social media will make you think you're a failure at the age of 18, scrolling through videos that only make you wonder why aren't I doing enough? He says being a millionaire at the age of 18 is so easy, anyone can do it, that you're stupid or on the wrong path in life, watching people in their twenties who claim they work from everywhere only a few hours a day, isn't that the dream? Or is that even true that will leave you wondering.

And let's present the other side, the one that destroyed many girls, comparing yourself to the image of the girl with the perfect waist, perfect leg, she again claims, she's eating healthily, she has a "balanced life", she has her life figured out, and I'm happy for her but does that leaves me with motivation or depression?

And let's present the other side which states: this is the best way to achieve your goals, this is how you become, if you want to be successful do these things, you stumble upon so many videos from so many faces that all you're left with is confusion, every other video you see contrast the one before, and after a while you realize you don't know these people, they could all be spreading lies just begging for views, I waste my precious time so they could make a living, and then I come back to my senses and that circle starts over again.

I will not state that social media is all poison, it helped me at some level, but is doing more harm than good, why am I feeling so behind with people I watch for 30 seconds? Why when someone says you have to do this, I think I have to do this, and it becomes an obligation, and the guilt I feel if I don't do it, if I don't follow a workout I saw online, it feels like a weight on my shoulder, but it's imaginary, because it's all in your head, and you chose that weight, you listen and watch those videos, you let them have that amount of impact on you, on your self-esteem, on your self-worth.

How do I let it all go? It seems it has been there for years and won't stop pushing down, will it break me or will it make me stronger?

Lamija: Times I Knew You By

Things simply happen. Sometimes, they meet your expectations; other times, they happen when you least expect them.

I've lived many lives. Most people don't believe in the afterlife or reincarnation; to be truthful, I am one of those people. But I cannot recall where these memories came from—faces, voices. They awaken strange, undefined feelings, making me feel uneasy. So, let me tell you. Perhaps you will recognize my name or fill the empty space.

Before it was all about surviving, later on many things changed and I was in the east. Every life ended in luxury and beauty, didn't it? What if it was just a feeling? What if none of it is true? What if we live in an endless illusion? I wonder. Despite it all, I would always recognize one phenomenon. The moment they appear; music starts to play. And I sigh: "You are my muse, while I am your composer."

It was long ago when I first saw them. Heads up, I could never say 'they' so I will write directly to them. It was not love at first sight. I even refused to believe in it because love is a writer's myth. It does not exist, except for great tragedy. Maybe I refused because I didn't want to pull knives out of my back once more. Maybe I didn't want to be looked at strangely, as if I were ill. I'll because I loved it. It seemed as if love was more of a competition of manipulations, an interest, or a desire to look at someone for as long as they appeared beautiful.

But no one could surrender me to the fate of those like me because I was "the greatest." Yet, shoulder to shoulder, the smell of alcohol, papers with sketches destroyed, and a few unpleasant words from the bar's owner, there you were. In a mess. I stepped in, took your hand, and felt all eyes on me. I didn't know your name, but I knew all the rumors. I didn't know if they were true until you surely did steal what once belonged to me. You were a thief, a kleptomaniac, a person drawn to illegal work. To me, you were a snowflake, carried far away by the wind, only to land on my doorstep. Easy to melt, yet cold. You were impossible to catch. Once our eyes locked, I felt myself drowning in the seven seas.

It took a long time for you to realize that you didn't have to be a vagabond to be free. And from that moment on, I was never alone. In madness, happiness, sadness, or arrogance, you were there; unwavering, not a bit afraid.

Your death hurt me the most because I still had a few more journeys to take, and you weren't there to ask me which pigment I wanted to use for an angel's eyes. If someone had told me that the day while I was in my own hell, I would go to a bar to meet the person I would cherish the most, I would have laughed it off. But every next time it was even more bizarre. I entered the copy shop, back when copies were still made by hand, at the order of a duke. At that time, I hadn't printed my works yet. A little out of dissatisfaction, and a little out of a secret insecurity that they weren't worth it. People would come to the play where I acted. Not because of me, or somebody else, or because of the play, but to show off. "High Rise," that's what it would be called. I always laugh at ridiculous gowns and wigs behind the curtains.

A lady, beautiful as rosy tulips, and brown eyes greeted me politely. She was not wearing one of those gowns but something simple. Her family was known for supplying the kingdom, but as always, I did not know then. We spent time lounging around, as all young people do.

Ages were just a number, and she woke up the courage in me to show my first work. We were a mystery to humanity. Mostly, we were a mess because I moved far for work while she stayed at home. Before that, we had married while our first child was already on the way, so they thought we married out of principle. To others, we were perfect, and to very few, we were nobody. Distance made my longing for you more, and every thought and word somehow, secretly, was about you and our kids. I still remember your letters through poems, verses written in me, and I promised then I would find you in every life.

Love then became a line that was between life and death of mine. Once a dove dies, its partner dies by its soul until the time comes.

For a century, we were separated. Loneliness ate me alive. Parts of me were missing, and I did not know which. I did not remember the previous memories. I was desperate and hopeless. It was a terrifying madness. I developed a power of empathy to come closer to people, but they called me a "madman."

Today, kindness is taken for stupidity, and rudeness for smartness, but then kindness was for mad people. In that spin to get to your senses, never raise a hand above your head with a holding blade. People will always look at themselves not understanding a word you say. Things simply happen. Sometimes, they meet your expectations; other times, they happen when you least expect them. However, sometimes you have to climb a dead tree to reach a living seed.

The 20th century, which was the dead end, I was with a soul that only put me down to bring himself up. I was working back then as a model but actually gathering information to get a few things here and there fixed in my book. He found out and burned it all. Furious and hurt, I left. I slept that night at my cousin's apartment. The next morning, he came under the window to apologize. I refused, but he told me that he had someone important that he would like me to meet. It was a middle-aged man, already started turning white, a bit taller than me with average weight and full of humor and serious talk. My new friend was also a writer but more successful than me. Not long after it; on a boat in a small town, a young man approached me while I was waiting for him to bring out some materials for work. The man was tall, nicely built, but none of it mattered then, only his eyes. I've never seen bright green eyes like those. They were neither blue nor brown. Blue shows feelings. Brown you trust blindly. While green is truthful.

He told me: "Between them are obstacles for horses. A horse dies if it breaks its leg. Be careful not to trip."

It took some time to process if it was a threat, but then a sentence that was living deep under layers and layers of skin, muscles, and bones came out to me: *"There was a time when I was alone. Then you came to take me home, but then home became wherever you go."* It was you once more. I left my previous partner soon because humiliation is not a human act. At the end, we parted ways again. I became an art professor, our daughter started university, and you were still wandering around, writing to me about what was new in the world. Life was beautiful… Until the letter that was not written by you.

Waves are often turbulent, sinking even the best-constructed boats. With them, dreams and hopes sink… hopes and desires for a warm, gentle embrace. But by the time the letter arrived, I had already plunged deep, deep beneath the surface of the sea, together with you. In infinity. It was lovely, I was 73. Today, I remembered. Why and for how long, I cannot tell.

But one thing I surely know is that the place I am drawn to the most is the place where I will find you once more. Isn't it? I cannot wait to hide in your chest and let go of all the tears I've been hiding, all the fear that was slowly tearing me apart, regain belief again, and finally fill every crack with reinforced cement. Now, you have to promise to be the one to me that we will never part because this is the last. Things simply happen. Sometimes, they meet your expectations; other times, they happen when you least expect them.

Sometimes, it is upon others what you'll become. The right person makes you fall three times: once with them, once with yourself, and for the last time with life.

Maybe it will take a time, maybe a lifetime or few but it finds the way. I forgot to tell you. Do not be afraid, but do you know why I write about tragedy more than comedy? Because life consists of birth, the living line, and death.

Every death, whether natural or not, is a tragedy, and that's reality. But the living line is comedy, so life is a tragicomedy. However, every birth is transitory, a transformation, but it is followed by different expressions.

Not even once did I think I would live for love and for living lines with unexpected events.

Lamija: Butterfly

Fly me to the stars, like a butterfly. I am not afraid to stand in the rain, or in the middle of space, as I change my mind every day when I fall in love.
As colorful as wings should be, I would fly through changes while your thoughts Wouldn't leave a print.

Love has many ways; one of them is a curse. I broke my legs and everything that makes me *me*, Forgetting you are blind and perfect.

Fly me to the stars, Like a butterfly. Through the mess, while calling her name, seeing my face.

I'm the greatest, I'm a royal fool, Full of rage, anger, yet I still forgive you.

Fly me to the stars, Like a butterfly. Raise the net, but now I will escape. Love has many ways, so do it right. I have a right to be a beautiful, lonely fool whose name you never truly knew, Because you are more occupied with elegant style than what's inside.

Part III: Teacher Voices

In this section, we hear from our teachers: Druze, Jewish and Palestinian teachers from all over Israel, who made time to meet weekly on Zoom, and share their own powerful written impressions. Their writing explores personal scars and identity, family, current challenges, and thoughts about the past, present and future, before turning to personal reflections about war-time experiences, and positive inspirations that get us through the most difficult days.

I Am From

Amal

I'm from a limited wide, dark round space.
Captured by a long rope, in a complicated maze.
Trying to get to the exit, as fast as in a quick race
Till I got it and realized my mum's face

I'm from a family of warm love that gave me too much care.
That almost is not found nowadays in this world of unfairness.
Taught me to appreciate others, calling them ma'am and sir
Taught me respect, and how to plant trees of hope everywhere.

I'm from a society that follows the traditions of the old man.
Greeting others is necessary, to make all people friends -is the plan.
Taught me that friends are diamonds of Laura, Diana, and Hanan
They are the tasty spices of life and together we are loyal fans.

I'm from a place that plants good manners in the minds of small kids.
Teaching them that understanding and containing others kill the mess.

To achieve goals and realize dreams needs challenging work to achieve success.

A place where educating people to be good members and decreasing evil to less.

I'm from a group of those who live in the space of lovely homes and school.

Getting as much knowledge to educate members to cancel the name of "fool" -

Who believes in the "love of power, not the power of love" and gets it a useful tool?

Not tolerance is the weapon to break the limits to get the light and feel so cool.

 I'm from then and now, from here and there.

from a place where its past is present everywhere

telling a lovely bedtime story to expulsion nightmare

to relax worries with a smile and say, "Thank you sir."

Rivkah

I am from a different culture, a different standard, a different age, a different world.

I am from defending my identity to simply living it.

I come from the red, white and blue – and from kachol v'lavan.[4]

I come from canned soup

    but have evolved into homemade recipes.

I come from science and law –

    a fondness for both and a desire for neither.

I am from quips, anecdotes, storybooks and novels

    that transport me to times long ago and others yet to come.

I come from community conformity

---

4   Blue and white–the colors of the Israeli flag

standing alongside fierce individuality.
I came from judgement and high standards,
    yet I choose tolerance and acceptance.
I am from organized chaos and chaotic organization.
I am from independence – physical, mental and emotional.
I am from a people with a complex history,
    a community with a code of honor,
        a family with a rich heritage,
            and a personal eternal hope.
I am born of love, have developed with love,
    practice love and preach love.
I come from deep roots and weightless wings.
I am from generosity of heart, hand and head.
    I am tethered to the past,
        stand firmly in the present
and courageously face the future.
I come from the realm of unending possibility.

Samar

I am from a small town nestled between rolling hills and winding rivers, where the scent of wildflowers fills the air in the springtime.

I am from a tight-knit community where neighbors are like family, gathering on front porches to share stories and laughter under the glow of the setting sun.

Naftali

I come from the sea,
From the endless infinity
Where the horizon merges with skies
To an endless azure that never dies

I come from the sand.
From the golden grain of the land
Warm and soft but hard to remove.
Pressed and squeezed in every groove.

I come from the heart.
From what sets me apart
From the blood rushing in my veins
From every desire I reign

Shatha

One, real and fair, the other, cruel and unkind. I am from ink-stained fingers and dog-eared edges, From cracked book spines plucked from dusty shelves, A life folded between pages, Where consonants and vowels dance like fireflies.

I come from a kingdom by the sea, A hidden world where words are my sanctuary, An unseen realm of imagined skies, Yet always, it fades too soon, A dream slipping from my grasp.

I am from a world where air smells of gunpowder, Where the horizon blooms with mushroom clouds, Where shadows whisper warnings, And speaking my mother tongue becomes an act of rebellion.
In one world, I am the dreamer, Lost in stories, cradled by hope. In the other, I am the watcher, Silent, wary, walking the edges of fear.
I am from two worlds, One a nightmare, the other a faraway dream. Yet in my heart, they collide— A battleground, a bridge, A story only I can tell.

Julia Mor

I am from generations before me, going further back than I know, and still discovering bits of information like hidden treasure.

I am from strong opinionated people, not afraid of following their hearts and minds.

I am from comfort food, celebration food and finish-that-plate-no-matter-what food.

I am from foreign tongues, which still pluck at the heartstrings despite fading away.

I am from hardship, struggle, ancient hate, and subsequent escape. And yet I am also from optimism, positivity, multiculturalism, and hope.

I am from a new land, bright, shiny, and hopeful, naive - but sometimes too light.

I am no less from an ancient land, rooted, complicated and beautiful, cynical - but sometimes too heavy.

I am from finding that balance, day in and day out.

Inna

I come from something I can't properly explain.
Which is the cause of this incessant pain,
because I come from crime and punishment and crime
Where human life just isn't worth a dime
I come from bitterness and hatred.
From that which is but pseudo sacred
I come from toothless anger, a strong swear.
Self-sacrifice that always breeds despair
I come from the monotony of days.
From petty struggles, shattered hopes,
lost causes, empty praise.
I come from mediocrity and vanity and fear.
Our only guidelines in this vale of tears
I also come from calm, surrender and relief.
From acts of courage, even if they're brief.
I come from cracks through which the light gets in

I've grown to really like them from within.
I come from words of love yet to be spoken.
From everything that is so far unbroken
And you who failed me.
And who got me through?
I still come from this stubborn faith in you.

Emily

I am from a broken home.
A home where sometimes hate trumped love.

I am from a small Jersey town.
The only Jew in my class, in my school

I am from a family of atheist, liberal Democrats.
A highly educated family.
A physicist mom and a law professor dad,
    who couldn't be in the same room together.
        so, I had two bat mitzvahs in two different states.
My two best friends were an atheist Christian and a Bangladeshi Muslim.
Our dads were colleagues and friends at the university.
It turns out the Christian is technically a Jew, but I didn't know that then.
I didn't know that Jews and Muslims weren't supposed to get along.
I learned that in college.
But I knew to be wary of Christians, sometimes.

I come from a religion rich with tradition
    with beautiful customs that strengthen family and community
    a religion that encourages learning and questioning
    and that loves unconditionally.
But I didn't know any of that until college either.

Today I come from a religious kibbutz in Northern Israel.
My community is religious but fairly liberal.
The school where I teach is religious and has a broad mix of students.
I love my home, my school and my students.
But there is a lot of anger and a lot of fear, especially today.
I feel at home, but not exactly.

I am from a community of Arab and Jewish English teachers.
    Who strive to live together in peace.
We share stories and learn skills and hope to bring these to our students.
We want to bring our students a different, better world.
We've been together for over a year, and it's been a hell of a year.
But when I am with them, I feel inspired, and safe, but not entirely.

Mimi

I am from… I am from Candyland and Clue and day school and friends.
I am from lots and lots of friends.

I am from Winter, Spring, Summer and Fall. I am from the backyard
and picking fruit and raking leaves.

I am from sleepover parties and phone calls galore. And walking to
friends to play. I am from learning how to ride my bike, and biking
all over the place.

I am from taking the bus to ballet and coming home.

Alone. Late. Walking home in the middle of the street… just in case.
I am from a loving family
I am from going to the shore in the summers. I am from barbeques
and lightning bugs
I am from having neat older teenage students stay with us, so they

could go to Akiba, and then having to say goodbye to them at the end of the year.

I am from having a great dog, who was always there to greet me and keep me safe, as he had the scariest bark!

and all of a sudden I am from Israel.

I am from not knowing how to call the teacher – what is HIS name? Hamoreh? But doesn't he have a name? I am from not understanding anything that was going on.

I am from finding a bunch of new American friends in Israel – but guess what? Everyone's Jewish but no one kept kosher! I wasn't even allowed to say God – without getting a dirty look.

I am from finding it really interesting to study the Bible like it was Shakespeare. I am wondering how it could be the same Bible that made this all happen?

and then I'm from the army. Uniform, and all. I am from a friendly foreign army … Nothing like the real Israeli army.

And then I'm from university. I am from women will run the world. We will show them. and then I am from work, lots of open space and noise. And who can concentrate?

And …. And … and that's where I am from -

Abeer

I am from names that draw suspicion,
Where faith is met with cautious glances,
A heritage woven in rich tapestry,
Yet tangled in the threads of fear.

I am from streets marked by divisions,
Where prayer and culture clash like storms,
Each belief is a barrier, each word is a weapon,
And my heart aches to bridge the divide.

I am from stories of ancestors whispered,
Their hopes wrapped in sacred traditions,
Yet here I stand, caught in the crossfire,
Identity pulled like a fraying seam.

I am from gatherings filled with warmth,
Laughter rising above the quiet doubts,
But outside, the world is a weighty silence,
Judgment cast like shadows at dusk.

I am from the fire of shared humanity,
Uniting in struggle against the tide,
Finding solace in the common thread,
Where love can flourish, unbound by fear.

I am from the resilience of my people,
A chorus rising to reclaim our place,
With every heartbeat, we break the silence,
Together, we weave a brighter space.

Robin

I am from a mother who taught me to be kind,
to be honest and generous,
to fight for justice and equality,
to sing *we shall overcome* with Martin Luther King,
and change the course of history.
I am from a mother, who didn't prepare me

for unkindness, selfishness, and arrogance.
I am from a mother who created art and beauty,
who shared delicious food, conversation and compassion.
I am from a mother, who never mentioned broken promises,
but fought for the oppressed, the other and all.
I am from having to grasp, that not everyone is like my mother,
not understanding why people are so harsh, cold and cruel.
I am from a mother who believed in the best, in fate,
and that in the end, goodness will prevail.
I am from trying to find my role in changing myself.
to be part of the world now that I know that I can't change it.

Steven

I come from Tel Aviv. Not the tall buildings and overpriced clothing stores part of Tel Aviv. The Tel Aviv where you can get a kosher shawarma at 3:00 AM, just in case you have a shawarma emergency. A place where Eritrean kids with crosses around their necks play football with Haredi Yemenite kids. Where Bukharian (Uzbeki) vendors speak in English to Chinese and Nigerian foreign workers, and in Russian to immigrants from Belarus and Ukraine.

Before that I came from NYC. But not the skyscrapers of Manhattan. I come from Brooklyn, the part where people live in homes with yards, each corner with its own synagogue and kosher pizza store. A place with people who come from every place on earth, speaking every possible language, rich with diversity. But where everyone lives in their own bubble, in communities separated by language, ethnicity, religion and culture.

Before NY, my roots are from Italy. Not the art of Florence, or the Colosseum of Rome, or even the glamor of Milan. I come from the grit of Napoli, where pizza was invented, and people still pay *pizzo*.[5] Where Catholicism and the pope reign supreme—unless they compete with football and Maradona. A place that feels to me like the essence of Italy, but where locals speak not Italian, but Napoletano.

Growing up I went to schools that taught us to read Hebrew, but never to speak it. We read about Israel, and prayed for it, but never visited it. We were taught about honoring our parents, then taught to ignore them, because the rabbis at school knew better. Taught that how you dress was more important than what you did, even when the texts taught otherwise.

I come from places of contradiction. I come from changing identities: First Alessio became Larry, then Robert became Avraham. I come from an American passport with an American name, and an Israeli passport with a Hebrew name, and in a few years, I'll have to choose what to put on the Italian passport. But I also found some common threads: I come from working class neighborhoods in big cities. I come from good neighbors, and good food. Families that take the bus or the train to the beach in the summer. I come from immigrants, and diverse cultures touching, but not quite mixing, just meeting at the edges. That's where I'm from.

Sassie

I am from Marin, and I am from Modiin.
I am from Redwood trees and olive trees,
Gardenias and tuberoses; morning glories and jasmine.
The scents of lilacs and baking bread and fresh-cut grass.
I am from Ross Elementary School, Redwood High School, and Yachad Modiin High School.
I am from family dinners
I am from Thanksgiving Christmas and Easter

---

5   Protection money paid to the Mafia.

Rosh HaShanah, Passover, and Shabbat
I am from burritos and kubeh
Chocolate chip cookies and biscotti
I am from the New Year's Day tradition of jogging across the Golden
Gate Bridge.
I am from Modiin and frequent visits home to Marin.

Monique

I am from……..
I am from an unknown place in the foothills far away where the
rivers run wild.
I am from a place that is dear to my heart.
I am now from this place that I call home and everyone knows
where it is.
I am from a place where I wear the mask of many and feel
comfortable in all.
I am a daughter, a friend, an educator, and a mother all in one.
I am from the unknown to the familiar, whichever suits me at the
moment I choose.
I am from a land of chaos and unconditional love.
I am from a place that has been around for all of time.
I am from a place that makes me flustered.
I am from a place that has challenged me daily and these challenges
are what have made me love it so
I am from a quiet soul always in search of peace and love amongst all.
I am from a place where humor is the best medicine.
I am from a place where a big hug and a smile fill my heart
with warmth.
The place where I am from is all of these and more, it is constantly
evolving as the days go by

Elena

I am from the border, have always been,
Hanging around boundaries and realities
Holding a different language in each hand walking down the
stream
Walking through the steps towards the Black sea vitality.
I am from page twenty something or thirty something.
In the enormous novel I've never finished
I am from tender candles and violent lightings.
From the distance - too short - from whispering all the way up to
screaming
I am from granny's spooky and hopeful tales.
Enrooted in the orchards which surrounded the Ukrainian village,
Half-hungry, half-dead, always half-step into some other place…
I am from where pain is becoming an image.
Of a motanka guardian doll which fails to protect
But it is being carried in your handbag forever.
I am from where too many better things are left intact.
From where the raven enunciating "Never…"
Is being bombarded by the silliest and the heaviest hopes.

This Scar Is From

Sassie

Do you see this scar
Hidden in my brain?
I thank my mother for this scar.
She has never stopped dieting.
Since before I was born.

My mother taught me so well.
When I was still a child
She brought me with her to Bod Squad
To work off any excess fat
With Jazzercise.

She instilled in me a diet culture.
From age 12, I have been aware.
That if I do not do as I should.
I may get fat, like her
And that's not good.

My mother encouraged me when I was 13.
And I bought the book.
Thin Thighs in 30 Days.
Vicious cycle of ice cream binges
And exercise purges.

When I was 14 and 15,
My mother was so helpful.
She let me drink.
Her Slim Fast shakes
In place of meals.

When I was 16 and returned home hungry in the evening
After running 10 miles in cross country practice
I grabbed the can of macadamia nuts.
"You might as well just put those directly on your hips.
Because that's where they'll eventually end up."

When I had my own children
I swore I would not pass this scar on to them.
I tried to hide my body image problem from my daughters.
I tried to make exercise into something fun,
Not something to control my weight.

But my girls are too smart for that.
They know.

Naftali

I look at this sign,
I see myself.

That long bar scaring the enclosure.
Two perfect half two perfect squares

In one, black and white shadows in outdated hairdos.
To the left is the color and the sound of life,
Splitting, bridging, the bar is me.

Stories from the old country, of fatal whispers carried too far.
Of tongue tickling kin no one knows.
Of keeping up appearances.

To the right
The free spaces and breeze,
The levity of the homeland.
And in the middle of me.

Samar

This scar is from my disability to undo things that I have done.
We often make decisions in a given situation and once you choose this
path, everything utterly changes, your destiny and your fate.
It certainly leaves a scar.
A scar of what could have happened if I made a different choice.
This scar is the consequence of my innocence not ignorance, it is the
consequence of my lack of confidence rather than selfishness.

However, this scar is responsible for who we are today.
It is a blessed scar.
It is here to stay and remind us of what we truly are and what we
have become.
Now my scar comes from my inner beauty, strong will and resilience.

Shatha

I have scars that go beyond my skin.
That has penetrated my body thoroughly.
That have lived and festered.
Growth never-ending.
But I have lived with them, carrying them as a shield.
I loved them as I loved everything with which I was faced.
So, I will carry them.
From now, until my last days standing.

Robin

This scar is from a long time ago.
Leaving my life behind
When taken to another place
Due to an experience that left him shocked.
Survivors in stripes, happily starving.
Staring at their saviors in red, white and blue
Begging to find whoever was still alive.
Inspired by the new Jewish state.
He vowed to help it one day.
And he did
Together with us
And we left everything we knew and loved.
Finding a hot, dry, tough place of conflict
Which became our new home?
Becoming a sabra
Leaving who I had been aside.
Only to emerge every now and then
Wondering, am I me?
Never will I know,
Since what if isn't

Rivkah

I have a scar, hidden away. It is a wound that has reopened a number
of times over the years with varying degrees of pain – mostly to
me, but sometimes to others, as well. The gash healed long ago yet
still aches from time to time. The scar can't be seen and it has not
prevented me from building a family, establishing a successful career,
or contributing to my community - but it still rears its ugly head at the
most inopportune times – it still haunts me.

Looking back, I received countless "mini scars" in my childhood, but I didn't understand myself enough to register them. I didn't understand that they were self-inflicted and I didn't realize that I was building a tolerance for pain. The scar emerged from my youth, from a time when I believed in my own invincibility. I was too easily distracted by activities that provided immediate gratification. I was a hard worker – but only when I believed in the cause, or the person for whom I worked. I wasn't humble enough. I wasn't disciplined enough. I wasn't mature enough.

The first time the blade nicked my sense of self and I remember it actually drawing blood was at the end of my college years. I stood there, like everyone else, looking so fine in my cap and gown. My parents and grandparents cheered proudly as my name was called and I walked across the stage. I took the folder they handed me with a big smile on my face - but there was no diploma inside because I had failed a course. Summer school awaited me.

I know what you might be thinking…so what? Lots of students fail classes. Lots of students have to suffer through summer school. That may be true, but at that point in my life, I wasn't like "lots of students." This was new, it was painful, and it was completely my fault. Yet the pain was painful enough – so the blade continued to knick and cut until I reached a point where the strike was actually a gash.

At the end of my master's program, I again felt the sting of poor choices and ineffective prioritizing. I either overestimated my ability to bluff my way through what I had deemed to be a fairly meaningless final assignment, or I seriously underestimated my professor's pride in being all-powerful. Either way, this time, I donned no cap and gown. This time I received no empty diploma folder. Instead, my family traveled from afar just to sit in the restaurant where we had made a celebratory reservation – eating a tense meal DURING the ceremony rather than after it. For only after the arrival of parents, grandparents, and siblings, was I told that I would not be allowed to participate in the graduation at all because I had failed the one final assignment. My father assisted me in approaching the dean of the program where I asked for mercy. We pleaded with the president of the school. We pushed on all levels, but to no avail. I was barred from the final ceremonial honor.

I did graduate, after submitting the same paper with minimal alterations just a week later – earning enough for a passing grade. The professor had made his point, though – he had engraved his dominance over generations to come while I was left hemorrhaging. I had significantly disappointed my family. I had inexcusably let myself down. This time, the blade cut deep into my sense of worth – it lodged in my soul where it still resides to this day for, I have struggled with this behavioral pattern my whole life.

To be fair, I have completed many programs since that long ago degree. I have achieved a great deal and I am proud of all that I have accomplished. I have worked hard and earned the respect of family, friends, colleagues and students. Yet, like an addiction, I continuously fight that urge to procrastinate, to underestimate the time needed to complete a task, to prioritize the ease instead of the important. The scar still stretches and pulls, stinging me with its threat of reopening. It exhausts me. It humbles me. It highlights my shame. It mocks my vulnerability. It calls out my weaknesses. It lurks below the surface, ever threatening to denounce me as a fraud…

…but this scar and I have been together for a long time. I have learned to live with it – even to embrace it – as a constant reminder of the gap between who I am and who I am striving to become. This scar still aches, but it lets me know I am alive. It shouts out that my work is not yet done, my personal growth is not yet complete.

Anonymous

This scar is.........
This scar is from a place that I cannot hide.
It is deep and might never heal completely.
This scar is from him and the years of pain that were inflicted upon me.
This scar is mine
This scar is from the man who I believed to be my partner in life.
This scar at one time frightened me and made me doubt myself.
This scar made me hang my head and weep for my home.
This scar is mine
This scar has led me on a journey that most would not survive.
This scar has made me strong and I find the lioness within myself.
This scar has taught me more than all of my degrees combined.
This scar is mine
This scar on the outside is disturbing and makes most uncomfortable
This scar does not make me ashamed.
This scar is something that I choose not to dwell on
This scar is mine
 I have learned to accept the pain and discomfort that this scar has caused me over time.
I know today, unlike what I felt about it not long ago, that I am going to die with it, and not from it.
I wear this scar like a badge of courage and walk with my head high again.
This scar is mine

Inna

If a scar is a form of death
then I have died many times
When losing the innocence of childhood
And the naivete of adolescence.

And if a scar is also rebirth
forged from the ashes of experience,
then surely, I have come forth
renewed, maybe better or maybe worse.

 If a scar attests to suffering
of what type is it?
One that comes from pain
or one that stems from overbearing love?
Most of my scars are of every kind,
souvenirs of lines upon my face
Evidence of life
where all the scars are intertwined.

Steven

I have four scars–one for each grandparent.

This scar is for Grandpa Larry. It's just a small scar, very faint. You died when I was very young, and I can barely remember you. But my dad said that you liked to visit and teach me Italian, and I'm the only grandchild who got to really remember you. After growing up without you in his life, my dad was just getting to reconnect with you when you left us. I'm told that you loved to bargain with people, and we even have some art that you bought when an art store was going out of business.

This scar is for Zaydie, my mother's father. I had a scary dream one night–the next day they told me that you had a heart attack. But it was a few months later, when I was at sleepaway camp, that you had suffered the second heart attack. I was 12, and I remember that day, getting picked up by family friends and driven to the funeral, although I have no idea if I went back to camp after. You loved books, and your house was filled with them. We kept as many as we could, and they've filled up a house in New Jersey and a house in Jerusalem.

This scar is for Grandma Evelyn, my father's mother. You were tough to get along with. You used to cheat when you played games with my sister, because you weren't willing to let her beat you. And you banned two of my siblings from your house. But I cherished my relationship with you. It was hard for you when I moved to Israel. You were afraid I'd lose one of my limbs in a terror attack, like the ones you'd seen on TV. When you got sick, I was in Israel, and by the time we realized it was too late for me to say goodbye. You loved to write, and I kept most of your poems.

This scar is for Bubbie, my mother's mother. You were the matriarch of the family. President of your synagogue, the busiest grandmother I knew, always traveling with friends, or attending events. Your schedule was always full. We grew up with you in our lives, babysitting us, attending all the important events, sharing holidays and birthdays. When you had to go live in a retirement home, and then Covid hit, it was really hard for all of us. It's still hard for me to remember that. This scar is the newest, and it hurts the most, although not as much as it did two years ago.

Where I Am Now

Mimi

Where I am now
Where I am now, ….

Where am I now?
Where now am I?
Am I now, okay?
Not sure, hard to tell.

It's hard to see a great idea unravel, so many miracles go bad.
I'm thinking about how hard people worked, how much time, hope,
and energy went into making this idea work… and now it's all coming
apart.
But why?
I'm thinking a lot about how the ultra-extreme, just a few people, ultra
extremists throw the huge majority of good people out of whack. And
when things lose their balance, things turn tipsy turvy and the ship
begins to sway in the huge ocean… and then what happens.

I recognize my life around me, on one hand it looks like something
I know, but is it?
So many lives have changed since the hope at the end of the tunnel
is fading. Just fading.
This cannot go on forever.
If only I could do something to stop the craziness.
If only I could really do something to stop the craziness NOW.
That's where I am now.

Inna

I Am in That Place
I am in that place I can't define
except that it's a place of duties
to my family, my work.
I can't afford to be out of line,
procrastinate or waste my time or waste my time.

I am that mom
with that annoying sense
of not being enough.
And every day I tell myself: "c'mon,
they're doing fine, keep calm, keep calm."

I am that catcher in the rye
trying to save them all,
they fight me in the classroom,
they fail and seldom fly,
and so do I, and so do I.

I am that Israeli girl
who wishes just
to bring them home
subdued by such a heavy toll
I pray to bring them all, to bring them all.

Elena

I am where the night shelling doesn't reach me but might every moment.
I am where the neighborhood synagogue is in the shelter.
I am where people yell from the kitchen windows trying to comment.

On what's going on or just asking what's the matter.
I am where I occasionally fight with the rav.
Trying to convince him not to lock the shelter at night
I am where the moon is almost golden above.
Where I walk the street among the flickering lights…
Hold on… I am always in the blank space.
Filling it with colors, sounds, and feelings
Constructing the world that inhabits another place.
Trying to export from their hopes and meanings.
I am where someone is sitting in the armchair holding the threads.
Trying to weave something, anything that shows a way - home.
Even several steps in the midst of darkness and dread
I am where you're shaking but I have to go.
For there is always a distant promise to keep
For there is always a thread to pull through the woods
For the nights are long, untender, and deep.
All the way from Tel-Aviv to Al-Quds.
I am where I dream of destiny who's sitting in the armchair.
Weaving the threads she will throw us in the morning.
I am where life is real though not fair.
Where I have morning coffee right on the corner.

Naftali

Every evening, I walk down the road. I look down at my feet pounding the cobblestones and wonder how they had gotten so big. There used to be a time when I had to leap over an entire stone, barely making it to the other side. careful not to fall on a dividing crack and now breeze easily across.

At the very bottom of the mound there is a nursing home where I see my mom. The once proud head has bent, and the answers that were so available in my youth, are non-existent in her dotage. Yet it is not about her, it is about me.

There is a point where you have come full circle, and you can finally reach the beginning, and it all seems new to you. This isn't her sitting there, it is me, 40 years ago, and 40 years from now. powerless and clueless, looking to his elders for answers and solutions. I am at that point where I need to relearn about myself through that image of the future me sitting in that wheelchair.

I learn about my faults and my pains and my compatibility, and through this I become stronger and more robust. Just like in the giving tree, this may be her final gift to me.

Where am I now? I am there, and here, and in between. I am in the coming and going, in the presence and in the absence. Most of all, I am inside myself trying to burst out.

Steven

Where am I now? I'm on a bus, on the way to my friend's village to pay respect after their grandmother passed away. Me, a Jew with a kippah on my head, wandering around an Arab village, until I reached the mosque, where the men are doing their part of the mourning. Life is strange. I no longer feel safe to walk around in the city I grew up in, or go to the university I studied at, not with a kippah on my head, but I feel completely safe to walk around an Arab village. Then my Bedouin friend messages me–are you ok? There were rockets in Hurfeish, near you. "Yes, I'm fine, didn't hear anything." Of course, none of us is really "fine". But I don't feel unsafe. I feel lost, only partially because Google Maps keeps telling me I'm in Lebanon.

It feels like we are lost. In the first few days of the war, there was fear, there was confusion, there was uncertainty. But there was also unity. People stepping for each other. By now it seems clear that unity has started to crack, especially at the top. And somehow, after 8 months of war–yes 8 months of non-stop war, there's really no end in sight. Worse, there's been no real game plan, no strategy. It's easy to criticize this government, but even those who criticize aren't offering a long-term plan for peace and stability. President Biden unveiled a plan–and it would take us back to square one. So, what has everyone on both sides died for? What was the point?

I'm disconnected from Gaza. Here the war feels quieter, calmer, but I barely hear from anyone in Gaza, only those who have left. The ones who we do hear from say the situation is horrible, a nightmare. Before they wanted Hamas gone, now they're just hoping to survive, or worse, have stopped caring completely.

I'm not in Jerusalem. The city that everyone claims is sacred but all desecrate; the House of God that man fights over. There they are having the Jerusalem day march–what's supposed to celebrate freedom and redemption but has turned into an ugly mob. My friend is assaulted and beaten up when he tries to stand up to them. Is this what we fought for? Teenagers are brainwashed to hate. Is this what God wants? I'm glad I'm not in Jerusalem today.

I'm still in the north. Heading home, I stopped at my friend's house. Luckily, she's vegetarian, so the maqluba she made is kosher. We're in one of the only places left where a Jew in a kippa and Muslims in hijab can walk together peacefully. I realize I've answered my own question. Maybe we don't need some fancy complex proposal drafted by a think tank or policy wonk. The answer is right here in front of us. Isn't it better to live together in peace and respect? That's where I am now. Google Maps still places me in Lebanon, and I have another hour and a half of train ride left, but I'm no longer lost–I'm home.

Sassie

I fear we are in a deep and dark tunnel.
Being led by monsters who

Do not want what is best for our people.
But I try to hold on to hope.

Some days when I wake up.
I feel like I cannot breathe.
It is claustrophobic down here,
There is no air.

I am hungry and thirsty,
I long to embrace my friends and family.
I feel bugs crawl on me, I'm dirty,
I want to see the light of day.

The outside world cannot hear our cries.
With their loud cries for freedom and peace
They have no idea that we **all** are being held captive.
We **all** are in the dark.

I Wonder

Naftali

I wonder if when we close our eyes we will all seem equal.
I wonder if the dead see black or eigengrau. no I don't
I wonder if in the future we will find a common song.
I wonder if one day Jew would stop being a 3-letter word.
I wonder what tears a crocodile sheds when he is really sad.
I wonder why piano keys can play such lovely tunes with different colors.

I wonder if next year will be my last
I wonder if the only certainty is instability.
I wonder if the tunnel I'm driving through is longer than our people's.
I wonder how many lights   if any, are at its end.

Do the sun people talk about the earth set, and earth rise?
Or is it just a matter of might vs. Right
Forests, trees and hills.
I drive out of Jerusalem.

Home - ASHKELON

Monique

I wonder about......

I wonder why I wonder. Sometimes there is no point in wondering at all. It is as if everything has already been decided, or has it?

I wonder if the hostages will ever be released if they are even alive?

I wonder if the soldiers will be, ok? Will they all come home soon?

I wonder if the innocent people suffering from this war will survive, will life ever be normal for them, or for us?

I wonder why I need to question everything? I wonder why I don't have all the answers.

I wonder why people feel so much aggression towards one another, for aren't we all the same? Weren't we all given the same rights at birth?

I wonder how the future of my children will look, or my students or even my own?

I wonder if they will be happy and live lives full of love, happiness, and satisfaction?

I wonder why I or anyone around me has doubts, regrets, or shame?

I wonder why I let others make decisions for me, in the government or my place of employment? Don't I have free will? And if I do, why am I not using it?

I wonder why our creator made us suffer and celebrate, love and hate, think and feel? Or did they?

I wonder if man has made all of their own problems and no higher being has any connection to it.

I wonder about everything and nothing. Does anyone really know anything at all?

I wonder?

Inna

Your tender cheek upon my cheek
your lips touching my face.
It's early morning, I'm asleep.
You're next to me, my boy.
Charmed by your vigorous physique.
Your ever-growing might
I wonder what adventures you will seek.
I wonder what you will be like.

 Will you be able to withstand?
the filth, the pain and the abuse
which you'll find hard to understand,
and will the muscles of your heart
shrink out of sorrow for this land
when death of a beloved friend
you will experience it firsthand.
I wonder how you'll cope with that.

The southern wind is dying now
it's been a long, hot day
I'm finishing a cup of wine,
the mind going astray.
And I'm not whining, not at all
just trying to find a way
to settle remnants of the light
with dark that gets its prey.

It's midnight, I am on the rack
All this to no avail
I wonder whether they will come back
and are we to prevail.
I wonder if I've still got strength
to navigate this sail

and looking at my sleeping son
I know I cannot fail.

Amal

I wonder why people missed their belongings and chose to get emigration.
Why do they kill moments, lose memories, and cause one's immigration?
I wonder if birds are cleverer than people to look for warmth by migration.
Enjoying the cool sun, and lovely moments without losing the direction
I wonder why learners get sad when they fail and have no preparation.
I wonder why people suspect everything from God but they still creation.

Life and death are two stages that every one of creation must try and pass.
Each is once. I wonder why people do not spend life as easily and so nicely.
Worries are found, why don't they ignore them by jumping on the grass.
I wonder….
Why do people color their hearts black when they can be clean as glass?

I wonder why people go so deep in water while they fear one wave.
I wonder why roses are not found in far places of wild, wide-open caves.
I wonder about those who tease others and call for help to stay safe.
I wonder about so many things…
That may be answered after I am taken to my GRAVE.

Sassie

I wonder what God is.
I wonder if He ever regrets creating man and woman.
Is He happy with His creation destroying the rest of creation?

134

Sometimes I suspect that He is tired of this game,
And maybe He is letting us exterminate ourselves.
Letting us eradicate the human race slowly,
But for Him, it is the blink of His eye.

And sometimes I wonder.
How God can be omniscient,
And what does that really mean?
I don't see why He would really care about
Each and every thing that every being ever did and said.
Does He know what I'm thinking?
I'd like a little privacy with my thoughts.

I wonder if God is on my side.
Does He want what is best for me?
Or does He choose sides?
Does He have favorites?
Like, that does not seem very God-like
And the thing about Jews being the chosen people,
I think that might be wishful thinking on our part.

I wonder if we have a purpose.
Or if this is all just some cruel joke
I think maybe we'd better not rely on God.
We'd better take care of our planet.
And take care of ourselves.
And take care of each other.
And maybe that's what God is.

Two *I Wonders* by Elena

An attempt at"decomposing" Shakespeare sonnet 66

Still not too tired about the light I wonder.
For wondering about the future would be pathetic.
Just about the light becoming richer and rounder,
About the light that slumbers on my threshold.
About the silly light right from the fairy tales,
Naive in its simplicity but stronger than strength,
About the happy golden light that's filling the place
Hovering like a giant bee-swarm at arm length.
About the dangerous light, as sharp as a razor,
About the killer light annihilating your trace
About the saver light, nothing short of amazing,
About the dusty yellow light that starts my days.
Still not overtired about the light I speak,
About the killing and tender, majestic, and bleak…

I Wonder II

    I keep wondering about wandering in the woods.
Having lost the sense of truth and direction.
Stepping over branches, stones, and roots
Picking fresh disappointments for my collection.
Disappointments are a trifle sweeter than outright pain...
I keep wondering about the trail to the sea.
About taking the crowded morning train
Listening to strangers, a notepad on my knee.
I keep wondering about the threads of songs.
That come and skip and rarely develops into something real.

I wonder why they keep attacking me in the throng.
When the breadcrumbs trail is so painful and hard to bear.

Mimi

I wonder
I wonder a lot.
I wonder if others wonder as much as I wonder.
I wonder so much that sometimes I don't know how I get anything done.
I wonder why I feel like I want to share what I wonder about with others.
I wonder why others don't feel they want to share.
I wonder why the sky is blue and the sea is not blue all the time,
and how many grains of sand are on one beach
and how lucky we are that we can go to the beach, and I wonder how
it is POSSIBLE that there are people who have never seen the sea,
or the ocean....
and I wonder what my life would be like with no computer, no
technology...
Does technology offer hope and support or does it create stress and
too much knowledge about everything and nothing?
I wonder what happened to the Israel I knew and loved? I wonder
how a whole society can give up on its youngsters and not care if they
go to school or not?
I wonder how it is that power corrupts? I wonder what there is when and
why is a change in a person when they get power, become powerful.
Why is it that they can no longer compromise nor stay pragmatic?
Why is it that they become so sure of themselves and their beliefs?
I wonder if our leaders fear the future more than I do.
I just wonder...

I Wonder About Today, Tomorrow and the Days After

Monique

I wonder about today, tomorrow, and the day after….
Today I sit and wait…I wait for the sun to set and the air to cool down,
I wait for my son to come home on the weekends from the army, and
I wait for people to start smiling again and feeling like they have a
right to enjoy life.
Tomorrow, I hope to wake up and not feel sticky from the humidity,
I hope to see my son and daughters for Shabbat dinner, and I hope to
hear good news about our current political situation that will make
me and my nation feel like smiling again.
The day after I do not know what will be. I can only hope that the
weather has changed to make it more comfortable and will continue
to be that way. Also, I hope my son will finish his service and come
home safe and sound, my girls will finish their studies at university
and finally, the happiness in people's hearts comes back to stay. I can
only hope that the day after means - no one will try to steal our joy
and will to be, and we will find ourselves smiling again.

Robin

I wonder about Today, Tomorrow and the Days After…

I wonder about **today**,
Knowing that it is not the way it was.
And it is not getting any better,
I wonder what is going to happen today,
Maybe something nice, enlightening, bringing hope.
I wonder,
knowing that I can only wish, until another disaster
is announced by the calm voiced spokesperson,

or a rumor on social media,
which is later verified as true,
by the same calm voice of the spokesman in the evening news

I wonder about **tomorrow**,
How to hold on,
when everything I have ever believed in has been shattered,
as the slow, gentle, natural flow towards coexistence,
towards happily living side by side
has been erased, washed away, drowned out,
by the forces of evil leading us all,
to judge all as one, and one as all, as guilty,
are all to blame.
are all responsible,
for the crimes of others with dreams of grandeur,
fueled by disdain,
of those they do not know
Believing that they and we are all the same
and for that reason, we know that they are to blame,
and that is why they and we must all suffer.

I wonder about **the days after** the ashes will have settled,
the tears have dried,
and pain has diminished a little,
and the rubble has been cleared away,
disposed of into a deep hole that is not deep enough
to contain the overflow of smashed lives of people long gone,
like a small hill
that trembles in the wind
although it is covered with weeds and flowers,
prancing coyotes, foxes, lizards, snakes and butterflies.
I wonder if maybe then,
the forces of evil will have gone somewhere else.

Maybe then,
our small voice of belief in us
will prevail.

Naftali

Last day of school...
They say that God is in the details. In those tiny specks of irregularity
and surprise that seem to shine from an ocean of blandness. I don't
know whether I agree, but it makes me wonder.
I remember a time, not so long ago, when people were committed to
doing a good job, and not looking for ways to get the most amount of
money for the least amount of work.
When our high school teacher came into our class and unabashedly
told us that only 25 percent will graduate, and it's okay if you didn't.
I remember how unafraid he was saying this. Unafraid of tattling
students or from the parents' association, unafraid of competing with
other teachers, and fully dedicating himself from that moment to doing
a good job. It might have made a better story to say that everyone
passed due to his exceptional teaching skills, as the movies might
depict it, but it didn't happen that way. In reality success wasn't in
the final score or the final average, but in us the students understand
that in order to make it we need to adopt principles that will carry us
through life. Even those who didn't make it till the end, adopted these.
Principles like complaining do not change workload. Not looking at
your homework isn't going to make it go away, and everyone has a
weak side. What makes one strong is how you tackle it. These were
the days of yesterday, when we cared most about delivering a fine
product rather than trying to convince everyone that we were the only
righteous ones in Sodom.

Monique

Today I am walking into class in that teacher's shoes. Greeted by cellphones poised to film every blurt and post it on TikTok, pricked in the evening by phone calls from students and parents with outlandish excuses, and a tittering principle. I look at the students, free from any restraint, even the restraint of reality and I wonder about them. How will they learn values in spite of entitlement? They believe they deserve everything just because they are what they are. I see them bullying a boy, and all the other teachers walking away, not wanting to face trouble. We teachers have become phantoms nowadays, a far cry from the leaders in the days of yore. What will become of these students when they go and serve in the army? Will they report the sandy hills, or the lack of hygiene to their parents? Will they fire the sand dunes? Once they don't get their wish, will they bully the innocents who did not have the foresight to run away, just like in that school yard 6 months ago?

I wonder about tomorrow, coming on the bus and seeing that no one gets off his seat for the elderly. I wonder what these younglings are thinking. Probably "It'll never happen to me", "They deserve what they get". I wonder what our education will wield in the next calamity. In the pandemic the go to thinking was let's markup masks' prices 100-fold. In this war it was let's markup glass's prices. I wonder tomorrow in the future where they are planning to spend their money. I wonder why I don't wonder about myself. I wonder if this will make me a teacher...

Inna

It's half past one.
I'm on the run.
escaping my own self of yesterday

the temper and the discontent
impatience, anger, and regret
my shadow-cast black silhouette
agrees with every word I say.
I wonder if I can evade
my shameful double, my dark shade.

You are asleep
so very deep
so beautiful, so genuinely free
my little babies, my own soul
I hope that you won't have to fall.
and if you fall, you'll end up whole
surviving every single storm.
I wonder how you overcome
the hardships in the days to come.

The air is dense.
It's hot and tense
I hope to one day reconcile
the monsters living in my head
my sanity is hanging by a thread.
It's delicate the path I tread,
though children are my heart's resource
I wonder if I stay the course
so that my life will not be false.

We Are From

Yasmine and Rivkah

We are from the fresh and beautiful Northern region of Israel…
    one of us for our whole lives and
    one of us since our rebirth into a new life.
We are from green and mountainous places…
    baby hills with cool trickling streams in a warm and moist realm
    giant monoliths with deep lakes and rivers in a dry and crisp
latitude
        but no ocean beaches, please.
We are an Arab Israeli and an Israeli American Jew
    both female and feminine – daughters, granddaughters, sisters,
aunts, cousins…
    but not both mothers.
We are from loving and caring families rich in values and faith…
    one from a giant brood
    one from a smaller unit
    from a belief in the one G-d – regardless of the name.
We are from parents who preach and practice respect for others
    honesty and integrity
        belief in oneself and in what is greater than oneself
            faith in others and in what lies beyond our
comprehension.
We are forever our Daddy's only little girls.
We are the youngest and the definite oldest.
One is single with no kids and the other is married with children.
One admires her oldest brother – the clever way he thinks, the love
he shows his wife.
One admires her deceased grandmother – her fierce independence
and her fierce loyalty.

We are from vibrantly colored clothing and big dangling earrings
     one who loves to shop and
     one who loathes to shop.
We are from dresses and head coverings, pants and flowing locks.
We are from favorite colors like white and purple,
     favorite foods like Mexican and Italian,
          My favorite drinks like coffee and peach iced tea.
We both delight in salty and savory food
     but only one of us also indulges in sweets.
We are work-a-holics, family-a-holics, coffee-a-holics, chocoholics.
We are from a passion for English literature.
We are from the place where texts teach us who we are and who we
ought to be.
We were born into, grew up in, and give back to the realm of education –
     questioning what we learn,
          striving to understand,
               driven to pass it on to future generations,
                    making sure to enjoy what we do so that our
students will, too.

We are from an enthusiasm for and opportunities to travel
exploring new places and new ideas
     open to different narratives and different realities
          trying to see the world and its residents through
untainted glasses.
One would love to live in Germany and
one has no desire to live anywhere else but in Israel.

One of us is strictly obedient to rules
     in her society
          in her religion
               in her parents' home.
One of us is obedient…to a point.

We are from a belief that religion is neither good nor bad

But rather it is what believers do with the tenets that matter most.

We are from those who utilize the teachings of religion to better the world and themselves without the belief that there is only one way to do this.

We are dismayed at and infuriated by the prevalence of those who abuse our beautiful traditions, warping the meaning of the words and using the convoluted doctrines as justification for acts which are anything but holy.

We are at a loss for words for those who do not speak the language of justice.
We are the same yet we are different.
We are independent yet we are intertwined.
We are from different worlds
yet we are from heartfelt friendship.

Robin and Mariana

We are two friends from many worlds

We are from tick-tocks on the wall and videocassettes.
From laced curtains and country towels.
We are from a countryside cottage and a train apartment, both cozy, warm, and smelling of autumn fruit, winter smoke & pine tree essence, spring flowers and summer sweat.
We are from the clutter hidden behind the open doors - magic is another word for it.
We are from homes that always waited for us, our parents looking forward to the summer.
We are from the home we filled with books and kids; Noisy, crazy, love.
We are from weeds, white flowers, tiger lilies and trees of the endless

forest, so high we neither dare to climb down nor jump, not before our silence made dogs angry and impatient.

We are from New Year's joy, from no holiday, from the holiday of holidays, and from each day as a day to celebrate Christmas, Ramadan, Purim and Hanuka and Thanksgiving.
We are from our grandma's cozonac, chicken soup and kugel, our mother's cakes, and our children's delicious experiments.
This talent skipped us, or we were just blessed. We must have been blessed.

Staring at the laced curtain and looming shadows cast on our bedrooms by moonlight, taught us the illusion of a fixed perspective.

We are from *we are not the best and we don't need to be*, even if you're not Nadia Comaneci, or Ester Rot Shahamarov, it matters that we participate, not how many medals we get…
We are from learning how to lose - over and over and over again, from games of chess, tennis, and football, because we were the youngest cousins.
We are from the games we played on our own, where winning never mattered and the score was never kept - that's life now.
We are from playing games of remaining compassionate, fighting for human rights and justice, we will find the game that can still save the world

We are from teaching the things we never mastered - debating, public speaking, negotiating, from building bridges and falling underneath - Quantum physics and religion, finding out that there are a lot of people who are unkind, selfish and arrogant.

We are from Gepis, Oradea, Sakhnin, New York, Seattle, and Mishmeret.
We are from wild berries and the forest nearby, running creeks and

wild rabbits and deer
only in other parts of the world, and the dry brown hills radiating in the hot scorching summer.

We are from the kisses, love of our grandmothers Buna Mariska, Granma Lily and Ida and Buna Florica. We are from our father's resilience and stubbornness, a father- in- law's grateful wiseness and our mother's softness and innocence, believing the world will heal.

We are from mothers who taught us to be kind, to be honest and generous, Who created art and beauty, delicious food, conversation and compassion?
We are from not understanding why people are so harsh and cold. But we believe that in the end, goodness will prevail.

We are from scars and we are from dreams.
We are from trying to find our role in changing ourselves and the world.
We are from standing together, and together, we shall sing.
"We shall overcome" with Martin Luther King
"We" are two, we are many, we are one!

Monique and Inna

We are from opposing poles.
Singing hymns of our mother lands
Suspicious of each other
Ending up chanting the HaTikva
In the same time zone.

Even though we have spent a good portion of our lives in the scorching sun of Tel Aviv
An abyss remains unable to be filled by the Mizrahi music and a Falafel.
The oriental flavor is unnatural to our DNA.

Growing families through a creative betrayal
Making compromises in order to fit in and accept our constantly
evolving children.
What would our grandparents say had they witnessed
this metamorphosis?
We struggle to maintain a balance of culture and our mother tongues.
Vis-à-vis our offspring, who insist on the Sabra way.

Our passion and youthful spirit are ignited by the curiosity of those
we teach.
And being able to develop creativity within ourselves
Makes our profession gratifying.
Despite the system's trying to kill this fire
We come from a place of perseverance,
So, it's not that simple to throw us to the curb.
Even in the smallest cracks we can find the light.

There were moments when our light dimmed.
We didn't sink in our own tears.
Tenaciously reemerging from the enveloping darkness
Scared but not beaten.

Dreams of a better life weren't our primary motivation.
New beginnings not anchored in any ideology.
Except in finding a different path in a new country.
Who knew our paths would cross in this land?
Such an unlikely wonderful place for both of us.

After decades of rich experiences and floundering about
We find ourselves fulfilled and with an appetite for more.
Our journey is not complete and nor is our desire.
To strive, to seek, to find and not to yield.

Kreitzberg Edition (Sassie)

We are from Mom's words of wisdom:
"Life is not fair, it just is."
"God helps those who help themselves."
"Don't break your arm patting yourself on the back."

And
We are from Mom and Dad still totally in love and "going together"
after 70 years.
We are from parents who always back each other up.
Dad kissing Mom affectionately every evening when he returns from
work in the City.

And
We are from family dinners every night.
Family vacations in Palm Springs
Cousin camp every summer

And
We are from a sports family.
Pinning medals on Mom's chest at swim meets
Tennis every weekend at Ross Landing Racquet Club
Front row baseline seats at professional tennis matches
Family runs across the Golden Gate Bridge on New Year's Day

We are from a mom who was always dieting.
And a dad who would cut out ice cream and salad dressing in order
to lose 5 pounds before his upcoming Dipsea Race.

We are from traditional gender roles:
Mom always wore makeup, maintained stylish hair and clothing, and
was the one who primarily took care of the house and children

Dad worked, trapped rodents, mowed the lawn, and taught Mom and all five children to drive.

We are from complete, unconditional, undying loyalty. Even if someone in the family is wrong, Mom knows that we are right and the other is wrong. And if someone hurts Dad's feelings, she can be poisonous. She still believes Dad's driving must be fine because he believes that, and her loyalty in this case is life-threatening.

We are from parents who see things as black and white, so happy with the life they made for themselves and their children that they cannot imagine why anyone would not choose what they have, if they could. Why would Sassie and Tzidki want to live in Israel? Why would anyone choose to remain childless? Why wouldn't everyone want to have a gardener, housekeeper, and handyman? Why would anyone double pierce their ears or wear clothes that weren't ironed or choose to be a vegetarian?

And
We are from a family that made a migration. Leaving secure, comfortable New Jersey to try new adventures in California.
Viewing the Golden Gate Bridge and fog daily
Living in a very different community from which they came
Falling in love with a new life filled with new opportunities.

And
We are from parents whose parents' parents were not so far removed from an old world, across the Atlantic, where they were not always welcome. Those old people struck out, took a chance, came here to survive and thrive. We are from those people too, though they might not understand our world today. We are from those people who hope for better.

Elena and Lara

I am from a windy industrial city,
Famous for its watermelons, apricots, and cherries,
The bottom southern point where you can cultivate raspberries,
The top northern point where you can cultivate grapes.
I am from a colorful bilingual childhood,
From candies hidden in the cupboard
And apple pies on Fridays.
I am from books that lured and tempted.
Like deep clear waters.
I am from a mysterious silence of an audience.
 Before a performance starts.

I am from where I counted days to the sea,
I am from where you want to escape to a bigger place.
I am from the middle point between "to fly" and "to flee."
From where people are scared, they'd leave no trace.

I am from the places I lost and can't be renowned.
I am from the places I chose and came to love.
I am from olive groves, vineyards, and orchards,
I am from the Judean hills, from getting closer to the stars.
I am from balancing between several languages,
I am from starting my day from "Thanks god" and "god forbid".
I am from plastic cups of coffee on my way to work.
From trying to erase deep footprints of pain
Like I erase whatever my marker has written
On a board during a class…
I am from listening to roosters and donkeys,
From steps echoing: "Never… never… never give up".

I am from a family of strong women.
I am from their history, their experiences, their perspectives,
their reactions.
I am from two homes – three.
I am from the world called me.
My world has four hearts and two bright stars.
I am from English and French and Yiddish and Hebrew.
I am from green, water, seasons, and snow.
I am from foliage.
I am from a tall mountain that only I climbed.
My mother climbed the mountain but not to the top.
I am from very little – with so much.

We're both from quiet admiration of our tough grannies,
From stories, told and retold, twisted and smoothed again/
We're both from several languages echoing in the valleys,
From several homes, from old keys in the drawers…
From admiring fall foliage, from chestnuts, mushrooms, and berries
We're both from walking distances through the mountain wood.
Or in the open steppe…
We're both from listening to flowers and to water.
Probably, we're both from walking barefoot down the stream.
We're both from Hebrew,
We're both from Israeli roads and trails.
We're both from where a marker glides a trace on a board.
 Before it forms an idea…

Ella and Shatha

We are from a page of agonizing waiting.
Feeling stuck, the future a blur
Committing the art of escapism via our pens

Sending messages of hope to our loved ones.
Our unborn children and grandchildren
Who, nourished by the seeds of our endless
prayers
We hope we will live a life of carefree,
unconcerned and frivolous peace
A world apart from our lives now.
We come from the only place we know as home.
That is strangely safe in its fearsome danger.
For which we will fight
By all means necessary
Striving for precious and lasting
Peace.

We are from lines of poetry.
Disregarding the rules
Painting worlds of emotion
That leaves us cleansed.
Or sometimes at a loss
Trying to wrench our hearts onto the page
With words more powerful than fists.

Amal and Emily

We're from such a very wide space of stars and the moon.
We are from all times – morning, night, and noon.
We are from those who are still stuck close to the radio.
to get the news very soon.
That want to struggle and get their dreams real with a very painful bone.

We're from different backgrounds that goes between a broken home
and a family together,
A kid of simple workers and a kid of a law professor and physicist mother.

That taught us to respect others as they are with whom they belong no matter who.

In order to spread love and care and be the helping hand for each other. Ignoring the differences between creations and hoping and praying for better.

We came from different places that plant good manners in the minds of small kids.

That accept and respect their religion and take traditions as a lifestyle of success.

In the past we were raised that people are the same and that killed the mess

Till we get to the immediate moment and become the worriers to decrease evil to less.

We're a group with the responsibility of raising generations in the space of lovely homes and schools.

Teaching them that nationalities are fake names that split people from the tree of cool.

Getting them down from the top because of the lie that was drawn by cheaters and a fool.

That supports differences in the name of politics until we are separated by those who rule.

We're the fighters of this agenda who want to spread love and peace and go through tolerance as a useful tool

Mimi and Naftali

I am a teacher surviving the end of a difficult school year.
I am a teacher trying to survive and get a decent income to live a respectable life and support my family.

Am I tired myself or is the school year and everything in my environment that is tiring me out?

I'm jaded, I'm tired and I need my flame to be rekindled. My joy of life needs watering.

I am a parent truly worried about the future of my 3 daughters… What will be here in the future?
I have sick people depending on me that I must take care of.
What kind of culture will survive this terrible war?
I have been fighting a legal system that has tried to marginalize the infirm dependent on me.
    Now, I am dealing with the idea that we will have to be in combat for a perpetual future.

My silence is part of where I am now. I don't talk too much.
I am NOW - well yesterday - at least - I enjoyed and was touched and cried - with the collective - over the returning of Noa Argamani - because her beautiful, feminine, young, naive, contorted frantic face was with me for these past months as the kidnappers captured her. She was so beautiful, sweet, gentle to be with her father.

But throughout it all I realize I am alive enough to never stop charging ahead. I'm proud of how hard I worked to get where I am now.

Chapter 2

As life marches on, four hostages have returned but eleven soldiers have been killed.
Soldiers? Students! Who was one year out of high school. How can we continue teaching?
I look at my 10th graders and wonder what the future holds for them. I cringe on the inside. Yet on the outside I tell them to get off their smartphones.

And life Marches on.

I look out of my window and see the open highway. I see cars travelling unto the endless expense, and realize the future is undecided. Every morsel of good news fuels me and moves me ahead. Hope is a potent fuel indeed.

Hope is life, I wonder to myself if there is a language in our world, where actually the word hope itself means life.

Even if there is not one, we need to make that language up, and maybe, just maybe change our world for the better. Maybe we should reverse the tower of Babylon and have everyone speak the same language again so they stop quarrelling.

And I would ask the question: If we were all speaking the same language, would we really quarrel less?

We Are From Wells

We are from Wells.
We want to know each other.
Deeper than your name and what city you're from.
We believe in dialogue.

Some of us celebrate Passover, some Easter, and some Eid Al Adha
Some of us eat Maqluba, and some of us eat jachnun, and some
eat kneidlach.
But when we come together, we have salads and sandwiches and
fruit platters.

We are all curious about one another.
Some of us are afraid when we enter the other's neighborhood.
Some of us teach in the other school.
But we feel misunderstood.
Only some of our children compile a roots project in 7th grade.
Some of our children hardly know their own culture.
Some of our children barely speak the language of their ancestors.
Only some of us can speak freely without fear.

We are
Asaf and Natalie
Adi, Arine, Ayelet
Costa, Hagit, Marlene, Michal
Mona, Orna, Rafi
Sana, Sassie, Shabli, Sharon, Shibolet, Suhaa.

Writing Through War

Shatha: A Silent Scream

A mouthful of unsaid words is stuck inside.
Waiting for their release.
But a fisted hand keeps banging on my chest.
Keeps on knocking off my breath.
They keep me locked up in their ironclad cage.
Stripping me of my voice.
I let them stay,
I let them bang,
For I know,
When the time comes,
When my voice breaks free—
It will echo through the universe,
A roar that will rattle the heavens.
And the truth,
A beast in disguise,
Will be set loose,
A monster called humanity—
Bare and brutal,
Unveiled for all to see.

Amal: Between Al-Quds and Jerusalem

I fell in love with an Arab African American prince who I met in the land of so far away.

As I got the honor to meet my nation through his presence that I dreamt to meet one day

He is elegant, a gentleman and Arab king between the foreign princes, amazed me by his say.

When he greets others by Alsalamu Alaykum, like announcing his pride being Arab like the light of sun ray.

I watched him passing in front of my eyes, smiling and my mind kept the image of him.

I wanted to know him more so, he directed me to read history books, "you will know me from there" he wanted to claim.

Then he asked me where I am from and I replied proudly- from the land of each one's dream

The holy land that holds the history, the glory and the land of all religions and nations. I am from the land that ages millions of millennia.

Then I saw him surprised and he asked me again, so where are you from? Like he wanted to know if in the Dead Sea or Gaza Sea I swim

I got the point, and said I dive in both but I must practice more in order to get the Asian and African shores as the aim.

I saw him repeating my words and asking again- ok! But where are you from exactly? I admire you but need to adjust the stream.

I got that we have been in love for so many years throughout history but he wants to be sure if I am the daughter of Abraham or Ibrahim

I want him so much too, but he won't understand that I am the daughter of both fathers -Abraham and Ibrahim and I replied- "I am between al Quds and Jerusalem."

Elena: Reflections

Reflections will be definitely written with no conscious attempt at versification. However, an occasional rhyme might find its way into the writing, like a bird from another dimension probing our world with the tip of its curious beak. Everything around me is more or less similar to birds. The kettle whistles cheerfully like the first chirp of the morning. A mynah tries to imitate the initial notes of the alarm. Almost succeeds and makes several people jump in panic. I put a metaphor inside another metaphor, in front of a metaphor, beneath a metaphor… trying to create a protective fence, which is of course only a flimsy illusion of a defense. The beaks of our fears are all around us, just behind the walls. If they are hard enough, a stone has the strength of a writing paper. It can be easily pricked, too easily. I wish *hopes* could enter with equal ease. Or can they?

Ella: WE BURIED THEM

The sun glares fiercely on this cold, cold day,
The funeral procession winds its painful way.
With shattered hearts, we lined up the somber road,
Kfir Bibas, a father alone, how can we lighten your load?

Our nation grieves a triple farewell,
To lives extinguished by horror none can quell.
Wailed eulogies crash through self-absorbed spaces,
Farewell to sons with freckled, laughing faces.

We have no words to ease the despair,
For we, too, are broken beyond repair.
A grave where three become one in the ground,
And the arms of our people encircle around.

Somehow, somewhere, He'll give us the reason,
As winter withdraws for the hope of the season.
Rays of renewal on tear-dappled dew,
Turning our sorrow to strength no one can undo.

Abeer: Humanity

I will have a child and name him Adam, because names in our time are a charge. I won't name him Muhammad or Isa, nor Ali or Omar, nor Saddam or Hussein, not even Zakariya or Ibrahim, nor even David or George. I fear that he will grow up with racism, that his name might dictate his fate. To foreigners, he would be a terrorist, to extremists, a sinner, to Shiites, a Sunni, and to Sunnis, either Alawi or Shiite. I fear that his name will be his passport. I want him to be Adam, a Muslim Christian. I want him to know that religion is only what resides in his heart, what he believes and does, not just his name. I will teach him that Arab identity is an illusion, and that humanity is what truly matters. I will teach him that hunger is disbelief, ignorance is disbelief, and oppression is disbelief. I will teach him that God is in hearts before mosques and churches, and that God is love, not fear. I will teach him what our ancestors forgot to teach us. I will teach him that what we lack is what we have, and that what we have is what we lack. I will teach him that I began by saying I would have a son because women are still being buried alive, and that the imbalance still persists in society.

Inna: Personal Reflections from Oct. 7

I would have liked so much to tell you
that a catastrophe
one Saturday, a little after dawn
would cause an unimaginable pain

and things will never be the same
in life again
in life again.

I would have liked so much to tell you:
Be ready in advance
save anyone you can
because there'll be a lot of blood
it's now your only chance,
before the flood
before the flood.

But in that paradise destroyed
women were raped
families burnt
and children lost
under the sky that once was blue.
And I repeat this like a fool
what I'd have liked so much to tell you
what I'd have liked so much to tell you
what I'd have liked so much to tell you.

Shatha: Thoughts

Loneliness is a strange sort of thing.
It's a dark hooded monster that creeps in on you, quiet and still.
It sits by your side in the dark.
Strokes you by your hair.
Caresses you with its clawed hands.
It wraps itself around your bones, squeezing just enough to make
you uncomfortable.

It leaves your heart maimed and marred.

Lie next to you at night, leeching the light out of every corner.

It's a constant companion.

It wakes you in the morning and puts you to sleep at night.

Loneliness is an old friend that stands beside you, that looks at you in the mirror and challenges you to live your life without it.

Loneliness is a bitter wretched companion.

And sometimes, it just won't let go.

Amal: Daffodil

This is a very special poem that I wrote about my special sister who had special needs and whom I lost four years ago; her name was Narjes. Narjes is the name of the rose of daffodil in Arabic.

Does modern life give technology the right to change people's emotions?

Categorizing them into groups and names by the lie of globalization

To convince them that people are different peoples of more than a nation

which lets them live behind the screens, till they turn with no appreciation

killing the union of belonging and fighting to get it back by organization

Struggling not to lose containing the other through the coming generation

God created the universe putting his beauty and specialty into his creation.

And made all people equal and free but differences are found in education.

He prefers educated scientists who will treat sickness and passion.

Gave them to mind the brain, looking and searching for any information.

Teaches people about the beauty of special people of syndromes' situation.

And raised the feeling of containing and love for them with consideration.
They are "The Special Ones" that have ever found in the whole creation.

In one spot of the globe, there was a garden in an unknown location.
Roses grew up of lavender smell and one different rose got attention.
It was a daffodil between the lavender field, a foreign rose of creation.
flowers went far from jealousy and captured it in the prison of isolation.
Till the farmer came and defined its beauty that decorated the location
Watered it carefully and took care of it with a fear of coming pollution.
It was strange to feel like the daffodil calling for any communication.

The wise farmer got the gift from God as the specialty in differentiation.
And was showing off that he was chosen to get God's adoration.
To send him this daffodil that is not found in any other location.
decorates his simple hut to be a great castle in a world of imagination.

Teaching each one of us the meaning of being thankful with appreciation and being aware to value even the smallest thing that may cause a revolution that may change life for the better and gives the real meaning of "pure relation."

Shatha: Finding Light in the Darkness

I wish that a lot of my life was fictional.
Where war is a forgotten myth and happiness is an achievable dream.
Where I don't hate my army husband's job or loathe the time we are forced apart.
I wish that a lot of my life was a fantasy story, where I am the protagonist, picking daisies in a field and not waiting for the sounding of death knells and the beckoning of ruin.
But,
I live in the real world.

Where the sound of him coming home is like a soft caress in my heart.

And despite the weariness on his face and the feel of his sinking cheeks in my hands, he is healthy and whole.

I live in the real world.

Where I wonder if it was the right choice to be pregnant at a time like this.

Where all I think about is the guilt I will feel if my daughter is angry at me for bringing her to a world where hate and violence is the language we speak.

Where all I thought about is having a piece of him if anything went awry.

Because I want to see his nose, his lips and his eyes. His thick charcoal lashes and his wit and laughter.

I want to see them on her face, in her features, when I look at her. When I hear her voice.

I live in the real world, you see.

I live in the real world.

Where, despite the darkness, we need to look for the light.

Where his laughter, his voice, his smell are what bring me comfort.

Where waiting eight long years to hear the words "congrats, you're having a baby girl" is what brings tears to my eyes.

Where anticipating being a mom and a dad overrules what feels like a ticking of a clock.

We live in the real world.

Where light should always be found, even in the darkest of days.

Elena: A Day Reclaimed

A day reclaimed.

When I turn back in tears, I turn back in pain.

Looking at the valley, half-eaten by mist,
I imagine the day I wish to reclaim.
And recreate into a modest feast.
First the setting: a blooming village by the whispering sea
The warmest and the shallowest sea in the country,
The softest dunes you can imagine, the skies that sing.
And only stop singing to generate two or three lightings.
In the midst of the warmest shower in the world
First the setting... Then the feeling: barefoot, happy
Never kissed, never insulted, never taught.
To watch out. Everything is yet to come. Just let it.
When I turn back in hope... That's still the day to reclaim.
To make it happen afresh for five minutes each morning.
A day with nothing to lose and nothing to gain.
Which probably makes it the happiest and the strongest.

Ella: Hope

There are days when.
Hope warms me in its
Soft woven blanket of
Dreams, prayers, and legends
An endless pattern
The angora wool of
Soft spun light
I may shrug it away.
Preferring the itchy dread
Of darker days
Destruction, death
The daggers of hatred
A coarse hopelessness
Of endless wars
Friction with a capital F

Within and without

BUT
Somewhere in the softness
Of my beating heart
I know.
That I must be still
I must hold fast.
To the fabric of
Better days
To the comfort object
Clutched
As I sleep
Untouched
By the nightmares of hopelessness.

Amal: Change

CHANGE

People sometimes close their eyes to ignore what they have seen.
Hearts get tired of explaining thoughts and what spoken words mean.
Judging and overthinking kills pleasure and causes bodies to lean.
Stop suffering because it leads to losing everything that once
had been.

Get up! Get alive! Days run so fast, adding to the number of years
of age. Creatures are different, but all of them live together in the
same cage.It is the wild wide world that separates members by the
written page,Titling them with names of countries and nationalities,
from familiar to strange.

It tires the mind until brains are updated to break darkness by the

light of the sun, To cancel limits, pain, and hate and spread love everywhere, joy, and fun.To love each other, help, realize dreams, work hard, and act all as one.To close all the files of fight, pain, and war and throw them away with a sign of
DONE.

Amal: Hope

HOPE

To all the people that I know and have met during my life chapter.
A message of love I want to send for being a daughter, sister, wife, and a mother.
First, I want to say "alhamdulillah" for being me as l am and thanks to God for creating me in a good shape and complete picture.
I look to the skies so thankful for all the blessings that I get from You, Lord, calling, praying, thanking and asking that me to you become closer.
You always balance my life, even when I have the greatest worries and heaviest responsibilities, but you give me the wisdom to struggle and the power of a fighter.
It is the uniqueness of feeling others' pain, being the helping hand for those who need it and seeing all people as they are the same and not " judging the book by its cover"
I have lost precious ones in my life, I cried, got frustrated then realized Your generosity for choosing me to be the warrior and the winner.
For getting the best dad that can be found on earth, and a very special sister.
I got the honor to serve and take care of them, like You telling me to do the mission and go up higher.
To get the highest human degrees of being an obedient daughter, good sister, and successful fighter.
The prize is getting my mom's wishes to God to keep and protect

me from dangers by calling God "الله ي رضي عليكي" my daughter.

The best winning of a gold medal is getting a unique or even the best man on earth ever.

A loving, caring, sharing, and supporting husband and an amazing role model father.

That helps me raise four lovely roses in our garden of life by containing me and them and holding us together.

To face the rudeness of life and fight for the place to which we belong forever:

The holy place of The Holy Land that lived for so many years and was attacked by dangerous minds of haters.

Who wants to convince people to live in groups, split them from the tree of union, humanity and cancel the meaning of life if all as one matter.

Hey you! You are totally wrong! All as one, and one cares for all, that is the point that we must raise the generations at, so do not create a gap and make it wider.

I was born as a Muslim Arab, so I practice Islam and speak Arabic and live in the holy land; my best friends are Christians, Druze, Jewish with a pleasure.

Stop mixing cards together, acting the worst way and trying to show that things are different by judging the book cover.

Your tries will not be taken anymore because we realize that our differences create a unique figure.

You will not cancel me if I am the other, and I will not let you live the saying "the other is me", no it is a mistake dear hater.

Me is me, you must get this and respect me as I do by taking that you are the other and I do accept and respect with pleasure.

Shatha: Three Kinds of Fire

There are three kinds of fire, she decided.

The first is the fire of love, A blazing inferno where lovers burn madly,

No flood can quench it, No storm can dim its light. It roars and crackles, A warmth that consumes and creates.

The second is the fire of jealousy, A slow, smoldering heat, Born of envy so deep it carves scars. No gentle hand can cool it, No whispered reassurance can snuff it out.It clings like smoke, choking the air.

And then, there is the fire of hate, A wild, raging blaze, Fueled by loathing and resentment. It devours without mercy, Scorching even the sweetest kiss.No tender touch can tame its fury.

Three fires, each relentless in its own way, Each leaving its mark, On flesh, on soul, on love.

Elena (Israel) and Alla (Ukraine): We Hope

Alla

I hope simple kindness will prevail,
I hope war will be defeated by peace.

I hope everyone will feel some joy.
And every joyful day will be repeated!

I hope kids won't cry in bitter fear.
Imagining they will be buried young.
And greyish pain won't cover mothers' hair.
I hope death notices won't come.

I hope still to see the reason restored.
And help both to governments and to the people.
I hope to witness a peaceful flourishing world.
I do hope the villain will be defeated.

Elena

Four am. I wake up and remember that wars start at sunrise
before Eos touches the ocean with its purplish fingers.
She's dressed so brightly, it never matters if it's February.
I look at the window thinking: it's time to wash it.
I look at the palm trees, feeling, - not knowing.
That in your city the war has started.
And placed its ugly dragon paws on the Dniepro's throat,
And beats the snowy fields with its beastly tail.
And ruins the gardens that would bear cherries.
Six twenty. You went to bed an hour ago.
Getting the suitcase ready for your flight to Leipzig.
Six twenty one. The calamity on its way.
Six twenty two. I wake up to fetch a mug of coffee.
Six twenty three. Several kettles are boiling.
Six twenty four. Another dozen joins in.
Six twenty five. I open a thriller.
Six twenty six. You turn a pillow.
Six twenty seven. The coffee is hot.
Six twenty eight. The mynah is chirping.
Six twenty nine... My Gosh, another minute.
Six thirty. Six thirty one. You sleep.
The sirens don't wail.
Eleven am. Eleven pm. Midnight.
Three am. All's quiet.

Both

This is the silliest and the brightest of our hopes.
Coming on its mighty wings out of the blue.
Coming on its lighting wings out of tunnels.
Coming on its embracing wings from the debris...

Writing by Our Students

Inna: Hadassim (Even Yehuda)

Where I Am From

Shirah Arad

When people ask me where I'm from, I always say the same thing. I say where I live, where I physically am most of the time. Sometimes, I tell them about my birth town and where I grew up until I was three.

But recently, I have noticed I don't exactly tell them where I'm really from.

Where you are from has nothing to do with where you live, but it has everything to do with your thoughts, your mind and your emotions. A smart man said once: "you are where your mind is," and I believe in that. To me, it's more important what you think and feel, rather than where you live. I have always been the kind of person that gives a chance, that gets to know people before judging them. Only you is what matters to me, your thoughts, and feelings. If I like you or if I don't, it has everything to do with **you**, the inner **you**, not the outside **you**, not what you own or who your friends are.

The inside is all that matters.

So, next time I ask you where you are from, I'm not interested in knowing where you live.
I want to know where you are mentally.

Dana Tuch

I was born here in Israel, but I never felt like I am a real Israeli. You see, I was born into a Russian household, where I was raised in a different culture, different language, different everything. And because of that I have struggled a lot at school. I come from a house, where there are expectations, where there is a high standard, where it's hard to be free. My accent is different, my food is different and I am different.

Gili Sharon

Where I'm from, you ask? That's a question, the answer to which isn't known to man.

Often I say I'm from the place I currently am at, but that often changes constantly, leaving me with a chronic sense of belonging. I suppose I am from Earth with my heart split between seas and continents. My "Home" is never certain and concrete. I may feel temporary joy every once in a while, but at the end of each day, as I lie in bed, staring at the ceiling, I still question my existence and a point in being.

Amit Chaimy

I am from an uncommon culture.
But from a common city
But I am from a not so common a country.
I am from a small place.
A small place called Israel.
Israel may be small, but strong.
Strong such as twenty countries
We survived all of it.
I come from
The best place to come from.

Liya Medicks

I am from many things.
It's exciting, complex and sometimes it stings.
I'll start with my parents, the best in the world,
Whose hugs will forever heal me from the cold.
They brought me to Earth on a day full of rain,
And since then, they protected me from hate and from pain.
I love them so much and I will forever,
But there's something else that wipes off my tears.
It's not even a part of the big human race,
It's actually a beautiful, magnificent place.
This place will forever be a part of my heart,
And seeing it break is tearing me apart
But even if it's covered by a big, sad cloud,
No matter what, I will always stay proud.
Proud of the army that's making me cry,
Proud when I hear "Am Israel hai!"
Being a part of this is feeling surreal,
I don't take it for granted, I never will.
This past year was full of sorrow and misery,
Too many of us we lost in agony,
But even after all of that grief and pain,
I just know - we will dance again.

I am from many things -
It's exciting, complex, and it definitely stings.
I am from my parents, who treat me so well,
But firstly I am from my pride, my belief, my home - Israel.

Abigail Botser

I live in Israel, next to my grandmother in Even Yehuda. I wasn't born here. I was born in Chicago, though I moved to California when I was two and to Israel when I was three.

So, where am I from? Now, for the past eleven years - I'm from Israel. But it doesn't matter. If you ask me, half my heart is in Cypress with my long-distance best friend.

But, it's also in my writing. My ideas for books in the Victorian Era, or in the Medieval times; where the thief gets the princess; where they run away from the toxic family; where they find love only in each other; where they die together, where he chose her; where girls can be who they want to be; where the characters are everything I want to be; where the characters are more than just people - where the characters are smarter and stronger than me. Because I write it.

Ella: Tichon Or (Tzur Hadassah)

Noya Keshet

I am from a land where compassion moves like a steady river.
I'm from strength rises with the dawn, quiet yet unyielding.
I am from the tear-streaked voice of my little brother.
Whose cry lingers, a reminder of that day's sharp divide.
I am from the petunias scattered along the kibbutz paths.
Symbols of endurance, blooming in the dust of memory that I remember standing strong like we did I am from Shavuot's sacred ceremony, where we gather.
Hands clasped; hearts bound in the rhythms of the past I am from Tomer Arava, Aner Shapira, and Shi Li Atari
Their names are like stones.

that weighs heavy on my chest.

I am from "this kitchen is for dancing" which my mother told us to remind us that we bring life to life

"I Have a Chance" by Avitar Banai lifted me from the depths."

Its melody is a thread pulling me towards the light.

I am from Kibbutz Givat Brenner, and from Europe's cool winds and Iraq's ancient soil run in my veins The taste and smell of coffee and fresh cookies always take me back to the stolen. innocence in that day, and it's sad that I find my comfort in this food from Keshet's story, as my family name, who danced beneath the stars.

Only to have his light stolen by the brutal hands of fate From the resilience found in a single smile in the faces I paint, where the beauty of life continues.

Everything is etched in pencil on the walls of my heart.

Steven: Young Ambassadors School (Petah Tiqva)

I Am From

Maya Ilany

I am from a house, I am from a home.
Loving and kind, comforting and warm

I am from my future; I am from my past.
I am mostly from the present, fleeting too fast.

I am from my surface, and deep in my heart.
I am me at the end, I was me from the start.

I am from the moon, the stars and the sun.
I am from boring, as I am from fun.

I am from my pride; I am from my shame.
I am from my feelings; I am from my brain.

From my good, from my bad
My happiness or my sad
I did it for me, and for that I am glad.

Eviatar Haham

I am from peace and love.
I am from a family that loves to be kind to everyone.
I am from a nice family.
I am from a great country with peace and love.
I am from Israel.
I am from a place with happiness.
I am from my parents who love me.
I come from Petah Tiqva
I come from loving Shawarma–it's tasty!

M.D.

I am from here.
I am from there.
I am from anywhere.
I am from fear for my life everywhere I go.
I am from being the punchline of every joke.
I am from knowing that I am welcome nowhere.
I am running to a bomb shelter at four.
I am from the trauma.
I am from the pain.
I am from the standing alone in front of an entire school brainwashed
into hating me.
I am from the abuse.

I am from the assault.
I am from being the punching bag of every person I know.
I am from standing up for myself.
I am from art.
I am from music.
I am from the theater.
I am from everywhere.
I am from the West and the East
From Yemen and Hungary
The Khaybar massacre, and Dr. Mengele's torture
From the yellow patch and the pink triangle
From Dreifus's case and Turing's death
I am from fighting this and fighting that.
I am from wanting freedom.
But more than all I am from myself.

I Wonder

Amichay Kreimer

I wonder if other people like stuff as I do.
I wonder if other people appreciate moments as I do.
I wonder how different we can be from each other.
I wonder why people never really learn from the past.
I wonder if luck exists, how lucky am I?
I wonder why people fight about how something that is as old as we
can think about (the world) started.
I wonder if other people wonder as much as I do.

Maya Ilany

Sometimes I sit and wander for hours.
I wonder if love can be determined by picking the petals of a flower.

If bullies are too brave, or defenseless cowards.
Why are people's souls bitter and sour?
Would they act the same way if they didn't have power?
They had the chance to save people, why didn't they take it?
Can justice exist or will it remain an abstract concept?
Is heaven real? How do you get in?
Is it based on your actions, or based on your motive?
Are we all in a coma? Did we imagine our life?
If we are in a coma, will we survive?
Will we remember this when we wake up?
If we all live and die, why does it matter when and how?
Why do I wonder? Will I get an answer?
I'm sure my mom knows, I'll go and ask her.

Part IV: In Loving Memory of Principal Zeyad Abu Mokh

We held several writing workshop days at Ibn al-Haitham High School in Baqa al-Gharbiya. The writing in this chapter comes from Ibn al-Haitham students and is dedicated to the memory of Principal Zeyad—a passionate advocate for youth empowerment and a firm believer in fostering coexistence through education.

I Am From

Muhammad Dacca Ashrad

I am from a society where there is a lot of killing,
Where people don't love each other, and it changes your thoughts and your personality.

But I am still from society,
I am from the call to prayer five times a day,
I am from where everyone helps each other,
I am from a very nice person,
I am from the scenery of nature that you can only see if you are here with us,
I am from always standing out in an Islamic community despite seeing the lifestyle of the European people.

Karam

I am from:
I am from a place that is not safe,
I am from a place that I consider leaving.

I don't feel comfortable in this place.

There is so much violence in this place.

There is no one who has a solution to the violence in this place.

But.... I do not want to leave this place and can't leave this place.

I have my family and friends in this place.

There is no sea in this place and there is not a green area.

I am from a city that people say is a peaceful city.

But every two weeks we hear about murder and violence.

Every time I step out of my house going to school, I feel insecure and unsafe.

but I love my people because they are so generous and it is common to find luxury cars in my city.

The name of my city (Baqa) means a bouquet of flowers and it's located in the west.

I'm from a Muslim city and that is because we hear the adhan (call to prayer) of the mosque.

Salma Atamni

I am from a place where people take advantage of each other.

I am from a place where selfishness rules, and kindness is only valued when it benefits others.

But I am also from a place where, deep down, people still have good hearts. They try to live together peacefully even though they aren't perfect.

I am from a place where I look forward to the good things that can come, not to the bad things that are already there. I hope to see people reach a point where kindness is shared and truly lived.

Yosra

I am from a mom who was born and grew up in the north.
I am from a dad who grew up without his parents.
I am from a country that has no love in it.
I am from a city where there are no green places.
I am from a city where there is no quiet in it.
I am from a city where everyday someone is killed.
I am from a school whose principal was killed.
I am from loving my city anyways.
I am from wanting my city to be better than it is now.
I am from hoping for the violence to end.

Saeed

Where I come from is an Arab town located in the northern triangle of historic Israel. It is known for its rich history, fertile agricultural land, and it's warm, welcoming atmosphere. Its residents work in various fields, and the town is notable for the high level of education among its people. The town's geographical location, close to major cities, makes it an important connection point.

I have a deep love for this town—not only for its beautiful history and culture but also for its incredible food. Every dish here feels like a celebration of tradition and care, making my connection to this place even stronger.

This Scar Is From

Sameer Abu Hussein

Every time I look at my foot, I remember the good times. Back in 2012, I was at my cousin Ayham's House. He had bought a four-wheeler. It was brand new, and we came out to the street to drive around. After an hour or two I told him "Do some tricks, don't be bored" he tried to do a wheelie and we crashed into the electricity pole. He fell to the ground. Nothing happened to him, but when I fell, I got a small injury on my left foot. Now after it has become a scar every time, I look at it and I remember that accident back in 2012. I also remember back then what I felt at that moment, 4-year-old me felt pain but at the same time pleasure that I didn't fall alone and that Ayham fell with me, and now we both got that memory in our lives that we still laugh about to this moment whenever we see each other

Sham Laham

I feel a lot of pain when I lose something dear. So how much pain do we have when we lose our dear principal? This was the biggest scare that time left for me.

This is due to the fact that our principal Zeyad was a brother and a father to us even before he was our teacher, and he always wanted our success. This scar hurts so much because time will not bring him back. Also, the way he died was very terrible, immoral people murdered him. Now I feel a mixture of strong emotions: sadness, fear and anger. However, teacher Zeyad also left a great effect on our lives, and we will stay on his approach: faith, respect, peace, tolerance and education. These values meet together. This scar will stay alive in my memory.

Do You Really Know Me?

Tala Gnamy

I was playing Roblox with my friends, and I had a problem with my headphones, so I wrote in the chat in Arabic to tell my friend that I had a problem with my headphones. 30 seconds later I managed to fix my headphones, just in time for me to hear a group of girls insulting us because we are Arab.

I asked myself did I do something wrong? So, I asked them "what's the problem"? One of them answered and said "You are Arabs, and you don't deserve to live."

I told her, "Why does that matter? What is the difference between us, I'm human and you're human. You judged me because I'm Arab, but you don't know who I really am. The problem is in your mind if you judge me before getting to know me.'

Jana Abed

Do you really know me? Do you really know what I feel, or are you just judging me?

Do you know that I cry every day because I lost my cat? Why and how can you say that it's "ok" to lose your pet? Do you really know how much I was connected to my cat, that inside of me I feel like I lost a part of my heart? You said that I'm sensitive, but I'm not sensitive. You just don't feel what I feel, and you don't live my life. You cannot judge if you don't know what the other person is feeling!

Remas Abu Mokh

Don't say that you really know me if you can't see my real thoughts and feelings and what I really feel inside. Don't tell me that you understand me when you don't see the war deep inside. I don't need you to understand me, I just need you to let me feel the feelings I want to feel.

If you're really saying that you understand me, can you tell me what I felt when my grandmother passed away? Can you explain the pain I felt that day, and how guilty I considered myself because I wasn't with her when she said her last words? No, so please, do not try to understand me, don't tell me it's ok, because for me it's not. Don't tell me not to cry, because for me it's the least painful way I can express my pain.

Where I Am Now

Abd alrahman Masri

Where I am now: I'm in the holy land that is destined to be peaceful and don't use violence as a language
or am I in a land where people hate each other and despise living together because of the hate they feel towards each other?

Many say this is the holy land and many say otherwise.
Where I am, I'm in a land where justice is served or am I in a land that favors a specific group.

I don't know how to feel or think, each day I wake up questioning myself where I am, but it turns out I'm at home.

Mohamed Majdalawy

In the beginning of high school, I did not know most of my classmates, and I was confused by the subjects that we learned, which caused me to fail exams. I did not feel like I was in the right place. But then, after I got to know my schoolmates, they started to help me in school, and I was able to improve my grades. Since then, I feel more like I know where I am, and where I want to be in the future.

Salma Atamni

Now I am in a better state than I was before.
Now I can see the world with my eyes and not my heart.

Now I can see the two faces that everyone has.

Now I realize that I was too kind to people who did not deserve my kindness.

And now I have come to a point where I stopped caring about anything and anyone who does not care about me, my feelings, or my opinions. Now it is my time to care about myself.

Saeed Daqa

At the end of 9th grade, I wanted to change schools. Of course, it was hard for me to leave my friends there and my memories, but I had to move on.

When I came to my new high school, I did not know anyone. I recognized some students from back in elementary school, but I had no relationship with them.

I started to make friends, it was a little bit hard, and scary, but I overcame that feeling, and I made a lot of great friends.

The thing that I want to say is that it doesn't matter how hard or scary a thing that you want to do, you must never hesitate.

Mohammed Abosene

Actually, right now I am lost in the depths of Nowhere. I don't know where I am or where to go. Should I chase after my dreams or follow my comfort?

So many things‹ for instance: I don't know if I have to stay in my class and in my major in school. In addition, I became Municipal Student Council Secretary and now I feel like I am under pressure and I feel that I have grown up and the responsibilities have increased so much. In addition to this my personality has changed a lot.

In the end I wish that there is someone who can guide me to the right path and if you have someone who can guide you, don't leave him because he will change you into the best version of you.

Reflection: The Night Baqa Didn't sleep

Sameer

November 6th, 2024 was one of the worst days I have ever experienced. I woke up that day at about 7 AM. I was starting to get ready for school and I was happy because I had a programming exam that day. I was about to leave for school then suddenly I got a call from my friend Abd Al Rahman Shded. He told me that our principal Ziyad Abo Mokh was killed for no reason. In fact, he was killed for being good and kindhearted. They killed him using a car bomb that they planted in his car that same morning. Everyone in the city heard the explosion, when we heard it everyone quickly went to the scene to see what had happened. When I understood what had happened, I felt sad and helpless that I could not do anything and that I wouldn't even see him the next day at school. After some time, we went to his funeral. I saw about 10,000 people attending it. By that number alone you can see how good he was and how many people love him, and that proves that he was killed for absolutely no reason. That night will not be forgotten and it will leave a scar in our lives forever.

Light Through the Darkness

Baker

In this hard life, there is lots of darkness. Maybe hidden, maybe not, like this dark life. Life isn't fair. I find myself asking, "is this really me?".

Maybe if I were somewhere else, I could get more chances. But this unfair world won't tell me what I can't do. If each person follows his light, which calls him, he could be whatever he wants. If God wanted this for him for sure it would happen, but anyone who is determined and sets a goal to reach, God will of course help him to succeed, and he can become unstoppable.

Siwar

Every day I think to myself and ask myself many questions. Should I give up? Why do I have to go through this? Why me?

In life there are problems everywhere, and every single person goes through struggles. But the important thing is how you deal with it, and if you are headed in the right direction. If you go in the right way, then you become strong and unstoppable, but if you head the wrong way, then you will feel weak and like a failure. So, the main thing is to know yourself, and to understand yourself with respect to reach the right way to solve the problems.

Siraj Kadan

Do you really know when I was hurt? Do you really know when was that time that I was near death? Do you really care about me?

Did you really see me when I was in the darkness?

Did you ask about me, or was it only my mom who cared about me, when she helped me reach the light when I was in darkness? Is she the only one who saved me when I was close to death?

Is my mom the only one that cares about me? Is she just my light or is there someone else who cares about me –just tell me.

Meral

Every day I think to myself and I try to make a simple change in someone else's day or week. My focus is on helping others and brightening their lives. For that reason, I care about small acts of kindness, and I believe that I should spread them and make others happy.

Omar Abed

One night I was scrolling through social media. Suddenly a sports reel showed up on my screen. It was a volleyball video. I felt like my soul was telling me "You've never been good at sports, but this one could be different." I kept watching more videos, and every new video encouraged me more, so I decided to join a volleyball team. Unfortunately, there was no boys' volleyball team in my town, and my parents wouldn't agree to me joining a team far away from our town. This built a wall in my path. But my will is stronger than that. I got a ball and started training alone, or sometimes with a friend. I hope that someday I can play volleyball in competitive games and be proud of my hard work while holding a trophy.

Meral Taha Akale

Life often feels like a series of storms, moments when the world seems engulfed in shadows. Yet, within the deepest darkness, a glimmer of light often emerges, symbolizing hope, resilience, and the human spirit's capacity to overcome challenges. The idea of "light through the darkness" serves as a reminder that even in our hardest times, there is a path forward, often illuminated by unexpected sources.

In my own life, I have experienced moments where hope seemed out of reach. One vivid memory comes from a time when I struggled with overwhelming self-doubt. I was drowning in fear of failure and felt paralyzed by the weight of expectations. For weeks, it felt as though I was walking through an endless tunnel with no light in sight. However, one day, a simple conversation with a close friend changed everything. Their words, "You are stronger than you think," resonated deeply. It was as though a candle had been lit in the darkness, showing me the way forward. Slowly but surely, I began to believe in myself again. That experience taught me the power of small gestures and the resilience that lies within us all.

This concept extends beyond personal and societal struggles and touches on our intrinsic connection to nature. After all, dawn always follows the darkest hours of night. This natural cycle reminds us that life, too, is full of difficulties, but the promise of a new beginning always exists. The sun breaking through storm clouds, the first bloom after a harsh winter—these simple yet profound moments remind us of the cyclical nature of hope and renewal.

The concept of "light through the darkness" teaches us that no matter how overwhelming life's challenges may seem, there is always a way forward. Whether it's through personal strength, the support of others, or collective resilience, the light is always there for those who seek it. As long as we hold onto hope, we can find our way out of the shadows and into a brighter tomorrow.

Janna Abu Mokh

In life, we sometimes face tough situations that make us feel like we're in the dark. This happened to me when I moved from middle school to high school. I used to get perfect scores in math, so I thought I would do well in the advanced 5-units math class too. But when I got my first exam back, I was devastated to see a 63. I felt like quitting the class and leaving the advanced track.

Feeling lost, I went to my cousin's house. She had recently graduated from high school and shared that she also had a low score at first but didn't let it define her. She encouraged me to work harder and stay in the advanced class. Her words were the light that guided me through the darkness. With her support, I studied more, and my grades improved.

Part V: Hope

Writers Matter sponsored a writing competition inviting pairs of Jewish Israeli and Arab or other minority writers to submit original work—poetry, stories, dialogues, songs, or any other form—centered on the theme of **Hope**. An international panel of judges selected finalists based on creativity, strength of writing, collaboration, and depth of connection to the theme. This chapter includes all of the submissions, reflecting a rich tapestry of voices and formats. The competition sparked meaningful dialogue, deepened connections across communities, and reminded us all of the power of shared creativity in times of challenge.

Under the Carob Tree

Madian Marana and Rotem Rechter

Yonatan,

I miss you so much. I know it's only been a few months since you moved, but it feels like a lifetime. Not seeing you after school every day has been tough. I especially miss our coffee time on Fridays.

*How's New York? And your new job? I want you to tell me **everything** when you write to me!*

School's not been easy, but at least today we missed a few classes because of this new program, Beyachad. They bring a class from an Arab school and we have activities and discussions together. Today's the first time we do it so I was a bit nervous and no one really made friends yet. Some guys in class said we shouldn't make friends with Arabs but I know they're just brainwashed. Maybe you'll come back one day when this country has all its issues fixed. Anyway, dad and

I miss you a ton. Come visit soon, alright?

XOXO,
-Your smart and beautiful sister

Dear Aunt Layla,
I hope my letter reaches you well. Here, the winds shift, carrying scents of wild thyme and whispers of peace. The air is filled with chatter of hope; They say borders may open; walls may soften. For the first time, I feel that you might return, join us for the olive harvest, and walk our fields once more.
I wonder too, how would Grandma feel knowing I lead a peace program? Would she deny my right to be true to myself? Surely you can understand, I'm trapped, and so our hefty stories falter before my tongue, and I dare not utter. But for the first time in forever, I dare dream my children will.

With love,
Ahmad

Hey Yoni,
I just wanted to let you know that Dad and I are okay. I've been avoiding a few neighborhoods lately, we're both staying safe. Maya from my class lost her sister in the bus explosion last Tuesday. She has not been to school and Dad won't let me visit so I don't know how she is. Funny how just a month ago we started a peace program, isn't it? We ended up having only two meetings before the attacks began. Eitan won't stop talking about how he knew we should not have trusted "them." I know he is wrong but sometimes I can't help feeling he's got a point. Why should I be so terrified to go outside?

Anyway, write back when you get the chance, I want to hear how you are doing as well. Do not worry about us, we're staying safe.

Lots of love,
-Deb

I pray this letter reaches you, Auntie.
Our streets scream loudly with blares and flames. Just days ago, I stood in the chaos of Al-Aqsa, the farthest place of worship. Right before my eyes, stones met bullets, and chants for justice drowned in gas and smoke. With each dawn, more checkpoints are born and walls rise across our hills, casting shadows over olive groves, and blocking paths I once knew by heart. Buses smolder, fear surrounds towns, and like a prison our streets are kept apart.

The peace program I once believed in was forced to pause. More than ever, amidst darkness and chaos, I want it to thrive. Perhaps one day streets will reconnect, voices will rise, and dreams will be set free. Maybe then, when the olive trees bear witness and the younger ones speak up, Grandma will understand why I chose this path.

My prayers,
Ahmad

Yonatan, I'm sorry it's been so long.

Things have been so scary lately. There were three bus bombings just last week. Yoni, I am afraid to leave our house. Dad tries to drive me to school every day but sometimes he has to work early
I had to take a bus from school today. I noticed a group of Arabs in

the back so I decided to get off, but then I realized I recognized one of them. It was one of the instructors from Beyachad. He noticed me too, and after a few moments the driver asked if I was getting on or not, so I got on. I didn't go up to them, but I know he recognized me. I know nothing happened but I couldn't get that moment out of my head. For a brief second, I forgot why I was afraid.

Anyway, I really hope this'll all be over soon. Maybe once it gets quieter, you'll come visit?

-Deborah

Excuse my disregard, Aunt Layla, our days spilled into one another, soaked with sorrow and loss.

My heart aches, watching destinies sink beneath an endless tide of rage and grief. And I cling to a quiet light, to a young hope. Just last week, I caught a glimpse of a Jewish girl from our group on the bus. Like strangers, we stood, silent and distant, but I know she recognized me too. We were strangers, yet when I got off, I could still feel her eyes looking into mine.

The next day, they crossed paths again.

This time, she decided to go up to him.

"Hey, you're Ahmad, right?" she smiled nervously.

"Yes! You were in Beyachad, right? I remember your face." He replied.

"Yeah, I was. My name's Deborah, from the Nayot school."

Both were hesitant at first, a few moments passed, and then the ice was broken, as if a barrier had been split open.

"Ahmad, do you- Do you want to catch up sometime? I know this is weird, it's just- I don't really know any Arabs, and I think it is wrong."

She asked.

"That sounds nice, but I'm not sure my family would love that."
Ahmad said.
An idea struck him, "There is a clearing behind my house with a
carob tree. We could meet there. Bring some friends if that helps,"
he suggested. She hesitated, then smiled.

"Actually, what if you bring some friends too, and we have a big
meeting- Just like Beyachad!" Deborah exclaimed with stars in her
eyes. Ahmad could not help but smile back. "That sounds like a
wonderful idea." He answered.
Each went in an opposing direction. Ahmad, instead of going home,
went to his friend's house to invite him.
So did Deborah.

Two days later, in the clearing, beneath the Carob tree, three Arabs
and three Jews sat and talked for hours. It was awkward at first, but
by the time they all waved goodbye, it felt like they had known each
other forever.
The next week, there were ten of them. The week after that, twelve.

And so, amid the pain and despair, amid the blares and flames, a group
of teens refused to sacrifice their humanity for hatred. Fear became a
thing of the past, alienation made obsolete. Enemies, turned human,
turned friends. The meetings under the carob tree were held furtively,
as if hope was a crime they were all complicit in. And the carob tree
remains, well aware that the tides of humanity are ever-changing and
meaningless. Amidst the worst days any of them had known, they had
never been more confident; better days are soon to be led by them.

The end

Hope in a Flame

Mikael Yatskan and Teya Andria

When I think of hope,I see a vision so bright,
A beautiful girl who turns dark into light.
When all seems lost,
Her smile leads me to trust,
The journey, no matter the cost.
In Gaza's streets and Tel Aviv's night,
Where children's dreams are full of fright,
Two peoples' pain is strong and deep,
While hope gets lost in fear's dark sweep.
Even here, when grief clouds the day,
Hope finds a way to guide the way.
Through rockets' fire and sirens' call,
When fear and grief threaten to fall,
We are human first, before it all.
She paints my world with gold,
Changing what's grey and bitter to what is bold.
Times when my mind wants to give up,
She gives me her hand and helps me stand up.
Each mother's tears fall just the same,
No healing comes from placing blame.
Through trauma's maze and darkest night,
Some souls still dare to dream of light.
Hope has always been by my side,
If it's in the beauty of my family's love that does not hide.
If it's in my friends who guide me through the way,
When the path seems all bumpy and gray.
I see it in my neighbors, whose story seemed done,
Until I glanced out the window, saw them hand in hand, full of fun.

Dancing in the rain, with joy in their eyes,
A reminder that life can bloom, even under gray skies.
For peace must start within each heart,
We stand hand in hand, to never drift apart.
When all feels lost, her smile shines through,
Breaking the walls that separated me and you.
No matter the direction—left, right, up, or down,
Hope shall forever remain unbound.
Through grief and fear, hope will remain,
An unbroken thread through all our pain.

Did You Get the Balloon?

Shani Elkayam and Venice Zayn

Hello dear readers,

This book is attributed to all of the people who have been forced out of their homes by conflict. The soldiers, the families, and most importantly, the children and the hostages currently in Gaza.

We, as the team of creators, wanted to show people that even in these dark times, light can still shine upon the world. There will always be light amidst the darkness, and to us, children are the ones who carry the most light. This is why we chose to tell the story of Noah and Amal, children who are living in a world that was cruel to them, forcing them out of their homes and away from their families, and yet, they find their happiness and light, and most importantly, their hope in the future ahead of them.

We hope you will enjoy reading this book. It is a children's book, but it means so much to both of us. This isn't only a story for children, after all, it's a story for everyone.

May the hostages return to their homes, and may we continue to hope for a future full of light.

Amen.

Page One:
Waking up to your room ceiling is the best thing to wake up to [besides a holiday hotel ceiling]. That is what Noah thought about when he woke up today, but when he opened his eyes, he was disappointed to find that again, it wasn't his ceiling but his cousin Peleg's ceiling. He did not like this place; this was not his home. After all, he was away from his mommy and daddy." I'm sorry, Noah" his Auntie said "They can't come here, they have to work back home, "Auntie Anna said.

Page Two:
Noah was a smart kid. He knew they were trying to protect him but deep down, he knew what was happening, "I do not believe that. I know there is a war. I know they can't come here because they cannot leave the house. There is no place for them to live here, there's too many people in this house and mommy and daddy don't want to leave their work behind" Noah thought after recalling his talk with his auntie yesterday.

Page Three:

Despite the fact that Noah wanted to try to reach out to his mommy and daddy, to call them and make sure they are okay, this was not the time. He had to go to school like every other kid. "That's what it means to be seven years old", he thought, "Mommy and daddy have a job, and so do I."

Walking out of his new room, Auntie Anna met him. She was always so kind, but he never really got to know her. Looking down at him, she finally asked the question she had on her mind, "Noah, would you be interested in joining me today? I have something I want us to do together.", Noah nodded looking at his Aunty, who had reached her hand out to gently ruffle his dirty blond hair, not sure of what they were going to do.

Page Four:

It was Noah's first day at school and he could already feel the butterflies in his stomach, but Auntie Anna comforted him, telling him that it would all be alright. As they drove by the school, a girl caught Noah's eye. She had long chestnut hair and big, *BIG*! green eyes, the size of the tennis ball that daddy gave him for his birthday. She looked at him with shyness in her eyes. He raised his hand wanting to say hi, but she suddenly turned away, running inside the school.

Page Five:

The school day went by really slowly for Noah. The teacher introduced him to the class though he did not really care for it. The rest of the day Noah's mind was on his family, his mommy and daddy and about the Lego toy he forgot to bring. When lunchtime came around, all Noah did was sit in his chair. He looked at the food, it was schnitzel and couscous, but his mommies were *WAY*! better. When it was time to leave and go back home his big sister Allona came and picked him up along with Auntie Anna, who had to be there since Allona cannot drive alone yet.

Page Six:
"Allona's birthday was a week ago. She turned seventeen this year and I gave her the best gift ever! It was a ring made out of a leaf vine with a flower in the middle. She was so happy that she gave me a kiss on the cheek, but I don't think she was really happy, because mommy and daddy were not here to celebrate with her this year. I even heard her crying alone in her room after the party ended" Noah thought.

After they arrived home Auntie Anna told him to get ready, she said they were going out on that mystery trip, but he could only go back to his previous thoughts about his big sister. She sacrificed a lot to be with him. She left her school, her friends, and her family to be with him to guarantee his safety. However, Auntie Anna interrupted his thoughts. She told him it was time to leave, and after they got into the car, all he really did was stare blankly out the window.

Page Seven:
It was not the place he pictured, he thought Auntie Anna would take him to a playground or something, but instead he was standing in front of a tall and big building with a lot of windows more than he could count." What is this place? "Noah asked with confusion written on his face.

"It's a place where kids that are far away from home like you gather to support each other in these hard times "Auntie Anna said with softness coating her eyes.

Page Eight:
The place from the inside was unfamiliar to Noah but at the same time warm and welcoming. When he walked in, a voice immediately greeted him, "Oh! Noah! Please, come inside." Inside the room there were drawings on the walls, drawings clearly made by kids and there were bean bag chairs organized in a circle where other kids sat, chatting away with each other as they waited.

Page Nine:
Noah saw a familiar face sitting between the other kids. He recognized those big eyes immediately, how could he ever forget? Those big green eyes. It was the same girl he saw earlier! But before he could actually say something, the "teacher" spoke up.

"Settle down kids! Since Noah is new to the group, I want every kid to introduce themselves" One by one, the other kids started introducing themselves, but Noah wasn't really listening to any of them. Until that girl with the big green eyes spoke.

Page Ten:
"Amal", *she said.*

Page Eleven:
Soon after, the teacher spoke again, "Thank you everyone, now, today-" And Noah immediately stopped listening after that. He wasn't really interested in what the teacher had to say. Up until she finally spoke again, "Alright, I want you all to get into groups, okay? Amal, could you please team up with Noah?" The teacher asked, to which Amal nodded her head.

Page Twelve:
Noah walked over to Amal then he sat down beside her. In the beginning, both of them were quite awkward. Noah didn't know what to say to Amal. Amal spoke first, quietly, in a whisper, "I like your shirt", she said.
Noah turned to look at her, "What did you say?". He asked, as he had not heard what she said all too well. Amal stuttered in her words before answering him, "I-I just said that I like your shirt".

Page Thirteen:
Noah couldn't help but feel surprised, but he appreciated the compliment.

He was wearing a shirt which had some characters from his favorite show. "Do you know the show?" he asked, to which Amal nodded her head, "Yeah, I know the show. I watch it every Sunday". Noah got pretty excited. He loved the show! "It's the best! Isn't it?", he asked, and Amal nodded again in agreement.

Page Fourteen:
Before Noah and Amal could continue their conversation, the teacher walked over to hand them their assignment. It was simple, "Introduce yourselves", "Write three things about the person that they like" and lastly "Share one dream that your partner has shared with you"

Page Fifteen:
Amal and Noah talked for a few minutes, sharing their hobbies and their lives. When they finally got to the last question, Noah and Amal could both agree on one thing. They dreamt and hoped that one day, there would be peace.

Page Sixteen:
After the group's support meeting was over, Noah waved goodbye to Amal while walking over to Auntie Anna, who was just waiting for him to finish. "How was it?" Auntie Anna asked. Noah only had one response, "When are we going back?". Auntie Anna could only smile, then she said, "Next Wednesday".

Page Seventeen:
From then on, Noah went to the support group every week on Wednesdays. Every time he sat beside Amal, it felt like they could talk for hours. At school, Amal and Noah would play together every day, and they would meet up at least once a week. NOBODY could separate them, *nobody*!

Page Eighteen:
However, one day Amal came to school with a sad face. "What's wrong, Amal?" Noah asked, unable to ignore the sadness in those big green eyes. Amal didn't want to say anything, but Noah could not forget the sad face that she had on the entire day. For the rest of the day, Noah could only think of Amal and her sad face. Why was she so sad? What happened?

Page Nineteen:
At the end of the school day, Amal pulled Noah aside to explain why she was so sad, "We're going back home to the North and I don't know if I'll get to see you again", Amal explained. Noah was devastated. She was his only friend, his BEST friend! And now she was moving away.

Page Twenty:
Suddenly, an idea came to his mind, if this was the last time he was going to see Amal, then he was going to make it special. "Come with me Amal, I want to show you something". Noah took Amal's hand, making sure she was following after him as they ran to the Kiosk that was right next to the school.

Page Twenty-One:
Together, Noah and Amal bought a yellow balloon. Noah gave the cashier some money that he got from Auntie Anna, and then they went to a bench nearby. "What are you doing?" Amal asked, and Noah responded, "It's a secret!" he said, as he finished writing something on some paper.

Noah folded it up as neatly as he could, then he tied the note to the balloon with some rubber bands. "I want to go to the field, will you come with me Amal?", he asked, and Amal simply nodded, still very confused as to what Noah was doing.

Page Twenty-Two:
There was a field close to where Auntie Anna's house was, so Noah

and Amal walked back to where his house was, then they entered the field. Together, they walked deeper into the field, until finally Noah stopped. "You wanted to know what we're doing, right?" Noah asked. Amal nodded, still waiting for the big reveal.

I wrote this note for you! So that one day when it comes back down, you'll see it, open it, and read it! That way, you won't forget me"

Page Twenty-Three:
Amal was holding back tears as she answered "Of course I won't forget you, Noah! You are my best friend, *forever and ever*. Noah smiled, giving her the BIGGEST hug he could, before he let go and placed her hand on the balloon. "On the count of three, we let go"

Page Twenty-Four:
"One...Two...Three!" Amal and Noah let go of the balloon. Together, Amal and Noah watched, holding each other's hands as the yellow balloon floated into the sky.

Page Twenty-Five:

Back cover:
The story follows the protagonist named Noah after he was evacuated from his home near the Gaza Strip to live with his Aunt Anna, along with his big sister. His parents stayed behind. In an attempt to support Noah, Auntie Anna sends Noah to a support group where kids like him are also dealing with the war go to get some help and support from each other. In the support group, Noah befriends a girl named Amal. What do you think happens next? get some help and support from each other. In the support group, Noah befriends a girl named Amal. What do you think happens next?

The End

Two Stories of Hope

Nitzan Hyman and Lama Ali

The small State of Israel contains many groups of people: Jewish, Arab, Muslim, Christian, non-religious, religious… But this diversity is often accompanied by isolation, where each society lives its own life without knowing or understanding the other. However, we believe strongly that hope can break these barriers and bring all groups of people together. Here are two stories of hope from our land of Israel:

Story 1:
Once, in a small village surrounded by mountains, there lived a young boy named Sami. One harsh winter, a devastating storm destroyed the village's crops, leaving everyone fearful of hunger. The villagers, disheartened, said the land was ruined and gave up on planting.

But Sami refused to believe this was the end. Every morning, despite the bitter cold, he took a handful of seeds and planted them in the frozen soil. *"Why are you wasting your time?"* the villagers would ask Sami. Sami smiled and said, *"Because I believe the earth will heal, and spring will come."*
Weeks passed, and the snow began to melt. To everyone's astonishment, tiny green sprouts appeared where Sami had planted his seeds. The fields, once barren, were alive again. The villagers cheered and joined Sami in tending the crops, grateful for his hope that they saved them all. From that day on, Sami's story reminded them that even in the bleakest times, hope can bring life to what seems lost.

Story 2:
In the North of Israel two towns are located close to each other: Kfar Yasif and Nahariya. Mustafa was a young Arab boy who was born and

raised in the Arab village of Kfar Yasif; he grew up learning only the Arab perspective of life in Israel and was taught that Jews are dangerous. Yossi was a young Jewish boy who was born and raised in Jewish town of Nahariya; he grew up learning only the Jewish perspective of life in Israel and was taught that Arabs are dangerous. However, both children hoped that there was a better life, where religion and faith did not separate people, and people could live together and be friends.

Mustafa and Yossi did not know each other growing up. They first met as doctors in the emergency room working together in the Nahariya hospital. Their thoughts of Jews and Arabs were based on what they had learned growing up - a fear of Jews and a fear of Arabs, but each hoped that there was a better life.

When the great war broke out, all citizens of Israel were affected: Jews, Arabs, Muslims, Christians, non-religious, religious…everyone. For the first time, Mustafa and Yossi began speaking during their shifts in the emergency room while helping the wounded, regardless of religion or faith. They found things in common, such as a love for basketball and the Los Angeles Lakers, and Hip-Hop music. They built a friendship that lasted forever.

These stories reflect the power of hope in facing challenging odds, just as Sami, the child in the mountain village, did. When the storms destroyed the crops, everyone lost hope, except Sami, who began to plant seeds in the frozen earth, believing that spring would come. As the snow melted, the fields flourished again, and hope was restored to people's hearts.

Our hope is that from an early age as children, we can work together to help one another in every aspect of this challenging time and build a strong future together. Everyone helps everyone, regardless of their faith and religion. People getting to know each other, respecting each other, and living a better life together for today and for future generations.

Hope is the spark that drives us to continue, whatever the challenges may be. It is what makes us believe that tomorrow can be better. By believing in hope and working for change, we can build a better world, where everyone lives in understanding and unity despite our differences.

The Wait

Yaara Shahar and Sam Kenani
When I was young, I used to think,
along with every other blink,
if a fairy joined me for a strawberry drink,
would she possibly cling?
I waited.
Clinging onto a flame in winter,
The epitome of a light bringer,
One thought made me stutter and hinder,
"How does its light always linger?" I waited.
I linger as I realize I'm a part of a chain,
from which love, faith, and fear I gain,
Will it bring me grey rain?
Will this sun ever remain?
I waited.
Remaining on a long branch,
two birds on a lively dance,
"Look at the land" they take a glance,
Is that a border?" She says perchance.
I waited.
Perchance for as long as I've waited,
all souls became jaded,
If I give up, I'll be hated,
Will I ever say I've made it?
I waited.
"I've made it" I yell with a smile,

As I look at the filthy devil,
Envisioning the future I desire,
With whom do I reconcile?
I waited.
Reconciling is a big word,
People often prefer fields of gold,
Over a future where lights unfold,
Even if young hands stay cold.
I waited.
Cold haunts my heart as I witness a red eye,
Where I've seen angels die,
High above in the blue sky,
Is this actually a goodbye?
Please be a lie,
Please be a lie,
I waited.
"A lie" she says, "you're not the one chosen",
To wait for a future where all shall be broken,
Where the truth is unspoken,
Where doors never reopen,
I waited.
Reopening the curtains of light,
As her heart with light I ignite,
I could've caught the next flight,
I could've left those in plight,
But I waited as I recite,
Waiting is hope, dressed in contrite. I waited.
I'll always wait,
Because of hope,
That is all there is,
All there will be,
And all there ever was.
Because of hope,

Is believing snow will come,
If we manage through the fall.

A Glimmer

Tamar Haleva and Ghanomi Baghdad

The sky hangs heavy, a canvas of ash,
While cities crumble beneath war's cruel lash.

Echoes of sirens pierce the chilling night,
And bury dreams deep under the rubble from the fight.

The fields lay barren, their whispers stilled,
Once vibrant with life, now the bodies are chilled.

The air carries cries, both near and far,
Each tear's a testament to war's deep scar.

But despite all that, there was still a glimmer,
It was ray or a twinkle, something unfamiliar,

Something fascinating, a feeling new and inspiring,
It was the dream of the unknown, truly aspiring,

That during those times provided a relief,
And a reason to keep fighting, a sparkle of belief,

Despite all the horrors that feeling was there,
Pushing through the sorrow to breathe some fresh air.
Like watching the sun setting, leaving the skies,
Yet still picturing the morning light of sunrise.

The people crying for the fallen tree in grief,
To see the young sapling grow its very first leaf.

It was the earth fighting through the winter's gloom,
So that back in the spring it'll be able to bloom.

And all freezing almost dying in the electrifying storm,
To feel the rays of the sun again and finally be warm.

That feeling was hope.

With every step we take together, the world will slowly heal,
And humans all with hearts once cold will simply start to feel.

The light will shine and scare away the heavy clouds and rain,
And glow and light and cheer all up and bring an end to pain.

From an arid ground, dried up and cracked, soon new life could grow,
And farmers back will plant and make a brighter path to know.

Hope stays alive in difficult times, through the darkness and the light,
It will lead us safely in the shadows of the frightening night.

The Walk of Peace:
How to Develop a Peace-Promoting Mindset

Sivan Ben Ami and Nour Istaitih

On the evening of Rosh HaShana, one year into the war, a woman by the name of Nava Levit Binnun decided to go for a walk. She didn't know what it was that made her do this—perhaps it was the new front with Lebanon that brought back memories from her youth.

At any rate, Nava felt that the horizon of peace was only getting farther away from our society, and that she had to somehow bring it closer. She later described it as "a strong feeling that I had to do something."

This walk was, in fact, the very birth of Nava's movement. In the brief time since the beginning of October, this initiative has appealed to dozens of enthusiastic supporters who all walk together for the shared goal of developing a "Peace-Promoting Mindset". Through a few simple principles that take inspiration from Tibetan Buddhism, Nava has become a sort of guru for those worried about the war-oriented mentality that has developed in Israel and want to do something about it.

"I felt that we just had to make a movement that consists of responsible adults," Nava told us when we sat down to interview her, "who start walking and say: we are not going to give up on peace. We understand that if we don't start doing things now, peace will only get farther away.

So how do we bring the peace horizon closer? Nava calls this "cultivating the field of consciousness." The way she sees it, a peace-promoting mindset is like a field that constantly needs to be cultivated. This cultivation is achieved through the four "contemplations". During each walk, the listener is invited to think of four basic principles that are related to the field of consciousness and cultivate them:

1. The human consciousness is a vast and valuable resource.

2. The world is a dynamic system, although we perceive it as static.
3. The world is composed of complicated webs of interconnected events and it calls for our humility and recognition of the limitations of our mind in grasping its complexity.
4. Pain and difficult emotions signal a confrontation with what truly matters to us.

Nava, a neuroscientist, noticed that the human brain tends to categorize things in a dichotomous way, even though the real world is much more complicated than just black-and-white. Her four contemplations aim to remind us of what our primal brain tends to forget, and through them, she aims to eliminate the oversimplified, binary thinking that can cause a lot of harm.

"Our usual, automatic way of looking at things in the world is actually extremely limited. One of the things that we try to remind ourselves of in this walk is what a superpower the human mind is when we go beyond our narrow mind."

Nava mentioned the small, narrow, and hopeless mindset that believes that people will never change; when in fact people do change, communities evolve, and even the smallest situations can randomly transform everything. Nava gave the example of World War One, which started because of a pure coincidence. Gavrilo Princip and his co-conspirators were part of a poorly organized plot, which failed at murdering the Archduke of Austro-Hungary. But, by sheer chance, that same day the Archduke's driver took a wrong turn and arrived right at the arms of the killers. It is amazing to think how something so insignificant as a wrong turn can lead to a world war that lasted years.

With every step she takes, the ground beneath her feels the weight of purpose, she strives to instill a mindset that goes above and beyond, breaks the limits of our societies, and challenges the lessons history has failed to grasp. And she's far from alone on this journey, people from every corner of the region gather to follow her, believing in change, and living for hope of it all.

"Every time I come to the walk, I get surprised at how many come and join me; Jews, Muslims, Christians, and Druze"—Nava says. Cultures come together in this walk to comprehend the story of humanity, in this dark and uncertain time. They won't give up hope and peace, fully aware that a resolution remains a distant horizon, and that the lane forward is fraught with obstacles and requires patience and perseverance. Yet, they press on. Creating an impact—one that may not be recognized immediately but will, without a doubt, be rewarded.

It's no secret that peace has long been absent in this region. Yet, as Nava insightfully explains, peace isn't as far out of reach as it might seem. It begins with redefining what peace truly means. Peace can be understood as a state within a complex system where equilibrium and stability dominate. By working toward creating that state, we are, in essence, moving closer to peace.

Nava emphasizes that achieving this doesn't require emotional detachment but rather the ability to channel creativity and harmony in our actions. For her, the walk symbolizes more than just a journey; it is a ritual, a transformative practice where individuals adopt personal growth. It is about developing from the mindset of a helpless child to a mature state of accountability where each person takes on the responsibility to improve the system that they are part of.

When everyone commits to this shared responsibility, the system itself will naturally move toward balance and coherence. Therefore, what if more people join her? What if those who follow her are not just adults, but also youths who will one day rule this region? A movement where they walk, not with the heavy weight of political burdens that divide us, but with a calm resolve, free from the lines that separate us. Maybe this is the answer, this is the solution we've been waiting for, and as humans who, despite the inhumanity that surrounds us, still possess the capacity for change.

As one neuroscientist, Anil Seth, suggests, what if we truly understand that we are, at every moment, living within a carefully orchestrated illusion, a collective hallucination we all share? When many of us see and experience the same thing, it becomes what we call reality. —Perhaps we have the power to choose what we hallucinate. Thus, perhaps it's time for us to collectively hallucinate peace, and certainly, that is what we call *hope*.

Two Sides, One Theme

Liel Shabtay and Nour Mansour Khateeb

When do you feel hope? When you hope to get some gifts for Christmas? Maybe when you hope your grandparents come to visit?

After October 7th, the concept of hope changed. A family that once had shelter and a warm home now finds itself searching for refuge and a tent to flee to, as the suffering worsens day by day …. This is the situation for the "Abu Sel" family, who were displaced under harsh and difficult humanitarian circumstances. They moved from one place to another until they reached a large tent consisting of basic materials, fabrics, wood, and concrete blocks. This tent provides these families with some protection from the summer heat and the winter cold. Many people are living in similar conditions due to the war that erupted after October 7th.

The elderly displaced matriarch of the family spoke about the extremely difficult conditions they are enduring. She said, "We are sitting in tents and surrounded by tarps, and when it rains for just ten minutes, we have no choice but to live in the damp environment." She is here with her sons and daughters, holding onto the hope that gives her strength—her hope being her grandson, who was born during the war.

When he was born, there were no clothes for him to wear, so she begged other women for something to cover him. She eventually found herself asking people for money to build a small tent to live in. On some days, she doesn't even have a bite of food to eat, and when she does find something, she gives it to her little grandson. She also added that her daughter and son-in-law, the child's parents, were unable to flee due to the dire conditions. They decided it would be best to send the child with his grandmother. As a result, the grandmother remains steadfast, doing everything in her power to provide him with a better life despite the challenges.

After all the hardships she endured and the departure of her husband, who never returned, her only wish now is to reunite with her daughter's family and live with them under any circumstances. This is why she clings so tightly to her little grandson, who she sees as a piece of her daughter. Without this child, the elderly woman wouldn't have the hope that keeps her strong and holding on to life. She dreams that this child will one day live peacefully with his parents in a safe home.

At the same time, in Israel, on the other side of the conflict, there are hundreds of families who lost family members, hostages who are waiting to come home and many other victims of the war.

On October 7, 2023, the day began like any other in Nir Oz, a peaceful kibbutz near the Gaza border. Families gathered for their morning routines, children played, and the community embraced the tranquility of the day. But as the sun climbed higher in the sky, that peace was shattered. Rocket sirens blared, and within moments, reports of armed militants breaching the border filled the airwaves. The once serene kibbutz became a site of unimaginable terror.

In the midst of the chaos, nine-month-old Kfir Bibas was abducted alongside his parents, Shiri and Yarden. Their home, a place of safety and love, was violated as Hamas militants forcibly took them. The family's relatives, friends, and community were left in shock, their lives forever altered by the abduction.

For weeks, the Bibas family's fate remained a painful mystery. Kfir's bright smile, captured in cherished family photos, became a symbol of lost innocence. The nation grieved and prayed, rallying around the plight of Kfir and the many other hostages taken that day. Vigils were held, candles lit, and posters bearing Kfir's face were displayed across Israel, each one a testament to the hope that the hostages would return.

As days turned into weeks, news of ongoing negotiations trickled in. While the uncertainty was agonizing, hope persisted, fueled by small but significant signs of progress. Then, in January 2025, a breakthrough emerged: Kfir was named among 34 hostages that Hamas agreed to release in a potential deal with Israel. For the first time in months, a glimmer of light broke through the darkness.

The announcement brought cautious optimism to Kfir's family and the entire nation. Shiri's sister, Galit, spoke to the media, her voice trembling with emotion. "We've held onto hope every single day. Kfir is a fighter, just like his parents. We believe they'll come home." The potential deal also reignited efforts to secure the release of all the hostages, uniting Israelis in a shared mission of resilience and solidarity.

For Kfir's relatives and supporters, the news was a reminder that even in the face of profound suffering, hope can endure. The community of

Nir Oz, despite its wounds, found strength in unity, working together to rebuild and support one another. Across Israel, the story of Kfir became a symbol of the nation's unwavering resolve to protect its children and honor its values.

The journey is far from over, but the possibility of Kfir's return rekindled hope for countless families enduring similar pain. It is a testament to the resilience of the human spirit, the power of community, and the belief that even in the darkest moments, the light of hope can guide the way forward.

Just like these families there are many others who hold on to hope because it's the only thing that makes them feel strong, the only thing that keeps them smiling, the only thing that helps them remember the good thing they're waiting for.

Hope is a light that never goes down, even in the darkest times, because when it does, you become the weakest version of yourself.

It's Possible

Zidan Ismael and Agam Avinun

Here I am, waking up again to go to work. I won't deny it—I wake up reluctantly, but I still rise day after day. Whenever I think it's not worth the effort, my subconscious mind takes me back five years. Back then, I was lost, having gone bankrupt and lost all hope in life. I spent my days waiting to join my murdered son, day after day. I had lost my family, my home, and my job, but the greatest loss of all was hope.

Once determined to achieve the impossible, I found it impossible to even stand on my feet again—or so I thought at the time. I surrendered, raising my white flag and letting fate toy with me however it pleased.

Whenever life's waves hit, I drifted like paper in the wind. Whenever I heard of a successful person, my hatred grew, and my despair doubled. Once resolved to bend fate to my will, I now bowed beneath life's burdens.

One day, as I wandered the streets, bitter and angry, looking for someone happy to ruin their joy, or someone sad to deepen their sorrow, I saw what seemed like the perfect target: a small child selling lemonade. I directed all my anger and hatred toward him, storming over and spilling his lemonade. I waited to hear him cry so I could feed my broken ego, but I heard nothing. I waited and waited, but instead of tears, he smiled and said, *"Maybe today's lemonade wasn't good. I'll make some fresh juice."*

My anger and hatred grew, but so did my astonishment. I couldn't continue spreading misery that day for reasons I still can't explain. The next morning, I woke up filled with hope, inspired by that child. I had forgotten what hope felt like. I spent hours trying to make sense of my emotions. The hatred that had consumed me for years still fought fiercely to snuff out every spark of hope within me. But I stood up, lowered my white flag, raised my sail, and began sailing against the tide. Today, after docking my ship, I continued my journey with steady steps and unwavering hope.

You may think I'm a fool for losing everything because I lost hope. I used to believe hope didn't exist, that it was just a concept invented by philosophers to disguise their negativity in better words. But here I am today, walking my path, leaning on the crutch of hope. And here you are, reading my words because of the innocent, hopeful words of a child.

A human without hope is a being without ideas, ambition, or passion. They care only about ending each day as quickly as possible, inching closer to death. A human without hope is no more than a soulless machine, without a heartbeat or a will to drive them.

Perhaps you think you don't need hope because you have no desire to improve your life. That's a trap many fall into. Even if your ambitions are modest and you're not striving for change, you need hope—to see the possibility of things staying as they are, for even that is never guaranteed.

And if you're hoping I'll finish soon, I won't disappoint you. I'll end with a question I once asked myself during my darkest moments, a question I couldn't answer until I stood back on my feet. A friend had asked me what advice I'd give to everyone in the world if I were standing at the edge of my final moments. It took five years of suffering and despair to find the answer, but now I have it, and I offer it to the world:

"Keep your hopes high, and work to ensure they're never let down."

The Sun of Hope Never Ends

Yuval Louzon and Jana Ali Nasser

Hope is an interesting thing. It slips in quietly often when you least anticipate it, finding its way into the cracks of the emptiness of a lost moment. It asks for little, just a thread of faith, a small step forward. But its impact can be immense.

In a small town, lived a young girl named Yasmin. Yasmin loved her grandparents dearly and spent a lot of time with them. Her grandmother was a wise and interesting woman who always had a story to tell, each filled with lessons and deep meanings. But this story, in particular, is one that Yasmin will never forget. It's a story that will stay with her for the rest of her life.

My grandmother once told me the story of a young girl whose entire existence was defined by her art. Drawing was not merely a hobby, it was her whole identity, the thing that provided her with purpose and hope in a world that often felt uncertain. However, her world came crashing down when an accident left her with a devastating injury, she lost her arm. The shock and trauma of the accident sent her into a coma where despite being unable to respond she could still hear the voices of those around her.

She slowly became aware of the harsh truth. Her arm was gone. The one thing that she cared about most was now gone forever. This realization shattered her spirit, leaving her feeling empty inside. She felt as though without her ability to draw; she no longer had a reason to live. The feeling of giving up washed over her.

Yet, in the stillness of her coma, a gentle and familiar voice began to break through her despair. It reminded her of the goodness she had brought into the world. It spoke of how she had always been a source of light for others, offering comfort and hope in their darkest moments. She remembered the joy, the laughter, and the simple acts of kindness that had made others forget their pain, if only for a brief time. The voice reminded her that her life was not only about drawing. It was about the people she loved, the shared moments of happiness, and the impact she had made on the lives of those around her.

But as she began to grasp this truth, another, harsher reality came in. She was still in a coma. If she were to wake up, she would do so without her arm, unable to ever again create the way she once had. *Was life still worth living?* she wondered. *Could she find purpose if the one thing that had defined her was now gone?*

And then the voice returned. "You are the only hope to continue my life. I cannot live without you."

At that moment, everything fell into place. The voice was not some distant echo. It was Noah, her dearest friend, the one who had stood by her through everything, the one who had been her pillar of support. She knew this voice. She had felt its warmth, and now in her most vulnerable moment, it was reaching out to her. It reminded her that her life still mattered. That she still mattered.

Do I deserve to live? she asked herself. *Am I worthy of another chance?*

In the profound silence of those questions, the answer became undeniable. Yes. She did deserve to live. She had given love, kindness, and hope to the world, and she was worthy of the chance to receive the gift of life once more. Her heart swelled with newfound strength, and she felt the surge of that belief course through her. And with that, her eyes fluttered open.

As her vision slowly cleared, she found herself surrounded by the faces of those who had loved her, who had waited for her, their presence a testament to the deep connections she had made throughout her life. At that moment, she realized just how much she would have lost if she had not chosen to fight. If she had given up, she would have left them behind. But she had chosen life, and that choice was her greatest gift.

A few days later, as her strength gradually returned, she noticed a piece of paper and a pencil resting on a table beside her. With all the energy she had, she reached out, pulling the table closer. She grasped the pencil with her remaining hand, her heart racing, and began to draw.

To her astonishment, she discovered that she could still create art. Her ability to draw had not abandoned her. Though her art was no longer as it once had been, it was enough. She could still bring beauty into the world, even with only one hand.

And then, in a moment that left me speechless, my grandmother revealed something that took my breath away. "If that girl had not chosen to live," she said softly, "she would not be here telling you this story. Because the girl… was me."

In that instant, I understood that my grandmother's story was not simply about loss or tragedy or recovery, it was a story about hope. The belief that no matter how dark life may seem, hope is the light that guides us through. Hope is what fuels our passion, what gives us strength when we feel as though we have nothing left. It is hope that makes life worth living, even when it feels as though our entire world is falling apart.

The Peaceful Friendship

Farah Awwad and Lihi Cohen

Story idea:
One Palestinian the other one Jewish, with different political opinions. This story is about how they navigate their friendship between the different opinions they have.
The girls have been friends for years so the friendship will be important for them to try and save.
Jewish girl- Talia @smellyfrog210
Palestinian girl- Lama @theycallmeclowny1478

Summary:
In the heart of the Middle East, where the threads of history and memory are intertwined, two peoples have lived on one land, the Israelis and the Palestinians. For decades, the specter of conflict has loomed over them, leaving behind the bitterness of loss and the suffering of displacement. But one day, out of suffering, a ray of hope rose, illuminating a new path toward peace.

Talia- A Jewish girl who was raised in a Jewish family and a Jewish belief, A BIG FAN of the show "LA LA LAND", Pizza girl, loves summer vibes, her favorite color is pink, Basketball girl and a math girl.

Lama- A Palestinian girl who was raised in a Palestinian family and a Palestinian belief, A BIG FAN of the show "LA LA LAND", Pasta girl, loves winter vibes, her favorite color is white, volleyball girl and an English girl.

Prologue:

It was 2am when Talia was scrolling through a chat forum of her favorite movie, La La Land.

She loved talking about it, but none of her school friends watched it so she had to make more friends online. She's been on the chat for hours when a friend request popped up from " @theycallmeclowny1478 "Talia laughed at the username before accepting the request and adding her back. It wasn't long before she got a message.

@theycallmeclowny1478- hey girl! cool profile

@smellyfrog210 - thanks ha-ha, love yours too. Are you a la la land fan?

@theycallmeclowny1478- yeah! It's my all-time favorite movie. lol

@smellyfrog210- no way mine too! I'm Talia, what's your name?

@theycallmeclowny1478- I'm Lama.

The story-

After a long day in high school, Talia came back home excited to finally text her best friend of 3 years Lama. They've never met in person before, but they've grown closer than ever over years of staying up all night and chatting with each other, making sure to update one another on every single detail of their day. Even though Lama lived so far away Talia didn't care, she was just happy to finally find someone who shared the same interests as her. Ever since that day Lama texted her they've bonded over their favorite movies, bands and hobbies. They were practically the same person.

The second Talia finally got to her room she made sure to close the door and open her computer to text Lama.

@**smellyfrog210**- hey girl! you home?

@**theycallmeclowny1478**- yeah, just got home. Movie time?

@**smellyfrog210**- do you even need to ask? be right back.

Talia and Lama had a tradition; every Tuesday they would watch their favorite movie on call. With snacks of course. After Talia went to get her snacks, she called Lama and they started watching the movie.

@**theycallmeclowny1478**- this was so fun, as always

@**smellyfrog210**- ha-ha yeah, we do this so much but I can never get enough of this movie

@**theycallmeclowny**- lol me too. Well, it's late, I should probably get going.

@**smellyfrog210**- okay yeah! bye girl

Later that night Talia was scrolling through her phone when she saw a new Instagram story movement about the hostages and decided to participate, this meant a lot to her since she's overly sensitive about it. She uploaded the post to her story and went to sleep.

Lama was scrolling through Instagram when she saw Talia's story. Why would her best friend post something like that? She knows that I'm Palestinian… right?? and anyway, why would she even side with them? Lama stayed on that story for a while, stuck in her thoughts when her mom entered her room. "Lama, its late honey goes to sleep. What is on your phone? Are you following an Israeli girl?" Lama seemed a little panicked before sighing and replied, "um yeah... this is my friend, Talia." Lama's mom looks surprised "you. Friend? you don't mind that she's Israeli?" Lama sighs again "well I didn't know until now. I have to think about this. I really like her; she's my best friend. but with everything that's going on lately. I don't know anymore." Lama's mom sits next to her on the bed and pats her back "Lama, I think you should talk to her. you said she's your friend, right? maybe you two can work this out."

"Thanks mom. I'll see"

Two days later after what happened between Thalia and Lama, Lama opened the chat for the first time since what happened between Lama and Thalia, and she found **Billions** of messages from Thalia.

@smellyfrog210-Girlll

@smellyfrog210-where are you?

@smellyfrog210-what's happened to you

@smellyfrog210-Are you ok

@smellyfrog210- Are you dead???

@smellyfrog210- Girl where are you!!!!!!

@theycallmeclowny1478- oh hey girl

@smellyfrog210- Finally you're here, where have you been?

@theycallmeclowny1478- I was sick

Lama didn't know how to explain herself... so she decided to avoid it.

@smellyfrog210- are you sure that's it? You seem a bit off.

@theycallmeclowny1478- well actually…

@smellyfrog- what is it? you can talk to me

@theycallmeclowny1478- I saw your story the other day. Are you Israeli?

@smellyfrog- yeah actually, I thought you knew. why?

@theycallmeclowny1478- I didn't know. Talia, you know I love you; you're my best friend… but I don't know if we can stay the same after that.

@smellyfrog- wait what? why?

@theycallmeclowny1478- I'm Palestinian, well my family is anyway. I don't think I can be friends with someone who hates my people.

@smellyfrog- oh. well, I don't hate Palestinians.

@theycallmeclowny1478- wait. you don't? I thought you would because of the war.

@smellyfrog- just because I don't support the ideology of their leaders doesn't mean I hate them. I don't care if you're Palestinian or not, you're my best friend and I don't want to lose you over something like politics.

@theycallmeclowny1478- are you sure? we probably don't share the same opinions about the war. don't you care?

@smellyfrog- yeah, I'm sure. You can have your opinions and I have mine, I respect that. Besides, we didn't start being friends over our political opinions so I don't think we should stop being friends over that.

@theycallmeclowny1478- yeah, you're right. Thanks Talia, I'm glad we talked it over.

@smellyfrog- no problem. me too. Well anyway! early movie night?

@theycallmeclowny1478- hell yeah! you read my mind.

A Love Beyond Borders

Moataz Abu Ahmad and Abigail Rubanenko

(**Khadeja**) It was the day I had decided to tell my family about David, the Israeli soldier I had been secretly seeing. My heart raced as I stepped into the living room, only to freeze at the sight of my family watching Al Jazeera, their eyes glued to the screen. I couldn't focus on the words being spoken, only on the images flashing before my eyes, was David, okay? Was he alive? A voice on the TV caught my attention just as my mother gasped, her hand over her mouth. The screen showed my brother's lifeless body, sprawled on the ground, a victim of the violence we had lived through for so long. My world spun as shock and grief collided. How could I tell them about David now? The thought of it felt impossible. A week later, gathering all the courage I could muster, I finally told them. The shouting and disbelief erupted immediately; my father's words cut through me like a blade: *"A Palestinian can never be with an Israeli."* I ran to my room, tears streaming down my face as I FaceTime David. His face appeared on the screen, and his voice instantly filled with concern. *"Khadeja, are you okay? What happened?"* I managed to choke out the words, "I told my father about us, and he won't approve." Before I could say more, I heard shouting from his side of the call. His parents had just found out about us from the conversation, and they were furious. *"David, what are you thinking? You can't be with her!"* They screamed at him in Hebrew, and I saw the pain in his eyes as he hung up abruptly.

(**David**) I got a call from the army telling me I had to report to duty in Gaza. With little time to spare, I quickly packed my bags and headed there. Every day, while on duty, I made sure to bring Khadeja and her family food and supplies, anything I could to help them survive.

Even though our families would never approve of us, we hadn't given up. We still talked every day, and our connection was stronger than ever.

Now that we're both in Gaza, we're planning to meet up. I've been thinking about it for a while, but the war really confirmed it for me: she's the girl I want to spend my life with. I want to propose to her, to make it official, because I can't imagine a future without her.

With the sound of every missile that falls and every bullet that is fired, my heart trembles with fear for my only love, Khadija. I can't imagine my life without her; she is the one who made me discover who I am and what I truly wanted to be.

One day, after we were ordered to search the displaced people from northern Gaza, my military unit stopped a Palestinian family. I was standing a little farther away when something urged me to approach. As I came closer, I was stunned, it was Khadija. Her bright eyes, long hair, and beautiful face were unmistakable.

Fear struck me that she might be harmed or treated badly. I quickly separated her from her family, pretending I needed to search for her alone. When we were finally alone, I could hear her heart beating with joy. She hugged me tightly and said in Arabic, *"How could I have missed this beautiful face?"* Overwhelmed, I replied in Hebrew, *"Hello."*

At that moment, it felt like the world around us disappeared. The destruction turned into green hills filled with flowers. We talked about our dreams and how, for the first time, they felt like they were coming true. The dream we had always shared was finally becoming a reality.

For the first time, I took out the ring I had carried with me since the beginning of the war. It was meant for her, for this moment. In my happiness, I forgot the snipers watching us around the clock. As I knelt down to propose, a voice crackled on the walkie-talkie: *"This girl killed him. Shoot her now."*

Before I could think, I stepped in front of her, taking the bullet meant for Khadija. I collapsed; the pain was sharp but the knowledge of her safety was stronger. Khadija fell to her knees beside me, crying hysterically. Through her tears, she said the words I had always told her: *"Hope is the only thing we have."*

(**Khadeja**) "It's been 60 years since I lost the love of my life, David. And now, I have the honor of participating in the Israeli Independence Day torch lighting ceremony."

I paused, looking out at the crowd, my heart swelling with both pride and sorrow.

"I've decided to tell you this story right here, right now, so you'll remember one thing: never lose your hope. Hope is the only reason I'm standing here today, the only reason I can share this story, the story of the love of my life.

Hope is what kept us going, even when the world was against us. Even when our families, our nations, tried to tear us apart, we always held on to that one thing: hope. We hoped that one day, we could love openly, without fear, without shame. Even though we never got the chance to do that, our story opened doors. It gave others the courage to love, to unite, to believe in peace, Palestinians and Israelis, Jews and Arabs, all around the world. Our story made it possible for them.

Many lives were lost in that war, but we grew stronger. We learned what was truly important. And through it all, hope was what carried us through the hardest moments.

So, I ask you now: never lose your hope. If you take nothing else from my words today, remember this, nothing is impossible if you have hope."

Ropes of Hope

Jack Lubavin and Tom Yaari

Do we have hopes?

Sure, we have hopes, but we are not sure they are real.

Do we truly believe people can be kind? I personally don't believe it exists. Well, I have hope it exists- I hope people will live in harmony and stop singing the symphony. While other teens hope to pass their classes, we are the broken ones.

We? We hope for friendship, not witnessing any dead bodies, to get to hug our yellow friends again. I hope women can walk on the street while not being scared. And I hope people can see others past their differences. I lost hope- then found it. No! You don't understand, I really lost it, where can I find it again? Where can we find hope and innocence again? Will we ever be able to find it? It takes one person to find it again, or to never believe it again. We got lost, not seeing any hope anymore. Will one person be our Savior, will he help us find hope, or will it be lost forever?

Up in the sky, our families are waiting, out there in the darkness, with the small light. A really small light that comes from each star, that gives us another light to see. We are the broken ones, yet we still hope.

A Lost Soul: Connecting the Soul to the Body

Emily Shalbi and Matan Behar

The first time the light entered our eyes was also the first time we ignited, the first time we 'gained' consciousness. That is the moment we officially became part of this universe and its vast life. Philosophy calls it welcoming an intellectual mind, a pure soul, and a healthy body to the universe. Psychology, however, defines it as another entity, another variable in the great equation. We were all kids, with joyful smiles, immature yet curious minds with one big loving heart. We were unaware of the world's flaws and only set to embark on a bright journey. We all had one common wish: "I want to grow up". Growing up was our biggest aspiration, yet we were roses unable to grow our thorns. How could something so beautiful be so dangerous? Little did we know that those thorns were the soldiers of every soul existing, preventing any damage that might cause the disconnection between the body and soul.

We explored the world with our little eyes and tiny steps, consumed by the present and its details. No yesterday, no tomorrow just now. Used to forgive people easily, not for being naive, but for trusting human nature. At the end of the day we live for the moment, don't we? Our angelic innocence lit up every room we entered, leaving smiles on the faces of those we met. "Sometimes I feel sorry for adults, they must be going through hard times." "I just don't understand why they are always so worried, so focused on the future." "I wish someday they will just focus on living in the moment without overthinking, just like all my friends and I do." "I wish I could grow up to show them it's not a big deal being an adult."

Unfortunately, however, we never had a sense of the future as kids. We always sought the moment, never giving thought to anything past tomorrow. Temporary happiness was our goal, even at the cost of future bonds. We would sever friendships over broken toys and inflict harm for inconsequential reasons. But that was all okay, because we needed to learn to prioritize the present before we could learn to plan for the future. We were budding flowers, yet still realizing our potential, following only the shining rays of light emitted by our sun. Growing up, family gatherings were filled with people of all ages, so was school. We used to see students older than us on a daily basis, ninth graders, tenth graders, and ones who are about to graduate from school. Wondering what it's like to be in their shoes: Teenagers, mature, sophisticated, and tall. The one and only question always popped into our minds: "Are they able to grow out their thorns?". We were still roses with no thorns, "beautiful" inside out, all we had to do was wait. We wanted to grow up for the sake of growing up, to be like our parents. They were our only role models, and the people in our lives we could see a future with. But other than that, we never really had a goal. We had not evolved enough to find what brought us joy and interest and thus could not dream of such a future. Though even rudimentary, happiness still highlights its importance. We paid no mind to grief and set away our worries. But however prevalent and welcoming our physical life was, the mental avenue still lacked progress, and our body came to be without a soul.

In the blink of an eye, the years went by. We used to normalize blowing off candles on our birthday cakes and wishing a wish. However, the candles of our thirteenth birthday felt different. They marked the ending of our childhood era and the beginning of an unknown era called "teenage years". Suddenly we are in middle school, now teenagers don't only have a body but also mixed feelings that managed to develop a little soldier deep down within our hearts, our souls. For now, all we have left is our soul, our body is simply a nostalgic history that belongs to a different timeline of ours. History is something that we will always treasure but it's just that, history.

And puberty hits us all, however inconvenient. It is an integral part of our evolution, but not one without drawbacks. The changes awaken an insecurity, disgust aimed at ourselves. Darkness crawls up our spines, turning what used to be love into hate. Our focus shifts to appearance, and we value the elementary. But curses and blessings are contrast and harmony, and though we change, we still inherit the innate child-like wonder we used to have. From joy to sadness, and days of future past, a larger vision of life we have, one with our dream cast.

Being in our rooms all day long felt like entering an infinite asylum created by our own will. We subconsciously have mastered becoming roses with thorns, not because we are ruthless nor ugly, but because this universe gives you beauty but it will always give you pain in order to balance the scales within you. The journey of teenagers is nowhere near easy, thus we learned how to protect our soul by growing thorns. Anxiety became the successor of all the happy innocent feelings we had as kids. Staring at the sunset automatically brings flashbacks of our childhoods, the sound of the loud happy laughs, costumes we used to wear, playing with friends, tea parties, becoming temporary angels flying in the snow, or even building sandcastles on the beach. We could be walking down the street, then seeing a little girl or boy with their parents and get hit with a Deja Vu kind of feeling, a happy tear leaving our eyes, wondering why we desperately wanted to grow up. One question lives rent-free in teenagers' minds:" Are we still able to live for the hope of it all? Or is adulthood something that cannot be romanticized?".

Locked in stasis, a prison of time. One of our own makings, one of a soul benign. Fact and feeling clouded alike. Body and soul, like spikes and thorns. Pandora's curse of love and fear, followed dearly by a vision nearby. It chases us all, the hate and sorrow, for we know not the consequences of tomorrow. We become our own yet fear the unknown. Our soul we strike, as for conformity we strive. Inner changes occur as we grow, and uncertainty sprouts. Such causes disdain for the future and makes us wish for a way out. Sacrifices are inevitable as we develop a personality, though we are left with only a soul and nobody.

Molting is the process by which a snake routinely casts off its skin to facilitate new growth, sometimes life forces you to do the same. Mourning the loss of the kid we were once will lead us to nothing except for a dead end. Wishing we could have the possibility of being kids again is one big delusion that stops us from experiencing self-growth as well as learning life lessons. Life should not and must not be as ideal as we want it to be. It's okay to have a roller coaster of emotions, it's okay to experience ups and downs. At the end of the day, all that you have lost is all that you have gained. The universe does not leave you empty; it always balances the scales within you, for all that it takes, it gives. For all that it destroys it creates. Reassess all that you think is damaged and defeated within you. Every breakdown was just a step to your becoming, to finally being able to connect the body and soul, by being a firm believer in the power of hope and its capacity. Do not fear your evolution, claim it.

But as the storm passes, a light draws near. A soothing wave washes over all our doubts, all our fears. We learn to live, learn to accept. What makes us unique no longer renders us inept. We built relationships and found our people, creating a space for us to truly express ourselves. We found what we were good at and nurtured it into a source of happiness. We know not what the future holds, and so we savor every moment, every interaction. We spent our lives looking forward to, or fearing adulthood, and such drove us crazy at times. However, hard work pays off as the body and soul finally bond and evolve into what we call a 'person'.

Every story has its ending, and no one writes their own. To become one with yourself is a goal we all share. While few achieve it, those who do so can truly live their lives. Fear can paralyze us, preventing us from making hard choices. However, it is only once we choose to be bold that we get to witness the greatness of which we are capable. During hard times, when no one else is there, our connection with our own body and soul is what allows us to be overpowered whatever roadblocks stand in our way. No matter how bad life gets, how depressing or misguided, we will always have one thing. **Hope**.

The Beginning of Hope

Ella Regev and Dima Aboliel

Her name was Emma, she was extremely beautiful, extremely intelligent and talented, but her thoughts were not the same. Emma is a 16-year-old girl, her parents were divorced and she didn't have a lot of friends in her school, her grades were always high and she never makes mistakes in exams, but we couldn't say the same about her daily life.

So, what is happening to Emma? If she's that smart and beautiful, what is going wrong? Emma had a really strong struggle with food, she had eating disorders, although her body was quite healthy, due to her parents' and relatives' comments she was so insecure about her body, she thought that she was so "fat" and that this makes her look ugly. This is not a new thing in our society: many girls felt that they were not enough or that they are ugly just because they don't fit in the impossible society beauty standards, countless girls and women have gone through this experience, and Emma was one of them.

She walked through the school tired, pale, like she was throwing up in the bathroom the entire day, her classmates saw her as a ghost, she was always quiet and didn't do anything, like she had no soul! Or maybe a person without hope. Emma had no passion for life, all she thought about all day was calories and food, and she never had hope that she would beat these feelings and become a confident girl.

Until her 17th birthday, that day everything changed.

Emma never celebrated her birthday due to a lot of reasons such as that she has only two friends so it's not worth it, and mainly because she never had the urge to invite people to her birthday, she never had hoped that anyone would come besides her friends.

So, what was different about her 17th birthday? On that day Emma's friends decided that they should organize a secret party for Emma and they invited some of their classmates to it. Emma had no clue about this secret party.

It was a cold, crisp morning on Emma's 17th birthday. She woke up feeling as indifferent as ever, her thoughts circling the usual loop of self-criticism and exhaustion. Birthdays were just another reminder to her of all the things she felt she lacked—friends, confidence. She had no plans for the day, except studying or lying in bed, scrolling through her phone.

Secretly from Emma, her friends had been working on something special for weeks. They couldn't bear to see Emma sinking further into despair. They wanted to remind her of her worth, even if just for one day.

The day of the party arrived, and all of the guests arrived at Emma's house. Excited by Emma's reaction, everyone was hiding in a few different places, holding their phones in their hands, and waiting for Emma to arrive.

Emma arrived at her home, not knowing that people were there, she went to the bathroom to throw up as usual, and when she finished, she went to the basement to grab a book so she could study. When Emma entered the basement she froze, her eyes wide with shock. She saw the effort they had put into this, the decorations, the homemade cake, and the cheerful smiles. It was overwhelming. She felt a lump in her throat, unsure of how to process the kindness directed at her, it was her first time feeling that **she was worth it**. With a big smile on her face, she ran to hug her friends.

The party was small but meaningful. They played games, ate cake, and for the first time in what felt like forever, Emma laughed. It wasn't forced or polite, it was genuine. As the evening wore on, Emma felt a warmth she hadn't known she needed.

That night, as Emma lay in bed, she replayed the day's events in her mind. For the first time, she wondered if, just maybe, she was worth more than the critical voice in her head had led her to believe. It wasn't a miraculous, overnight transformation, but it was a start.
Her friends had shown her that she wasn't alone. And for Emma, that was **the beginning of hope**.

Hope and Action in Dark Times

Eli Klitsner and Narod Minassian

"A feeling that what is wanted will happen, desire accompanied by expectation." This is the dictionary definition of 'hope', but where hope differs from something such as 'optimism' is in the strong feeling of trust in someone or something outside of your own abilities that hope provides. Hope comes from an external source such as a parental guide or even a god, something out of your control. The fundamental law of 'hope' lies in how it can cause somebody to loosen his or her grip on the situation, such as a soldier operating in the hope that God or allies will come to the rescue, potentially causing him to act out of impulse instead of thought-out strategy. Hope often makes you feel safer than you truly are, which may result in a dangerous misunderstanding of a situation.

Joan of Arc is among the most iconic women in history, winning battle after battle for the French in the Hundred Years' War after claiming that God guided her. She led all those battles, and she was completely dependent on hoping or trusting that God would guide her in the right direction. She may have won battles, but she eventually started losing more and more until she was captured by the English and consequently lost her life in the most horrible way imaginable. Instead of developing a strategy to defeat the English, Joan depended on God and was blinded when going into battle with no strategy. This actually worked for a while, as the English were confused and unused to the new style of attack, particularly by a girl. She won battles for her country which led to the victory and freedom of France, but only after her death. During the war, however, she was captured, imprisoned, and put to death. After the French had achieved the crown, her people and the king whom she had helped to establish turned their back on her, deciding she was of no more use. She thought that God had sent her to save France, and was entirely committed to the idea that God would guide her through the correct path. On her last day, she was convinced that God would save her from the/m. She was ready to do what God intended for her. Her hope in God did not fail her; the people of the world did (a point Rabbi Jonathan Sacks made about Auschwitz), as she was condemned by the English and burnt at the stake for saying that God guided her.

This analogy can effectively compare the life of Joan of Arc to the wider question of this essay, which explores the possibility that hope is a misunderstood aspect of human existence. We want to understand how hope can be used in different situations, and whether hope is not necessarily a positive feeling; that while it makes us feel better, it can lead us to unwise decisions.

Although from different communities and backgrounds, we were both raised in this country since we were children. However, we grew up with different lives which have affected our points of view about hope. We think that it is vital for this essay that you, the reader, understand our points of view and understand what hope means to us in Israel.

Eli's point of view:

When the war first broke out all that time ago, everything felt so surreal. At the time I had my hopes higher than ever that everything would be okay as I hadn't yet truly faced the weight of these events, of the horrors going on in the world, so hope was easy to come by. A few months ago, however, the hope that had pushed me so high led me to crumble and fall even further down as my father's cousin, a man he had known since childhood, was shot and killed in Lebanon while serving in the army. This showed me how real war really is. This loss is personal, one I never before imagined happening as all of a sudden, the full weight of the war was dropped upon me and my family. My hope did not protect me; it just made the harsh reality that much harsher when it was destroyed. In the aftermath, I no longer wanted to hope, but soon enough little by little I began to hope once more. Then once more my hope betrayed me when my uncle was shot in both arms on his way out of Gaza and only narrowly survived, his survival was the only reason I have not renounced hope entirely, and the reason I can build up a little hope again for the future.

Narod's point of view:

Due to the fact that I am a non-Jew and non-Arab living in this country, I have always been looking at it from an outside point of view. Yes, I may be living in this country but I will never experience first-hand what each 'side' in the conflict has experienced. I have been aware of the conflict in this country but I have always hoped and thought that one day both sides would see what I see in them, two nations who can live and function in a great way, as long as politics, religion, and race are not mixed. I have always hoped that one day the conflict would be resolved, but I had yet to know the severity of the situation until October 7th happened. The day the war broke out I was woken up by the sound of the news playing. Still being half asleep, I asked what was going on and my parents responded with "a war has started and this time it does not look like it will be a simple one." Seeing everything on social media makes my heart ache for both sides, but unfortunately this war has pushed the hope for peace and resolution of the conflict to become a dream that might not come true. The anger and resentment that reappeared in this war are much deeper and stronger than at any time before, and yet I still see terrible things on social media. I also see many people coming together and pushing for peace, which is slowly making me hope and dream again that a solution is obtainable.

Meanwhile, my own community feels caught in the middle, with tensions over the sale of land in the Armenian Quarter of Jerusalem's Old City, although this sale was made without the community's knowledge and came as a shock to everyone. The younger generation could not and would not stand it. Through dedication and stubbornness, they came up with different ways to protect the land that rightfully belongs to the Armenian community: 24-hour surveillance to make sure that no construction takes place, chasing away the man who wrongfully sold the land, and going on news channels to get the exposure this issue deserves. The Armenians in this country go through so much but they are never given the attention like other people in this country do, due to the fact we are a small community and do not easily fit into one 'side' or another in the broader conflict. Seeing the community coming together, young protesters together with older women who come and bring food to boost morale and share their past stories and wisdom, gives me hope that maybe one day the land will come back to its rightful owners and Armenians will stand as equals alongside the city's other communities.

Another struggle that Christians face is the restrictions that are imposed on Christians during the Holy Saturday in Easter. Whether you are a Christian from this country, or a pilgrim from abroad, we get our rights taken away from us to walk freely and to attend church on the day of the Holy Fire. It breaks my heart to see that every entrance to the Old City is covered with police forces redirecting Christians away, sometimes violently, preventing them from attending church on one of their holiest days. Even though every year people know that going to the Old City on Holy Saturday will be challenging, thousands of Christians still go hoping that they will be let in. Seeing these people with such determination on their faces, gives me hope that one day we will get access to attend church in the holiest place on one of the holiest days for Christians.

Over the past year and a half, we have both experienced things unlike anything that we have seen before. Even with our different experiences, we are united by the fact that our hope can heal from the people around us. Whether or not we know the person on a personal level, hope can come to you, like seeing hostages come back home online or a relative making it out okay or even just a happy smile on a friend's face. Although hope can be 'false' or leave you crushed or betray you, it remains one of the most beautiful aspects of human experience: the idea that we can always aspire to something better.

Hope is a gamble that can take you to the highest of highs and the lowest of lows yet sometimes it can even help mend the wounds it itself has caused. Joan of Arc's story adds a crucial lesson, however: hope cannot substitute for pragmatism and compromise. As in the 'parable of the drowning man', God puts opportunities for peace before us, but it is up to us to take them. As the Armenian community has shown, 'hope' comes from the actions we take together to make our world a better place. You might say that hope is risky, but maybe, just maybe, a risk worth taking.

The Phone Booth At the End of Winter

Maria Muhmadat and Nitsan Ravid

The air was cold. The entire world was covered in that irreversible fact. And the boy just walked there, in the middle of the city that was burned, flooded, drowned, and ruined and finally… Frozen. He smelled like lilacs, there's only so much you can do to stave off the winter once you leave the indoors, but smelling like lilacs can't hurt.

It wasn't that sort of skin-cold that you get when you take a shower on a winter morning. This was a deep cold. A ''sitting naked in the rain for so long that you can't feel anything but the mud and your blood''-cold; a ''buried in the mines a thousand strides beneath the earth, still alive even though your every heat source died days ago''-cold; it was the dead cold. The ones living there weren't meant to experience it. It was the memory of death, and it stuck with you. Stay within your bones long after you're already being pulled to safety and warmth. It made anything not like the cold feel… Less real, somehow. Hollow.

What importance could any warmth have when deep within your body still lay buried that unmelt frost? It conquered you, marched over your soul with silent war drums that left nothing but frostbites and shivering.

243

That's why you got to put on some lilac perfume. It doesn't warm you or anything, but it does smell nice.

- - - - -

Manufactured silence raked on the hospital floor, pooling into viscous puddles. She couldn't hear the dozens of hearts beating out of rhythm, nor the short coughing breaths, she could barely hear her own thoughts. It was snowing outside, but the heater did its work.

This was about the state of the entire city. Always brimming with life; always *awake*; beeping, ticking, pulsating, spinning round and round like clockwork teeth on a child's neck. It could deafen you to these little human sounds; a kid crying by the sidewalk; the footsteps of a shoeless woman strolling the streets like a pre-mortem ghost, an old man whispering a muffled goodbye as he steps into the train tracks. Tick.

The kid thinks he sees his older sister on the other side of the road, he runs— Tick.
Frostbites climb up the woman's skin, her wailing strengthening until her body can no longer afford to spend warmth on tears, then, she— Tick.
The 23:30 PM train rushes into the station. Nobody notices a broken, bleeding—Tick.

- - - - -

Not that he can smell the lilacs, you know? He's holding his breath. It doesn't help much; the cold is already within his bones. Bones covered in little to no flesh, even less fat, and any scraps of cloth he could find and stitch into a patchwork cocoon of jackets lined with jackets. No, it wasn't pretty, but it was the only thing keeping him alive outside the shelter.

Outside of the lilac perfume and the coat, the boy carries two more objects —a small whale doll, and a coin. The coin was a tiny thing of cheap copper. Even before this country collapsed, the coin could've barely bought you a lollipop, now it is completely worthless. He holds it high, letting the dream lit night reflect off its well-polished surfaces. Held like this, the coin burned brighter than any diamond. Despite the weather, the metal was warm.

He's almost out of air now. The burning sensation in his lungs provides no heat. No matter how bad it is, it's always worse when the air is inside you. He clings to the doll closer. He imagines the moment. Maybe the dreading will help prepare him, somehow. When that lethal atmosphere collapses into your respiratory system, and the freezing floods your veins, blood flow comes into a stop. The boy falls to the side of the road.

A street light flickers dimly.

- - - - -

Mira closes the hospital window. Tick. She brews black tea at exactly 96.1 degrees Celsius, for no longer than 180 seconds. Tick. Dinner — cleared. Teeth — brushed. Tick. Eyes — closed. Tick. Tick. Tick. The hours of the night bled out slowly. Mira was lying in her bed, the only thing disturbing the silence were gigantic white machines, pristine and expensive, kept clean and in top condition. She was so Luc— *tick.* —so lucky to get this treatment. She was sleeping. She was supposed to sleep. She scheduled herself to go to sleep early, tomorrow they were releasing her back into the city. Her eyes were wide open. More and more moments— *tick.* —hours pass by. They always passed by. Her entire life just passed by, day after day, rhythm following schedule, psyche— *tick.* —projects blurring together, habits soli— *tick.* —habits freezing into perfect machinations that ticked in unbreakable unison. Forever.

This place was supposed to be a break — company mandated, of course — "spend some time in a quiet hospital by the sea, that'll fix it." Fix it. Because she had lost control— *tick.* —acted out of order. "Psychotic meltdown," the doctors said. She. Psychotic.

A meltdown? The thought refused to fully form within her mind without breaking apart. The ideas seemed irreconcilable. *Tick.* But company mandated is company mandated. She'll play along nicely, as she always does. Smile to the doctor, check the right boxes, and go back to her normal life— *Tick.* —normal life.

So that's what she was doing here, taking a break, getting better, "fixing it.' *Ti*— Her hand slammed into the monitoring glass. The shattering echoed in the emptiness of her room. Gears and metal springs were rolling all over the floor. Red pain screamed from her shard-covered fingers, the blood dripping downward, the ferrous smell spreading, her laughter was the first real sound she heard in so long. It was broken.

- - - - -

He tries to stand up. It's like riding a frozen motorcycle, his body refuses response, everything is slow and stagnant when—

The ice within his bone breaks, the momentum pushing him off balance. He falls back down, far harder than last time. He's too tired to even scream.

Why… not just… stay down? He collects his legs and the whale doll and the cloak and presses them all into himself. Above him, the wind screams like a siren; flattens the world; allows no sound to be heard.

- - - - -

The room was silent, truly silent this time. The blood congealed in spikey patterns on the floor, there was glass and broken plastic everywhere. This… This was a mess! What was she even thinking?! Her insurance wouldn't cover this! And what about, and if, and why would she, and— Her thoughts were spinning in an endless loop that coiled around itself into a hanging noose that tightened and tightened and—

At that moment, an insane realization came to her. She… didn't care. Not about the machine, nor about going back to her job, nor… What did she hope to find every day she dragged herself out of bed? What *did* she care about? It had been so long since she allowed herself to ask that question. She had a good life, a well-paying job, and loving parents. She was doing *great*.

She spent so much time doing great that she forgot how ''great'' felt, ''being great'' was the axiom of her life. It became a deafening background noise. She never noticed the pitch changing. Listening inside instead of out is not something they teach you to do in the city. After all, if you're busy looking in you might get run over by a bus. Now, in silence, she listened closely… Something was wrong.

- - - - -

He pressed his face into the soft doll and started whispering. The boy had a language, but he wasn't sure where it came from. He found things in the ruins, coins, dolls, scraps, the shelter, but the language… The language just found him. In gigantic neon street signs, in broken recordings that he replayed again and again until they stopped working; on the backs of canned preservatives that always run out too fast. The language found him behind every corner, and slowly, he started searching for it.

Now, the boy made a small whisper. He told the doll he was scared. It didn't answer. He asked it to help him up. It made no sound. He said he doesn't know how many more falls he can take. Again, it denied him any reply. Finally, in a voice so tiny that even the ruins couldn't hear, he asked the doll if he could stay here forever, to let the wind just wash him over. There wasn't a single sound. He loosened his fingers, letting go of everything, preparing for a last nap.

Then there was a little clink. The coin! He accidentally dropped it on the pavement when he— Oh never mind that! He had a coin to catch! He jumped up and started running, forgetting the doll behind. He followed the glinting song the coin made as it bounced down the streets, faster and faster, the song grew louder, it mixed with the boy's laughter, it rose over the wind.

By the time he caught the coin he was wheezing, breathing, and giggling all over. You didn't really have a reason to run in the ruins; you didn't really have reason for much of anything. He pocketed the coin and kept running, he had a quest to complete.

- - - - -

Mira tried repeatedly to recall how her tears felt. She knew she could cry; she had scheduled and archived instances of crying, remembering the events themselves made sense; but the feeling was gone. She was an observer, cut away from her own life and forced to watch. What decisions did she make with those hands? Skin bruised, bones shattered, and for what? To hold on to a boat didn't build, sailing to a direction she didn't know.

She traced the memories of her life with broken fingers, trailing along the edges of unfilled dreams and all too real nightmares. Everything lay in shards around her. She didn't know how to ''fix it. No more, she was letting go.

So why not run away? She dressed up, did her hair, and pushed open the hospital's door. At 23:30 PM, Mira sneaked out of the hospital. Nobody noticed.

- - - - -

The cold crawled and coiled around the concrete waste like famished vines, digesting gray walls until all that was left were bare steel ribs.

The air shattered windows to find.

more heat, sipping frost cracking down riverbeds until the entire ocean was left devoid of warmth.

The graveyard-city sprawled over the horizon, but it was not dead, it couldn't sleep or rest even after all that time. The ghost of urbanity. But the haunted ruins told stories, if you look closely, you can see the imprints that people left behind them: The items they didn't have time to pack were left in the wreck like scattered letters; panicked footprints like commas; evacuated houses left like torn pages, their skulls a nameless period.

A thousand forgotten stories told through absence.

He remembers how difficult it used to be to squeeze through those streets on a busy day, everyone so determined to get to wherever they needed to go; dense crowds fighting tooth and nail for every step. Easily running through it, the road becomes claustrophobically vast. The place is now haunted by the hordes of all the people that aren't there, that should be but were taken away. That loneliness swallows you.

But despite, or maybe, in spite, of all that ruin — the boy lingers on. Why? Perhaps to remember the stories of all those who are no longer with him, perhaps to tell a story of his own, living requires no reason at all. Or just because he wanted someone to talk to.

He slides around the corner, reaches the end of the street, and faces...

A phone booth.

That phone booth was ancient, its entire rusty frame stood proudly at the end of the street. It didn't make any sense that it would work after so long. But the boy hoped it would, and that was enough. So just like that, in the middle of a night darker than ink, he stood in front of the phone booth. It looked like a fallen star nested between the ruins, sharp neon letters spilling warm light on the street. They spelled out a single word, TELEPHONE, nothing less and nothing more.

He knew exactly what he had to do, now... If only he could figure out how to open that rusty door.

- - - - -

Beyond the electrical doors, beyond endless geometric halls, there lay the sea. The gentle curve of the waves rose and fell from horizon to horizon, there were no edges in the boundless waters, and the smell of salt felt like freedom. Nobody ever claimed there was something wrong with the sea. It could be cruel or calm, save lives or snuff them out, but nobody would dare to try and fix it.

She walked along the shore; the wind grew colder with every step. By the time she reached the sea the world had frozen still. Then she entered her leg. Wisps of frost

crawled up her skin. Mira took another step, her second leg entering the water. The sea caressed her feet with long icy nails. The water felt like acid. She wanted to scream. Another step.

The grip tightened around her knees, struggling not to lose balance. Another step. Saltwater pierced her wounded arm; prodding pain filled her nerves. Another step. She felt out of place; something was missing for so long — no longer. Another step. The waves became more violent, the air squeezed out of her lungs. No. This isn't what she wanted, she tried to step back, then the tide swept her over. The door finally broke open. The inside of the phone booth was… warm! A golden honey-tea-warm that he forgot even existed.

She felt the weight of the ocean force down her throat, her breath burning. Every warmth disappears. She shut her eyes; everything went silent.

The beautiful coin rolled down the slot, he pressed his fingers against the radiant buttons of the phone booth. If this was really a fallen star, he would make a wish. A loud ringing teared through the quiet, Mira coughed out saltwater and blood, shaking, half dead, yet… Alive. She stood up, a tiny platform floated atop the murky waters. On it, a phone booth.

The boy put his ear against the phone and waited. Nothing happened. Tears started streaming down his cheeks, he hated himself for that. This was a stupid idea, it was always a stupid idea. What was he thinking?! A phone booth in the middle of nowhere— She picked up the phone with a hesitant 'hello?"

Deep inside, a spark was lit, something began melting.

''Hello!'' He replied. And they began to talk.

Strings of the Past

Kristen Abu Nassar and Zohar Benkimhy

The echo of strings was heard across the walls at Manhattan school, Yousef's fingers plucked at the strings, practicing hours every day while pouring out his emotions in his playing. Even though guitar seemed to be the escape of reality for Yousef, he still felt empty. Music has always been his escape, his only outlet since the day he had learned to hold his first guitar, when his mother gifted it to him on Christmas day, it was through these strings that he expressed the quiet rebellion and the chaos that ran through his veins.

He has been in America for as long as he can remember, and yet he never felt home, He never felt like he belonged, his struggling mother being a Palestinian Christian who immigrated from her country and chose to live in the USA completely alone, having grown up without a father figure, all seemed to crush Yousef's mind everywhere he went. While practicing, he heard the handle of the door twist, seeing a figure out of the corner in his eyes, he had already figured out who it was, Yoav. His assigned partner for the end of the year performance, his assigned partner who he never felt at ease with, his assigned partner who he felt foreign with.

Yoav, on the other hand, felt the same uneasiness towards Yousef.

251

Yoav was known for his musical intelligence and talent, and even though they shared the same university, they had never been friends. Yoav was used to being the quiet loner, one who kept to himself despite the attention he garnered from his talent and his good looks. He had always felt like an outsider where he lives, like he doesn't belong and while having a Jewish dad who served in the military for some time and a mother who never showed up, which played a significant role on his personality for now. And for the history of these two, they never felt at peace being together.

Yousef's judging, disapproving stare during their first meeting only added fuel to the fire. The air between them was thick with racial tension, not outright hatred, but a deep, underlying discomfort.

"Your part is the intro," Yoav muttered, tapping his sticks against his knee.

Yousef nodded, not bothering to look up from his guitar. He already knew what his part was, it was the same every time. The rock beats, the heavy riffs, the quiet sense of revolt in every strum. He didn't need Yoav to remind him, in fact, he hated that Yoav reminded him.

For the next few days, they worked in silence, trying to put the feeling of discomfort aside, but something shifted when they began rehearsing together.

Yoav slowly felt himself starting to be mesmerized by Yousef's playing, he felt how Yousef poured his heart out into his playing; therefore, he started letting his guard down, started admiring his playing.

He saw a new version of Yousef he didn't think of, meanwhile, Yousef felt the exact same, and despite the coldness between them, he felt Yoav's rhythm pulling him in. There was a familiarity to it and an instinctive understanding that grew each time their instruments collided.

One day, Yoav decided to take a different approach.

"Hey, Yousef," he said, dropping his sticks onto the practice table with a clatter.

"We should try something. I was thinking of combining your guitar

with my drums... like... a mix of Middle Eastern beats and rock."
Yousef raised an eyebrow.

Surprisingly, a wave of happiness washed over Yousef, and he felt quite appreciated, since Yoav was willing to explore some of his culture and background.

And even though Yousef was surprised, which made him hesitate for a moment, until he cautiously nodded. "Alright, let's see what happens." For the first time, they actually began working together. It felt new and exciting, they were not only playing, but they were also having fun, which felt right. They found something unspoken but deeply understood. When the rehearsal ended that day, neither of them wanted to leave. As they packed their instruments, Yoav felt a strange impulse to speak. "Why do you play like that?" he asked, the question slipping out before he could stop it. Yousef glanced at him, surprised.

"Like what?"

"Like... it's personal," Yoav said, glancing at the guitar. "You don't just play; you feel the music." Yousef paused. There was a moment of silence before he spoke softly.

"I guess I do," he said quietly. "It's the only way I know how to deal with all the noise in my head."

Yoav could see the hint of pain in his eyes, and for the first time, he felt a flicker of empathy for the boy who had been a stranger just days ago. They stood there for a moment, the tension between them fading, replaced by a fragile understanding.

After a while, time flew by, and suddenly it was already the end of the semester. And in the meantime, Yoav and Yousef began to talk more, not just about music, but also about life, about family. They opened up to each other slowly, having found comfort in each other's companion, therefore their bond deepened, despite their differences. Yoav told Yousef about his father, Roy, the man who had gone to fight in Israel's war and returned after a few years, so he doesn't remember anything from his childhood other than the feeling of emptiness but having his father back after 2 years at the war felt like a dream come true.

And Yousef also opened up about his emotions, which he struggled to do before. He spoke of how his mother had struggled to raise him alone, how he felt lost between two worlds, not fully his own.

But it wasn't until the night before the performance that everything changed.

The night before their big performance, both Yoav and Yousef entered the music school's auditorium to run through their final set. The place was almost empty, the stage lights dimmed, casting long shadows across the floor.

As they tuned their instruments, they heard voices from behind the curtain. Two figures emerged, a woman with dark hair and green eyes, and a man with a strong, rugged presence.

It was then that Yoav's heart skipped a beat.

It was his father.

"Dad?" Yoav whispered, disbelief creeping into his voice.

The woman beside him was Meryam, Yousef's mother.

Yoav recognized the woman standing next to his father as Yousef's mom, even though he felt a little confused on why they're standing together, he brushed that feeling off.

He rushed to see his father before he performed yet when his eyes locked with the woman, Yoav's stomach turned, and suddenly he felt a surge of anger, confusion, and something else, something that could only be described as a deep, painful connection.

"Oh hello, up. What is this?" Yoav demanded, his voice breaking, just standing there feeling confused.

Yousef stood frozen, staring at the two figures before him. His mind raced. The recognition was slow but unmistakable.

Meryam's face paled, she had puffy eyes, it seemed like she was crying, meanwhile Roy looked equally stunned and vulnerable, they stood in silence for a long moment before Meryam decided to do what she had done.

Meryam stepped forward, her eyes filled with sorrow, and before she could think her arms hugged Yoav tightly, so tightly trying to make up for all the years lost, seeing his face and checking every feature, observing and appreciating Yoav... Her son. The son who she couldn't grow up watching over, the son who didn't have a mother in his life, the son who she thought about every night and every morning, cherishing him in her memory as a secret from Yousef.

In her eyes it was already a burden to carry all of that pain within her, therefore she couldn't place it on her other son, Yousef.

(my love... how I missed you) ''اشتقتلك.. كيف'' (ك اكاة فك ةا لا)
''حبيبي.. انا

Meryam's eyes filled with tears as she spoke in front of Yoav, while he was in shock.

Staring at her other son, holding his hand "The war... it tore us apart. I didn't know how to tell you, Yousef. I didn't know how to explain." Yousef stepped back; his guitar slung loosely over his shoulder. The weight of everything settled on him like a heavy cloak. He turned to Yoav, their eyes locking for the first time, no longer filled with confusion, but with something else, recognition.

Yousef was shocked to his core, he slowly started connecting the dots, slowly started to comprehend everything, meanwhile Yoav got emotional, it felt like he understood after feeling his mother's warmth. The warmth that was stolen from him.

"Maybe," Yousef said quietly, "we were meant to find each other again." Yoav nodded slowly. For the first time, he felt the pieces of his life clicking into place.

It turns out they are brothers. Yoav's father, Ron was sent to Israel to complete his duty at war during the second war with Lebanon in 2006, and suddenly he went missing.

While he was missing, he lost all contact with his wife, and with his mother who took care of Yoav. After finally coming home, it was too late.

He had lost all contact with his wife, Meryam, and even though he searched for her in every part of the city he lived in, in their old neighborhood, in their grocery shopping store, in their favorite park, he couldn't find a trace of her.

He settled for life's decision and accepted his 'fate', taking care of his son, Yoav, and moving to a different city for a new life, with the hope of meeting his first love again.

Meanwhile, since Ron was in the military, Maryam had lost all contact with him, having no idea about his whereabouts in Israel, and having no idea that he got missing, she just didn't know what to do, she waited and waited, waited and waited,

But after two whole years with no information, with countless thoughts at night, crying until the stars disappeared from the sky, she couldn't find a trace of him.

Therefore, she decided to move on with life, to take care of her now 3 years old baby, Yousef, and move on to a different city, with a new life, with the hope of meeting again someday.

And while they explained their story to their beloved children, they felt connected, they felt relieved and even laughed about how the meeting place is a mere university concert hall.

The two boys stood there, side by side, brothers by blood but strangers by fate. And as the lights of the auditorium flickered on, they took their places on stage, their instruments in hand, their music ready to tell a story of loss, reconciliation, and unbreakable bonds.

As the first notes echoed in the empty room, Yoav and Yousef played together, a symphony of past pain and new beginnings. They didn't need words anymore.

The music was enough.

The Painter

Yuval Shalev and Ruba Abo Raya

<u>Part 1: The Painter</u>

Between dusk and dawn stands still a despondent will, leaden through despair, shackled by unrest. The once arcane avenues now lay abandoned by the peoples they once abridged.

Under glistening summer skies, dusty ends intertwine with terrible beginnings, as star-crossed lovers are bound by shrapnel and shadows. Haunted by silence and its producers, the roads echo silently with memories of better days.

Tonight, these forsaken streets bear witness to a strange oddity. An IDF soldier, wearing some sort of oversized grey hoodie and a pair of blue jeans, sneaks out from camp at dead of night.

Grumbling about their "dang conscription," the energetic soldier haphazardly shoved their bountiful golden locks under their hood and marched on, their pale face glistening in the moonlight.

Holding a small brush in one hand and a glistening palette in the other, they sharply scan around for suitable "targets." The town's central plaza catches their eye, muttering to themselves, "Bin-Go."

Approaching a large, decrepit wall, their hands moved on their own. Their nimble fingers conjured intricate, expression-filled strokes, leaving Hephaestus stunned. Handcrafted murals promptly adorn their woeful surroundings, lighting up the abandoned markets with breathtaking phosphorescent hues.

They studied the painting, mustering a fragile smile. "Not bad, huh Abby? Not as good as you, of course... never could... but someone's got to keep the dream alive, right?" The voice wavered, teetering on a memory they refused to name. Clapping their hands together, they forced a bright tone; "Welp! Gotta go back to work, someone needs to tidy this thing up."

Their delicate brushstrokes whisper to the people, reminding them that even in the bleakest darkness, simple beauty can emerge, rekindling hope in a place that had long forgotten how to dream of a tomorrow.

Two eyes watched silently from afar, speechless in their admiration. Mouthless, although not ceasing to express.

An armed guard, equipped with a green headband, lurked hidden in the shadows, watching the soldier with an intensity he has not felt in years. A simple question sprang to his melancholic mind- "...why?"

Part 2: A Discovery

One unusually clear night, the sky shimmered with countless stars, their cold, steady light evoking awe in all who gazed. The soldier's mind drifted off, "Abby... she always dreamt of such skies back at Sderot..." they quietly uttered to themselves, void of their usual sparkle and vigor.

They stood near an old church's wall, painting a woman shielding a younger girl from an unseen storm, her expression enchanting. The image glowed with raw emotion, defying the darkness around it. The soldier worked swiftly, as if put under a spell, their brushstrokes rhythmic and precise, almost hypnotic.

Stepping back to admire the mural, a small plastic card slipped from their pocket, landing softly on the ground unnoticed. Nearby, the observing guard, who had been monitoring their activity for the past couple of days, silently picked the card up after the soldier left the scene, his calloused hands turning it over.

He examined it; a photo of a young, captivating woman stared back at him, confidence in her eyes. Beside the image, a name was printed in neat Hebrew: "Ariel Carter." Above it, a symbol caught his eye- a dagger entwined with an olive branch atop a shield.

His face hardened, his gaze drifting to the mural. Withering in thought, sweet yet dusty memories of his father resurfaced- sharp and agonizing, as if puncturing shards of glass.

He pockets the ID and walks away. His mind racing, his thoughts linger, her face... embedded.

Part 3: The Gazan Standoff

The following night, the bird took flight, vibrant with hope. Her long, ragged skirt accentuated her tall, slender figure as she trailed the dull dusk, her brush making rights of the wrong.

"Why?"

She froze. Shattering her lively composure, she stopped and turned, her bones filling with anxiety. She saw it- a man materializing from the shadows. His face obscured, a rifle pointed at her, and two piercing amber eyes gazing into her being.

"Why what?" she responded meekly in Arabic, her voice taut. The man stepped closer; his weapon aimed at her. Face illuminated, revealing a well-groomed stubby beard and messy curls. Fury etched in his features, narrating untold nightmares.

"You think your paint can feed the children!? Bury the bodies!!? Erase the past??!? Why are you fooling yourself???" His voice jabbed at the air; fury-soaked words left a feel of rot.

"What are you trying to show?!?" His voice snapped, distasteful and bitter, a whip cracking.

Ariel caught her breath, her chest tightening. "No... nothing..." Her voice is innocent. Gathering her scattered resolve, attempting to forge some confidence, words came from her mouth, each one a slight struggle.

"I... I just… I want to help. My sister drew to bring people together... and I... I want to keep that going...."

His mute, yet reverberating laugh filled in the birdcage. "For your sister? What lofty ideals. The moment we wore these uniforms; our deeds were sealed."
Her hands trembled.

"We were studying... arts, back home. My sister didn't choose her fate. I... I didn't choose this."

His grip loosened. "And I am a novelist who traded his pen for a sword, no one does." His voice loosened yet filled with frustration. "But we all pay the price. A price your paint could never substitute..."

She hesitated; something restrained her. The weight of his words sank in; it struck a familiar chord.

"I understand, But -" she attempted to respond.

"But what?" He scoffed out loud as he stared at her for an insufferably long moment, his eyes unyielding and unreadable.

Finally, his voice broke the silence, and he stepped back. "Just, just let me ask you this," his voice mellowing, gun holstered back.

"May I ask you something?"

Ariel, slightly confused and taken aback, replies, "O -? Of course!"

The guard, planting his gun, leaning on it, attempting to mask his emotions as he questioned:

"What do you do when you simply can't do anything, but, but there's nothing you can do...?"

Ariel replied softly: "You do what you can."

Before she could utter another word, a fleeting smile crossed his face as he turned and vanished into the same shadows he had come from.

"Leave, never come back. For I cannot guarantee your smile, nor your life."

His words echoed through the darkness around them.

Ariel stood alone, with too many questions, too many answers. Her brush trembling in her hand, pondering whether to even finish her work.

Part 4: Chilling Fire

The following night, Ariel, as always, quietly changed into civilian clothes and slipped out of camp unnoticed, ignoring what the man had told her. The streets were quiet as always, a charming irony for this reality.

She once more found a suitable target- a dilapidated hospital. "If only we were a bit quicker... I'm sorry..." she sheepishly commented, her face overflowing with regret.

This time, her brush manifested a brilliant phoenix, rising from desolate ashes, its wings lit ablaze with impossible colors. The mural took flight, burning through the night sky, fighting the suffocating emptiness, as if alive.

A small rustle behind her, too quiet to notice at first, suddenly made large "thuds." Before she could turn, something cold was pressed against her neck.

Ariel was brutally dragged into a dimly lit and dusty room. Her hands were bound tight to a pole inside, the coarse ropes digging deeper into her skin with every futile struggle.

As her captors surrounded her, their cold faces beamed, yet she remained unbothered. One of them growled at her, "Who are you?" His tone cut short any pleasantries.

Ariel, attempting to muster a false bravado, retorted with a smirk, "just a painter. A nobody." Answering in Arabic, she kept her voice steady despite the immense pounding in her chest.

"Two weeks in, never thought studying Arabic would pay this many dividends..." Ariel thought, chuckling to herself. Though the humor did not settle quite well with the captors.

One of them, stepping forward, delivered a blow to Ariel's stomach, forcing a painful gasp. "Don't play games. Who sent you?" The man yelled in her ears.

Yet unknown to them, Ariel had already called for help using a special distress beacon. Ariel, violently coughing, straightened herself and confidently uttered, "None. For passion follows no orders."

They searched her pockets as tensions ran high amidst the room. Finding nothing inherently incriminating, their glares told Ariel that her answers should change, and fast.

One of the men, the most imposing in stature, stepped closer to her, his presence dominating the room. He grasped Ariel's face firmly, turning it left and right, as though searching for hidden truths in her expression.

Ariel's responses, weary but unwavering, seemed to frustrate him. His voice grew harsher with each passing moment, words cutting like blades as he demanded answers she couldn't provide. Ariel's resolve remained steady, her silent responses an unspoken defiance that only deepened the tension in the room.

Part 5: Blue World

The chaos halted suddenly, as if the sun was at the Battle of Gibeon. An impeccable young man entered the room; his presence silencing, yet oh-so-familiar. With a simple gesture, the men left without skipping a beat, answering, "Yes, Youssef."

His face, unreadable, lingered on Ariel. The door closed; the two were left alone. The man stood, silent. Each second stretched into eternity as his eyes bore into her. He saw the fierce defiance in her expression, tenacious yet collected through the tense air.

"So, Youssef, is it? Seeing you in uniform and not just that funny bandana is hilarious." She sneered.

"We meet again... unfortunately my platoon got to you first... take it as your last warning, dear."

Ignoring him, with a rebellious attitude "My sister always quoted from Gerhard Richter that 'art is the highest form of hope-' "

"Ariel, it's no time to play poet," his voice sounding irritated, "forget about that darn sister, think for a second, look around-"

"Hast, thou killed and taken possession? 1 Kings 2—"

"Stop it ! This isn't the time for games," Youssef snapped.

"Pretty boy, you're letting me finish. Last time you got the wrong impression. Now shut up, or I'll show you the same mercy you all gave my sister."

"Alright, but-"

"Do not but me."

"I'm tired. Tired of your talk about choice and regret. You're nothing but hypocritical."

"You all act so divine, so righteous, yet you couldn't spare the life of an innocent girl?"

"The only reason I didn't blow you up is because of that damn sister you keep talking about with your rotten mouth."

"She was barely 19. She only preached kindness and love. She didn't deserve her cruel fate."....."Nothing to say? Nothing to comment on? No rebuttals? No remorse?"

"....." Youssef stood, his silence aching him.

"I am giving you a chance, Youssef. Let me go, let me paint, let me help."

He clenched his fists, his knuckles bloody. The ID in his pocket felt heavier than the heavens above.

Turn the girl in? Justice, or vengeance? Thoughts blended and dueled, morality and vendetta greying out, sparring like cats and dogs.

Yet outside, the men's voices rose, praising Ariel's mural. The warmth in their words was gentle but piercing.

For the first time in years, Youssef's world wasn't red with anger or grey with despair. It was blue.

His gaze softened; reaching into his pocket, he pulled out Ariel's ID and slipped it right into her chest pocket. "Leave," he said, his voice low but firm, unwavering.

"Go" he simply repeated.

Part 6: The Escape

Ariel hesitated, scanning Youssef's face for any sign of betrayal. There

265

was only weariness. She nodded, limbs trembling, as she attempted to stand.

Engines roared in the distance, startling her escape. Her heart dropped as she recalled the emergency message she had sent before her capture.

Gunfire erupted outside, followed by intense bloody screams. Youssef cursed under his breath, grabbing Ariel's arm and commanding, "Follow me!"

They moved like shadows through the chaos, darting past crumbling walls and empty stalls, as Youssef led her through a narrow alley she would never have found alone, his pace swift but steady amidst the violent chaos.

Near a hidden passage to her base, he stumbled, clutching his side. His clothes darkened blood. "Guess I got shot," he half-jokingly muttered. Ariel reached for help, but he simply waved her off.

"Hurry up, go." he rasped.

"I'm not leaving you," Ariel insisted vehemently.

"You have to. The fighting will spread here soon." His tone was firm, despite his failing strength. "I already made my ugly mark... scrubbing it away now feels pointless. But you? You have the whole world waiting for you, dear."

"No no no no Youssef." She frantically repeated, "Don't do that to me, I am not some sort of fairy tale hero, don't do that to me bud, don't leave me here."

His voice steadied. "A hero isn't defined by special powers or magical weapons, but by the hope they spread. It's about holding tight onto your wish, rising after each and every fall, and crying out all your desire. As one day you'll see, it's what makes heroes shine the brightest."

He shoved her forward, his smile lighting the gloom of the alley. Ariel's throat tightened with unspoken gratitude, but she knew there was no time to argue. She nodded and ran.

Youssef slumped against a wall, blood pooling beneath him. He smirked grimly. "Lying like this... You didn't deserve this, Father... though I do... irony."

His gaze drifted to a mural on the wall, its vibrant defiance mocking yet mesmerizing. "Even amid war and agony, fate writes on walls, turning tears into hope." He chuckled, coughing up blood. "At least I'll die as a writer... as me."

His voice softened. "May God grant you the success you deserve, Ariel..." His eyes closed; his final words lingered in chaos.

Epilogue: Whisper of Tomorrow

Ariel returned to the smoldering ruins looking for Youssef. The wind carried the faint scent of ash and paint, overpowering the fleeting fragrance of the once-flowering acacia trees.
She dug her fingernails into her palms; the weight of Youssef's final words lay heavy on her heart, searching for solace in them.

Finding Youssef crouched, lying next to a wall but smiling in peace, she sat next to him. Reminiscing of the ragtag memories he left her, she sat next to him, placing her head on top of his shoulder, droplets of rain hitting Youssef's legs.

Her lips brushed his- soft, fleeting, like dawn trembling on the edge of night.

In that final, quiet moment as the tears quelled and the break of day could be seen, Ariel felt it, felt Youssef's hope, vowing to bring it to all she could inspire.

Our Parallel Lives, Our Intertwined Destinies

Lidor and Abed

We are Lidor and Abd. I'm a 17-year-old Israeli Jew, and Abd is a 15-year-old Palestinian Muslim. Though we live close by, our lives have felt worlds apart. We grew up in different cities, with different family traditions and personal challenges. Yet when we started talking Online, we discovered that our struggles, dreams, and hopes are a lot more alike than we ever imagined.

Our conversations have shown us that hope isn't some far-off idea - it's right here in the everyday moments when we listen, laugh, and learn from each other. As we share our story, we invite you to see that even small sparks of connection can light the way to a brighter future.

I (Lidor) grew up between Haifa and Zichron in a home that was forever changed by my parents' divorce. The pain of watching my family split up taught me early on that life can be uncertain and harsh - but it also instilled in me the importance of seeking light in every dark corner. My academic interests led me to study political science and economics at the Open University after school hours, while my passion for debate and activism pushed me into competitive teams and even inspired me to run a nonprofit that teaches activist youth how to advocate for meaningful change. These experiences have fueled my dream of one day managing my own firm in London - a place where I envision a future free from fear and conflict.

I (Abd) come from Baqa al-Gharbiyye, where my days are marked by lively family gatherings with cousins and personal pursuits like cooking, running, and working out at the gym. I constantly challenge myself through Model United Nations conferences and other events that sharpen my English and allow me to interact with peers from diverse backgrounds - including Jewish youth like Lidor. My dream is to build a powerful business that brings both mental and financial peace - a vision of a life where hardship transforms into opportunity.

Even as we come from diverse backgrounds, the traditions we cherish have helped shape who we are. I (Lidor) celebrate the major Jewish holidays, especially Passover - a time that reminds me of our ancestors' arduous journey from Egypt to the Promised Land. Passover is not just a historical recollection; it's a testament to our resilience and the belief that every hardship can lead to a new beginning. I (Abd) celebrate Ramadan and Eid with my family. For me, these occasions are far more than religious observances - they are moments when our family comes together, sharing in a spirit of unity and reflection, and reminding me that hope can be as powerful as a miracle.

Language, too, has been both a bridge and a barrier in our lives. I (Lidor) grew up speaking Hebrew, English, and a bit of Russian - a linguistic mix that echoes my family's journey from the USSR to Israel. I (Abd) speak Arabic, interspersed with Hebrew and English, a reminder of the rich, multicultural tapestry that defines my daily life. Despite these differences, our shared desire to communicate and understand one another led us to connect through digital means - Discord and WhatsApp became the tools that helped our voices merge into one conversation.

Our collaboration began as a formal assignment - a mandate to work together on a project meant to bring hope and peace. At first, our exchanges were careful and measured; after all, we were strangers with histories that often cast us as adversaries in the eyes of the world. Yet, as we started sharing our personal stories - our family struggles, our dreams for the future, and the very essence of our identities - we discovered that beneath the labels of "Israeli" and "Palestinian" lie two hearts yearning for the same things: respect, dignity, and the promise of a better tomorrow.

We cannot ignore the weight of the conflict that surrounds us. I (Lidor) have often felt the sting of hearing opinions that challenge the very existence of my homeland - opinions that reduce my identity to a political statement. I (Abd) have heard stories of families forced from their homes and communities clinging to the hope of return, and those stories remind me that behind every statistic, real people suffer and long to be seen and heard. In our discussions about these issues, we haven't always agreed. I (Lidor) lean toward the idea that secure borders are essential for my homeland's future, with negotiations on settlements and governance occurring only under conditions that preserve our state's identity. I (Abd) believe that a just peace requires fully recognizing Palestinian rights, dismantling systems of occupation, and ensuring that those who have been displaced have the right to return. Despite these differences, our conversations are always grounded in mutual respect. We are not enemies debating policies from opposite sides; we are two young people who understand that peace can only be achieved through dialogue, empathy, and a willingness to listen.

Hope, for us, is not an abstract idea - it is a tangible force that emerges when we decide to work together despite our differences. I (Lidor) see hope as that unexpected ray of sunlight piercing through a stormy sky, a reminder that no matter how entrenched the challenges, there is always an opportunity to create positive change. I (Abd) view hope like discovering a cure for what seems incurable - a little miracle that reassures me even the gravest wounds can begin to heal. This shared belief in hope has transformed our formal project into a journey of personal growth, one where our intertwined destinies create a legacy of understanding and cooperation.

One powerful symbol that has emerged in our collaboration is the city of Haifa. I (Lidor) see Haifa as a living mosaic where Jews, Muslims, and Christians coexist - a place that embodies the possibility of harmony amid diversity. I (Abd) share this vision; in Haifa, I see real life.

example of how people from different backgrounds can live together in peace, side by side. This city reminds us that our differences need not divide us; instead, they can enrich our collective experience and pave the way for a future built on mutual respect.

In a letter to the future, we would tell the next generation that although today's world is fraught with conflict and division, it is also a time when hope takes root in the most unexpected places. We will write:

"It is a scary and challenging time, but do not lose sight of the possibility for change. Look for the small acts of kindness, the moments of understanding, and the bridges built between hearts. We are living proof that when individuals from different backgrounds come together, they can forge a path toward peace. Keep hope alive and remember that you have the power to shape a world where everyone is treated with dignity and respect."

Our journey has not been without its challenges. Reconciling our divergent histories and perspectives sometimes led to heated debates and moments of frustration. Yet, every disagreement became an opportunity to understand the deeper layers of each other's experiences - a reminder that behind every opinion lies a life shaped by unique struggles and triumphs. We learned that compromise does not mean sacrificing our truths; rather, it means acknowledging that our truths can coexist if we commit ourselves to dialogue.

Reflecting on our lives, we recall historical moments that have inspired hope. I (Lidor) remember the 1980s in Israel - a time when, despite ongoing tensions, there was a sense of possibility, a period when people could travel with fewer restrictions and meet across cultural lines with genuine curiosity rather than fear. I (Abd) find hope in the stories of the 600s, when the Prophet Muhammad taught that Jews were to be treated as peers without a trace of hatred - a moment in history that defied later divisiveness and celebrated our shared humanity.

As we continue writing our story together, we remain committed to the belief that our collaboration is a testament to the transformative power of hope. Our parallel lives, once defined by separation and suspicion, have merged into a shared narrative of resilience, understanding, and the courage to dream of a better world. We write side by side, our words interlaced with the understanding that every conversation, every shared memory, and every dream brings us closer to the future we both long for - a future where our identities are celebrated, and where the light of hope dispels even the darkest shadows.

We are Lidor and Abd, co-authors of this journey, united not only by our differences but also by our shared vision for peace and a brighter tomorrow. Together, we continue to build our narrative - a narrative that proves hope is not just a distant ideal but a reality we create every day, one message, one laugh, and one thoughtful conversation at a time.

Part VI: Gaza and West Bank Writers

As we were preparing this book, Steven initiated a new writing group of young writers from the West Bank and Gaza. These writers are very promising and have much to contribute to our writing initiative. With new writers joining our sessions every week, we find these students most willing to share their personal stories. Their individual experiences illustrate personal trauma and the way they are coping with the reality of their lives. Their messages are powerful and most importantly, they are willing to share these experiences. Thes young writers have found writing to be a productive way to deal with their fears. We have included all the writing pieces completed to date.

Reflections

Malak

I am Malak, a Palestinian girl from the Gaza Strip. I have a modest dream, like any girl in this world — to pursue higher education and work in the field I love. This is my vision for the future. But... is this what happened?!

Before the seventh of October, I was working toward this dream. But after that date, everything changed. My world turned upside down. On that fateful day, the 7th of October, the first displacement occurred. Our first destination was Deir al-Balah. We went to my uncle's house. There were nine people in my family, along with five other families living in the same house. The total number of people in the house was 60. Do you have any idea how much daily suffering we endured — with food, drink, clothing, and hygiene?

The house was next to Al-Aqsa Hospital. Then they threatened to storm the hospital, so we fled to Rafah, to a place where meals were being prepared for displaced people. We stayed there for two months — two months sleeping on sand, two months of extreme hunger, two months of bitter cold, two months of daily fear from what was happening around us.

Then we were ordered to evacuate immediately, so we went to Al-Bureij. It was a four-story house. One day, something terrifying happened — something that we will never be able to forget, no matter how old we get. It's etched in our minds. A drone started firing at the fourth floor. My uncle told his children to go down to the ground floor, hoping things would calm down.

We were sitting together on the second floor, drinking tea and talking. Suddenly, my cousin said he would go to their flat to pray *Dhuhr* (noon prayer). They lived on the fourth floor. My cousin finished his prayer, and then the house was hit by the first shell. We were frozen in fear. My aunt was next to me and burst into tears, screaming, "My son is still upstairs! What happened?! What is going on?!"

Then, in less than a second, my brother went up to rescue him — and the house was hit by another Israeli shell. Tragically, my brother's right arm was next to him, and his legs… God, it's heartbreaking… but he was still alive.

My uncle saw that his son had been martyred and that his nephew was still alive. He ran down and shouted for help. Then the house was hit by a third shell.

That was the strike that completely ended my brother's life.

That was the strike that took him — even though he was only twenty years old. Life was still ahead of him. But we say Alhamdulillah (praise be to God) in all circumstances.

We ran barefoot out of the house, fleeing over the rubble. We went to a relative's home, where they tried to comfort us and give us strength.

At that time, I didn't know that my brother had been martyred. We left the house knowing my cousin had been martyred, and we were incredibly sad — he was kind-hearted, cheerful, with a beautiful smile, always lifting people's spirits. He was truly a wonderful human being.

My aunt kept screaming and crying, saying he was still alive, refusing to believe he had been killed.

Then suddenly, my older brother arrived and said, *"Enough. That's it. Mohammed and Bahaa are both gone."*

That was the shock.

I knew my cousin had been martyred, but I didn't know my brother was with him too.

It was truly the hardest and most painful moment I've ever experienced in my life.

Since that moment, and to this day, life has become suffocating.

Enough… truly, enough.

We've been through unbearably heavy days. A year so dark in every sense — a year in which we lost so much. A year in which we saw humiliation, degradation, hunger — and the worst of all, *loss*.

The most loyal is gone. The most tender-hearted is gone. The one who understood me the most is gone. A piece of my soul left with him that day.

May God never bless those who turned their backs. *Hasbi Allah wa ni'ma al-wakeel* (God is sufficient for me, and He is the best disposer of affairs).[6]

Baraa

I am Baraa, 16 years old.

I was raised to the sound of bombing, not music. I opened my eyes to a world full of fear, but my heart never knew submission. Every airplane sound increased my resilience, and every tear I saw in my mother's eyes was a fire that ignited strength inside me.

I am not a victim; I stand with my head held high. I never broke, even when we lost our homes, even when we lost dear ones. I stayed standing because the children of Gaza stand strong.

Do I dream? Of course, I dream.

But my dream is not small.

My dream is to continue my education, to build my country, to raise its name in front of the entire world.

I dream of being free, living with dignity, and telling the entire world: I am from Gaza, and the impossible is just the beginning for me.

Rayan

My name is Rayan, a child from the Gaza Strip. I grew up with a love for physical sports and excelled in karate. I started practicing at the age of six under the guidance of my father, who was one of Palestine's

---

6   A reference to Quran 3:173,

champions in karate. I became attached to this sport, distinguished myself, and despite my young age, I became one of the karate champions in our camp, the Al-Bureij Camp. I earned the yellow and orange belts in a record time that no club in the Gaza Strip had ever witnessed, due to my determination to achieve my goal of becoming one of Palestine's champions and representing the Palestinian national team in international events... But then...

My dream was interrupted because of the war on October 7, which made it difficult to reach the club. However, I continued my daily training at home with my father, Mahmoud. But the first displacement made the dream stop for the second time, and I ended up living with my grandfather, my mother's father. My father, Mahmoud, was captured by the Israeli army.

My father was held captive for a full month of torture and abuse. After being released, his injuries were severe, preventing him from continuing his training. To add to that, the main training club was bombed and completely destroyed.

Here, my shock began: my sports dream froze, my physical fitness declined, and all I could think about was how to get water for my family and how to bring them food. It became hard to find due to the food shortage in Gaza.

Can it be possible for a child like me, who hasn't yet reached twelve years old, to bear all these burdens?
No dream came true.
No safety in my life.
No education available.
I am just a talented child with a completely destroyed mindset.

So, in your opinion, after reading this story, my story, what is the solution for me!? What is the solution?

I Am From

Shahed

I Am From...

I am from a land whose name is written in blood and patience,
from a homeland that carries the face of the sun despite the clouds,
from a house that still stands in memory, even if its walls have fallen.

I am from Gaza, from a city that learned to embrace its people even in moments of loss,
from a street filled with dust after the bombing, where I still planted a rose from my soul.

I am from my mother's arms that became my homeland when the homeland felt too tight, and from my brother Bahaa's laughter — the last thing he left me before he was gone.
From the hand that held mine and said, "Don't go,"
then let go… taking a piece of my heart with it forever.

I am from a moment that became a wound that never heals,
from a memory suspended between sky and earth,
from a gasp I survived yet never truly survived.

I am from a voice I use to write, because crying is never enough,
from silence I used to resist the noise of helplessness,
from a heartbeat that still chooses life, even when life chooses to test me.

I am from a homeland that never forgets me, even as I try to run from

278

the grief within it,
from a key kept in memory, and a home still standing in my heart,
from a dream of peace that doesn't break — even when everything
else does.

I am from there… from Gaza, from Palestine,
from a pain that taught me how to endure,
and from a love that taught me never to leave.

I am from Bahaa…
and from the laughter that will never die.

Mousa

I'm from there, where I once found my heart. When I was born, I was
incredibly lucky to be born in the city of peace, and it was also lucky
for me. I'm from a country that never sleeps, with the sounds of stones,
churches, and mosques. There's a synagogue a few meters away, and
I've always wondered where it came from. I'm from a country with the
sad sounds of street vendors, the beautiful voices of children, and the
frightening sound of dust. Everything here is special, and everything
that's special makes it different, and everything different is something
beautiful. Plants can grow everywhere, and so can I. I can see my
heart everywhere here. I miss what was from me and I was from it. I
miss the place where I first fell in love. I miss my first school desk,
my first kick of football, my first caress of the sea on my feet, my first
bite of ice cream. I'm from there, where no one knows where it goes.

Malak

I am a woman who does not break, even when everything around
her shatters.

I am silent when words fail,
the light when electricity disappears,
and life itself when life refuses to be lived.

I come from a land that teaches patience without asking for your consent,
a land that makes you fight without a weapon,
and love life, even when it doesn't always love you back.

I do not beg — I deserve.
I do not wait for pity — I carve my chances from the rubble,
and plant seeds of hope in soil still trembling from the sounds of war.

I am the one who learned to rise every morning despite sleepless nights,
to work with short breath,
to smile while holding a thousand unspoken wounds in her heart.

I am not a sad story to be told,
I am a lesson in survival to be written.

I am a woman carrying a world of burdens on her back,
yet she walks.
She leans on no one, complains to no one,
because she simply cannot afford the luxury of collapse.

When I'm weak, I stand.
When I cry, I write.
And when I miss life… I create it with my own hands.

I don't wait for the light — I become it.
I don't seek salvation — I am it.

This is me.
And here I stand.

I am not just me. I am the echo of thousands of broken stories.

Noor

Where am I from?

Someone asked me:
"Where are you from?"

– I'm from a place that's not often mentioned in the news, but its voice never fades from the hearts.
– From a land not measured by its size, but by the weight of its tears and dreams that refuse to die.
– From streets that pulse with life despite the walls, and homes that never shut their doors on hope.

He said: "I don't understand… Can you explain more?"

– I'm from a land known by history, yet some try to erase it from the present.
– From a place we don't just leave… We carry it with us wherever we go.
– From a dialect that holds traces of weariness, and a laugh flavored with defiance.
– From the scent of thyme at dawn, and songs sung despite the shelling and the silence.

"What's the name of this place?" he asked again.

– Its name is sometimes spoken with fear, but always with pride.
Its name is Palestine.

– I am not just from a map…
I am from a story, a people, a survival.

So if you want to know me, don't ask for my passport…
Ask me about my roots, the key that still hangs, the song yet to be sung.

I am from there… from Palestine.
And that's all I need to say.

Where I Am Now

Malak

"Where am I now...
I am in a tight, dark place, as if I'm stuck in an endless corner.
The faint light from my phone is the only thing that breaks through this stillness, as if it's a weak ray resisting the darkness. This light, barely visible, follows me all day, but it fails to erase the darkness surrounding me on all sides.

The only sound I hear is the sound of ambulances passing by on the street, as if they're playing a tragic tune that penetrates deep into my soul. It feels like the entire world is moving quickly, while I am here in this place, living in an endless circle. I think about everything, but I can't escape the thoughts that slowly consume me. The thoughts chase me, disturb me, and intensify the darkness. Every time I try to breathe deeply, the air feels tight, as if every breath I take is an additional burden. I am here, amidst walls that don't allow me to move freely. I see no space for hope, as if the horizon has closed in front of me.

I need to escape this tightness, to breathe freely, but how can I when I am here!? In the walls of this dark place that always reminds me of everything lost, every unfulfilled dream, and every moment wasted in time...
I am here…

Mousa

I often asked myself: Is the place the place, or are we the place?

Who decides that this place can be classified as a place? It's us!

The place cannot be separated from our bodies. It is a part of our bodies, and indeed, it is the most important part.

I am now inside my body, touching every cell of it. I am the one who creates the places, and our brains are the ones that give us the images of this place. Each of us can see the place from our brain and heart.

Every moment of emotion can change the place we are in. When we take the place with us, it captures the heart and makes the soul dance with joy, as if the whole world has gathered to present a unique show. I now carry the place with me to begin a story, a word, a new beginning that makes me feel refreshed.

I just wrote something about this place:

A caravan of noise is passing through my language now

To ignite the laughter of words... The land of the place is in my lungs.

And I remain the owner of the place in this weary expanse...

And my doctrine remains in the place... To live without doctrine.

The shortest definition of where I am now is:

The place is me, and my places are with me. I drag them wherever I want. I do not rest in one place... Rather, places to rest in me...

Shahed

Where am I now?
I am in a place unlike any other. Between the rubble of war and the pulse of life.

Each morning, I open my eyes to the heavy sound of reality, carrying in my heart an unconquerable hope.

I live in the heart of a merciless war, in the eye of a storm that never calms — and yet, despite everything, I still write my story with determination.
I still open my books, prepare my coffee, and chase my dreams as if there were no war.

Where am I?
I am in a place between the ruins and the school notebooks covered in dust.
And in every moment, I choose not to bow down, but to lift my head to the sky — that same sky I believe holds a place for me, even as the echo of missiles tries to convince me otherwise.

I have lost the dearest person to me   my brother, my support and companion —
He left as a martyr, leaving a void in my heart that cannot be filled, and a will that will never be forgotten:
"Keep going, Shahed. Don't stop."
That is why I am here — studying, working, building myself —
As if he is still watching me, as if his voice still whispers to me: "You are capable."

I am not just from Gaza — **I am Gaza itself**: strong, burdened, sorrowful, but standing.
I carry my pain and my country's pain, and I weave from tears threads of determination,
And from the rubble, bridges of dreams.

Where am I?
I am on the road to glory, even though the path is laden with pain and

the sky is heavy with tears.

I am in every moment where I choose light over darkness, knowledge over ignorance, and life over defeat.

Where am I?
I am in the dream... in the will... in a tomorrow I will create with my own hands —
Not waiting for someone to save me but deciding that I will be.
I am in the sky, because my ambition resides there,
Because my spirit is too great to be chained by the walls of war.

Where am I now?
I am in the middle — in the point where destruction meets life.
In the moment when I am shattered inside, but choose to smile, to rise, and say to the world:
I am the daughter of Gaza... the daughter of resilience.

Finding Light in the Darkness

Mousa

Light...?
Light takes me to its paradise.
So, I became a bee sleeping over honey.
Light buries me in its soil.
So I return carried on the shoulder of hope.
Light is the key to joy, its secret.
Light is a window overlooking pain.
Light is the sultan of all creation.
And you see it trembling in fear like the servants.
Light is like the soul, an obscure matter.
Light is the bell of the beginning and the rejoicing of the clay in the water of nothingness.

Light is the battle of birds of prey.

Light is like poetry, a wild female.

Light is a squawking wind.

Light is Ishtar, in whose love the universe is slaughtered and creatures roar.

Light is the cold of its fire.

Light is the hammer and thunder of God.

Light is the artery of prophecy in my hands.

Light is the collar of a white dove above the deserted and forgotten wall.

Light is to live life as we wish.

And to say to anyone who has transgressed, "One."

Light is to forget eternity and its grass.

To forget the titles of the end and eternity

Light is a woman who massages her night...

And she closes her eyes in fear of envy.

Light is the anklet of the poem

When it dances in the foam

Light is not our standing and wailing above the crumbling ruins.

Light is a fire in sleepy lips.

Light is like you; its face is a spark.

And darkness is like me; its face is miserable.

Light is like you, soft and smooth.

And darkness is like me, wild and fierce.

Light is a ritual of spiritual worship.

Light is the pulse of water in the pain of the soil.

And in the blossoming of a rose

And in the fragility of its magic

And in the cheerfulness of its prophetic face

Light is what the stranger said to his flute.

O flute, O whisper of the flowers rising to the streams

O flute, O homeland that nests in the eye sockets

Light is what the prophet said to his trunk.

O light, embrace me and do not fear my separation

Light is our sight and our radiant gaze in supplication.

Light is our hidden ladder to heaven.

Light is what the martyr whispered and confided in

To a martyr at the hour of bombardment

"It is the most beautiful of deaths, our death together.

So come, my death."

Light is a Sufi who covers his night.

And says, O letter, go away. How ignorant you are! My country's light is beseeching its Lord, and crying out, "Loving you, my master, is my love for you."

The light is a star wandering in a star, and says, "Rejoice, so that the heavens may rejoice."

The light is a cat averse to a cat, and so its cat closes the doors, and meows, and then says, "I come, come to you."

The light is for me to glance at it stealthily and see an angel walking in the two gardens.

It is for us to fly, you and I, in the smoke of life like two butterflies.

It is my joy, despite the bent back, despite my fragility in love. It is for me to tell you, "I adore you, O light of existence." The light is you and I, O fragrance of existence. It is for me to tell you, "If I am absent, forgive me, for I will return."

Malak

In the depths of darkness, where there seems to be no hope on the horizon, where our footsteps echo in the void and the sounds around us fade, this light is born. But this light does not come from the outside, nor does it wait for others to light the way for us. This light comes from within, from our unseen strength, from our belief that darkness does not have control over us. When worries accumulate, doors close, and everything seems deep in the dark, remember that inside you is a courage that the eye may not see but that you feel in every moment of struggle. This light we are talking about is not just light; it is the

288

determination to move forward despite obstacles. It is the ability to stand again after every fall. It is the hope that never dies, no matter how many steps stumble.

In this world, many will try to extinguish your light. They will talk about you in your absence, and they will doubt your ability to continue. But when eyes are closed, you will still see with the eyes of your heart, because you know well that this light can't be extinguished by anyone as long as you insist on being stronger than the darkness.

Darkness comes to test our resilience, to teach us that strength does not lie in avoiding pain, but in facing it. You are capable of being the light that resists the darkness. You are the one who carries in your heart the ray of hope that can light the way—not just for yourself, but for those around you too.

Always remember that the light within you is not the result of perfect circumstances or a life free of challenges, but it is the light you ignite within your soul after you learn that life is filled with darkness. But you will not let it rule you. You will continue to create light in every corner and shine in it every moment.

The greater the darkness, the more beautiful and powerful the light you create will be. And do not let a moment of weakness or pain make you think it's the end. You are the light that will never stop, no matter how fierce the storms are. And in the end, you will discover that in this darkness, you were the light, and you were the light everyone had been waiting for.

Noor

In a time when darkness multiplies around us, light remains the undying hope—the vision that guides us when paths blur into one another.

And because light is not merely something seen, but a soul that is illuminated, I share with you this text that touches the essence of words and draws from their glow the meaning of life.

Among the most beautiful things ever said about light is the saying of God Almighty in His noble Book:
"Light upon light. Allah guides His light whom He wills."[7]
It is a light that transcends the limits of sight, reaching into insight, with which God guides whom He wills of His servants to the paths of tranquility, purity, and guidance.

And how could light not carry such majesty, when our Lord said in the decisive revelation:
"Allah is the Light of the heavens and the earth. The example of His light is like a niche within which is a lamp…"[8]
A divine light—not perceived by our senses but seen by souls attached to truth and guided by it through the maze of life.

Light… a word that holds in its letters the secret of life, the music of serenity, and the fragrance of hope.
Light is nothing but a beginning to every dark ending, a promise at the heart of pain that nothing lasts forever—not even darkness.

Light is not just sunlight. It is the spark of hope in a chest worn by sorrow, the smile of a heart that chose to shine for others even as it faded within.

It is the sound of a prayer in the depths of night, reaching the sky with confidence, returning as light into the heart—even without words.

I've learned that light cannot be bought, nor borrowed. It is born within us when we believe that every darkness has an exit, and every

---

7   Quran 24:35.
8   Quran 24:35.

trial holds a space for relief.

Light lives in sincere intention, in a gentle word, in a beautiful coincidence that changes the course of a gloomy day.

Sometimes, light is a person who passes through our lives like a breeze—not staying long but leaving an unforgettable trace.

And sometimes, the light is within us, though we do not know it. We light the way for others with our presence, our patience, with a story that no one has heard.

Light is what pierces your heart at the height of darkness.

It may come in the form of a prayer, a kind word from a stranger, or a smile you weren't expecting.

Light isn't always a beam… Sometimes it's a person, a moment, a dream.

In moments of brokenness, you need nothing more than "a small light."

Be the light—in your words, in your patience, in your kindness. Even if the whole world is dark, it's enough to be a flame for someone, and to carry within you a light that never fades.

Let light be your path—not only what you see, but what you see with. And be among the people of light… those who mend hearts with words, and grant peace through silence.

Light cannot be extinguished when it comes from within. Storms cannot erase it. Winds cannot put it out. For it is not just light, it is a creed, a soul, a purity. And so, light remains the most enduring legacy in pure hearts, and the unforgettable message in times of confusion.

Let us be among those who carry the light in their eyes and hearts—not to be seen, but to illuminate. For true light is the one that never dies, because it was born from within.

Shahed

Light Through Darkness.
In Gaza, darkness is not just the absence of electricity.
It stretches further to include the absence of safety, the loss of comfort,
and the fading outlines of tomorrow.
There, in the heart of siege and death,
light is born from the rubble of pain.
It is crafted by people who carry life despite its cruelty,
who believe that within the heart burns a flame no war can extinguish.

The mother in Gaza is not just an embrace, she is a fortress.
She bakes with patience and weaves hope from threads of suffering.
She is the homeland when the homeland cracks,
and the light when all the lights vanish.

The father is the pillar that never bends,
even if his back arches under the weight of oppression.
He is the tree that no wind can uproot,
even if fire scorches its bark.

The doctor is a miracle walking on earth.
He heals without proper tools, saves without rest,
faces death face to face and returns to save yet another soul.
He is the light in hospital corridors when darkness consumes all,
the voice that tells us: "We still have a pulse… we still endure."

The journalist, the bearer of truth in a time of deception,
writes in blood, films beneath bombing skies,
and screams truth into a world accustomed to silence.
He is the eye that never blinks,
the conscience that never compromises.

And I…
I am the one who lost a piece of her heart when my brother Bahaa left.
He held my hand and said, "Don't go,"
Then let go leaving my hand to hold emptiness, and my heart to cradle grief.
But I did not fall, and I did not hide behind my tears.

I faced life head on
carried my pain in my palms,
and went on writing, learning, resisting,
planting light from my tears.

In Gaza, we do not wait for light at the end of the tunnel.
We carve it with our own nails into the walls of darkness.
We create it from the smallest things: a child's laughter, a mother's patience,
a cry for justice, and a story of survival.

This is the light that cannot be extinguished.
a light born from ashes… unlike any light the world has ever known.

Looking to the Future

More than a year into this project, we can reflect on how far we've come—and look ahead to where we're headed. Our teacher training program has introduced the writing to twenty educators from schools across Israel, who have successfully implemented and adapted the materials for their own classrooms. Our teen workshops have engaged dozens of young people from Israeli, Palestinian, and international communities, with their blog posts reaching thousands of readers worldwide. Our writing competition, *Hope*, brought together forty students and resulted in 20 unique co-written pieces. The writing also provided a vital emotional outlet for teens at an Arab school in Israel following the tragic murder of their principal.

Our work has gained international recognition, featured in a Yom Kippur program at a synagogue in Houston, Texas; presented at a United Nations Office on Drugs and Crime (UNODC) education panel in Vienna, Austria; and highlighted at the Museum of Intercultural Dialogue in Kielce, Poland.

Looking forward, we plan to grow both inward and outward. We've recently launched a writing group in Gaza, beginning with facilitator training. These new facilitators will soon lead writing workshops for Gazan teens in both Arabic and English. We are also expanding our presence in the West Bank and plan to include more schools and cities within Israel. The theme for the 2026 *Writers Matter* writing competition will be announced soon.

Our approach to collaborating with schools is evolving. We'll begin pairing Arab and Jewish schools, enabling students and teachers from neighboring communities to connect and collaborate through writing. We also aim to integrate our international youth writers with Israeli and Palestinian teens into shared writing cohorts.

At the same time, we're exploring new partnerships abroad. Plans are underway for a *Writers Matter* course at a youth peace camp in Kosovo this summer, led by Steven. The course will bring together Israeli and Palestinian youth alongside Albanian, Serbian, and American peers. It will also be presented at a panel on Youth and Peacebuilding at the United Nations in Vienna in July. Additionally, we plan to offer in-person writing workshops in Germany, Poland, Sweden, the United Kingdom, and across the United States.

If you are part of a community or school that would like to hear from our writers or participate in a workshop, we would love to hear from you. We've seen firsthand how powerful this writing can be—and how deeply it resonates with audiences who engage with the voices of our courageous young writers.